Canada's Enemies

Canada's Enemies

Spies and Spying
in the Peaceable Kingdom

Graeme S. Mount

Dundurn Press
Toronto and Oxford

Editor: Avivah Wargon
Designer: Shawn Syms
Printed and bound in Canada by: Best Gagné Book Manufacturers, Louiseville, Quebec

The publisher wishes to acknowledge the generous assistance and ongoing support of **The Canada Council, The Book Publishing Industry Development Program** of **The Department of Communications, The Ontario Arts Council, The Ontario Publishing Centre** of **The Ministry of Culture, Tourism and Recreation**, and **The Ontario Heritage Foundation**.
Care has been taken to trace the ownership of copyright material used in the text (including the illustrations). The author and publisher welcome any information enabling them to rectify any reference or credit in subsequent editions.

J. Kirk Howard, Publisher

Canadian Cataloguing in Publication Data

Mount, Graeme S. (Graeme Stewart), 1939–
    Canada's enemies: spies and spying in the peaceable kingdom

Includes bibliographical references and index.
ISBN 1-55002-190-7

1. Spies – Canada. 2. Espionage – Canada – History – 20th century. I. Title.

FC549.M6 1993   327.12'0971   C93-094431-3
F1034.M6 1993

Dundurn Press Limited
2181 Queen Street East
Suite 301
Toronto, Canada
M4E 1E5

Dundurn Distribution
73 Lime Walk
Headington, Oxford
England
OX3 7AD

Dundurn Press Limited
1823 Maryland Avenue
P.O. Box 1000
Niagara Falls, N.Y.
U.S.A. 14302-1000

Table of Contents

Acknowledgments

Any author owes tremendous debts to many people, and I am no exception. These include my parents, Stewart and Bunty Mount, and my father-in-law, Allan Biggar, who helped with the proofreading; my wife Joan, who encouraged this project; my son Fraser, who taught his father to be somewhat computer-literate; my son Andrew, who tolerated my absences on research trips and shared some of the travel; colleague Edelgard Mahant and her friend Grace Maurice-Hyam at the National Archives of Canada, who gave me the idea; William Glover of the Directorate of History at the Department of National Defence and Professor Norman Hillmer of Carleton University, who read or listened to sections and offered comments; colleagues at Laurentian University's Department of History (especially Dieter K. Buse) who read and discussed sections; students Paul Derro, Gordon Dutrisac, Michael D. Stevenson and Earl Reid, who assisted with the research; Deans Michael Dewson (Laurentian) and Douglas Parker (Université canadienne en France) who wrote letters of introduction to various archivists and provided moral and financial support; Ashley Thomson at Laurentian's Jean-Desmarais Library and colleague Carl M. Wallace, who introduced me to Dundurn Press; Richard Heller, a former colleague at the Université canadienne en France, who retrieved the necessary documents on Agent X at the Provincial Archives of British Columbia; Jean-Yves Grenon, another former colleague at the Université canadienne en France and a retired diplomat, who commented constructively on the sixth and eighth chapters; Rhodri Jeffreys-Jones of the University of Edinburgh, who has given encouragement and sound advice as I prepared manuscripts on espionage history; Claude-France Hollard, who established the appropriate channels with archivists in Paris and in Nantes; Michael J. Mulloy, whose assistance in picture retrieval proved invaluable; the staff at Pictures Now in Sudbury, whose skills revived ancient pictures and rendered them acceptable for publication; Avivah Wargon, the copy editor at Dundurn Press, who caught ambiguities and sought clarification; and Rose May Démoré, Secretary of Laurentian's History Department, without whose computer and photocopying skills the preparations would have taken considerably longer. Employees at the various archives I visited rendered invaluable assistance. Any mistakes are, of course, my responsibility.

Introduction

Many books about Canada and its involvement in foreign espionage have become available in recent years. In 1981, Major S.R. Elliott produced *Scarlet to Green: A History of Intelligence in the Canadian Army, 1903–1963*. Great Britain's F.H. Hinsley makes some references to Canadian intelligence in naval warfare on the Atlantic in his *British Intelligence in the Second World War*. Providing comprehensive coverage of the past half-century is J.L. Granatstein and David Stafford's *Spy Wars: Espionage and Canada from Gouzenko to Glasnost*. Thanks to the Access to Information Act of the Trudeau era, an insiders' history of the Mounted Police and its role in security until 1966 has recently become available – Stan Horrall and Carl Betke's *Canada's Security Service: An Historical Outline, 1864–1966*. Another book, *Security and Intelligence in a Changing World: New Perspectives for the 1990s*, edited by A. Stuart Farson, David Stafford and Wesley K. Wark, deals with Canadian intelligence since 1976.

There are several other works on Cold War espionage. Robert Bothwell and J.L Granatstein co-edited *The Gouzenko Transcripts* in 1982. Donald Avery has written about Soviet espionage in Canada during World War II in "Allied Scientific Co-operation and Soviet Espionage in Canada, 1941–45." One of the casualties of the Cold War was Canadian diplomat Herbert Norman. In 1986, two authors presented contrary opinions, James Barros (hostile to Norman) and Roger Bowen (sympathetic). Most others who discuss Canadian foreign relations in the 1950s also say something about Norman. In *Spy Catcher*, the book that Margaret Thatcher tried to ban, Peter Wright states that in 1955, after the Soviet embassy in Ottawa burned down, RCMP agents assisted by MI5 personnel from the United Kingdom bugged the new building while it was under construction. In *Men in the Shadows*, John Sawatsky tells of questionable Cuban behaviour on Canadian soil since the revolution of 1959.

In 1990, Victor Ostrovsky, a veteran of Israel's Mossad, published his memoirs in collaboration with journalist Claire Hoy. Hoy and Ostrovsky demonstrate that Mossad gathers intelligence from Canadian troops in the Middle East under United Nations command, and that Mossad agents travel on phony and stolen Canadian passports. This book was so devastating that the Israeli government tried to prevent its publication. Similarly, Charles Taylor and James Eayrs accuse Canadian troops who served in Vietnam as part of the International Control Commission (1954–73) of spying for the United States.

Dealing with the present rather than the past, Richard Cleroux has written a critique of the Canadian Security and Intelligence Service (CSIS), while

Jeffrey T. Richelson and Desmond Ball describe Canadian electronic surveillance of the Soviet Union in a study of UKUSA (the intelligence alliance of the United Kingdom, the United States, Australia, New Zealand, and Canada).

These books by ex-spies, journalists, and professors are eye-openers. Canada is an interesting place after all, both for what Canadians do elsewhere and for what foreigners do in Canada or while posing as Canadians. Soviets and their Cuban allies saw Canada as a base from which to study the United States. Soviet-bloc, Yugoslav, Indian, and Israeli governments wanted to know what their dissidents and adversaries were doing in Canada. What hijackings or assassinations might they be planning? What funds might they be raising in order to promote change in their lands of birth? In few other countries could such diverse people meet and scheme with so few restrictions, so many opportunities.

Most of these books deal with Canada since 1945, the period most familiar to the reading public. Elliott's *Scarlet to Green*, the principal exception, focuses on military rather than civilian intelligence. Long before 1945, however, Canadians and their friends spied in foreign countries and foreigners spied in what is now Canada, on civilians as well as on people in uniform. There are articles on such matters: Jeff Keshen's on Canadian agents inside the United States in the Civil War era, who monitored Confederate terrorists and Fenians; my own on spying in Canada during the Spanish-American war, now revised as the first chapter of this book; and Wesley Wark's on Canada's entry into cryptography during World War II. Unfortunately, non-specialists rarely read articles and remain unfamiliar with the events they describe until they appear in book form.

Moreover, new materials are constantly being declassified, not only about Canada in European archives, but within Canada itself. Professors Gregory S. Kealey of Memorial University and Reg Whitaker of York University are now publishing a series of volumes of RCMP security bulletins, two of which appeared in late summer 1993. Their introductions describe RCMP surveillance of suspected subversives and RCMP efforts at counter-intelligence. Materials that have long been accessible in archives in the United States, the United Kingdom, and Germany are unfamiliar because nobody has examined them. This book should fill some of the gaps, demonstrating that Canadians have a history of foreign espionage, both by and against them; that unsung heroes have made a difference; and that Canadian history can be exciting, even humorous. It should also demonstrate that Canadian espionage has been a plug-the-gaps variety. On the whole, Canadian authorities were prepared to allow first the British and then the Americans to be their windows on the world. As long as these allies were doing their job effectively, nobody in Canada seemed to care that Canada was not conducting its own foreign espionage. Only serious failures on the part of Canada's two mentors led Canadians into foreign intrigue.

Until World War I, Canadian spies complemented British ones. When they operated on United States soil, they did so with the tacit approval of American authorities but with limited help from them. Likewise, Canadian authorities turned a blind eye to American spies on Canadian soil, and the Americans operated inside Canada without serious regard for Canadian law.

Active Canadian-American intelligence cooperation began during the 1920s and intensified during World War II. Since 1945, as other writers have shown, the United States has replaced the United Kingdom as Canada's principal intelligence partner, although through UKUSA and other fora, Canada does work with both. This book includes one chapter on the post-1945 period, based on newly declassified materials. Chapter 9 should offer a sense of perspective. While not everyone would share Brian Mulroney's unadulterated enthusiasm and praise for the United States, very few would consider it an enemy. Certainly this author does not. Nevertheless, once readers have seen the kinds of activities in which friends engage, they may be less surprised about what enemies have done.

1

The Secret Operations of Spanish Consular Officials during the Spanish-American War*

I solated as Canadians often feel they are – the only people between the United States and the North Pole – they have often found themselves involved in the problems of people from other continents. In April 1898, Spain and the United States went to war, ostensibly over the liberation of Cuba. When Spain's colonies on the American mainland gained their independence in the first quarter of the nineteenth century, Spain did manage to retain control of two Caribbean possessions – Cuba and Puerto Rico. In 1895, Cubans rebelled against Spanish rule, and over the next three years, many in the United States came to see distinct advantages to the liberaton of Cuba. When the Spanish government refused to abandon the island, President William McKinley asked Congress for a declaration of war against Spain; Congress obliged. Battles were also fought in Puerto Rico and in the Philippines, both of which the United States formally annexed (along with Guam) at the 1899 peace conference in Paris.

When Spain and the United States went to war, they severed diplomatic relations. American diplomats in Spain returned to the United States, and British diplomats assumed responsibility for American interests in Spain. Key Spanish officials posted to the United States did not, however, return to Spain. Instead they crossed quietly into neutral Canada and reported on the war from there. Suspecting the Spaniards of espionage, the U.S. Secret Service watched them carefully. Americans and Spaniards focused their activities on Montreal, although they operated across Canada, from Halifax to Victoria. With the availability of Spanish archival sources in recent years, it is now possible to understand the events of 1898 more fully than in the past.

In particular, Spain's Montreal spy ring of 1898 deserves another look. The episode surrounding its operations demonstrates that Canada was

*Reprinted, with changes, from North American Spies: New Revisionist Perspectives, ed. Rhodri Jeffreys-Jones and Andrew Lownie (Edinburgh: Edinburgh University Press, 1991), by permission of the publisher. The author wishes to express his gratitude to the Social Science and Humanities Research Council of Canada for financial assistance with the research of this chapter.

already and almost inadvertently developing its own foreign policy – one of close cooperation, within limits, with both the United Kingdom and the United States – a policy that would be a hallmark of Canadian foreign relations throughout the twentieth century. It demonstrates that as long ago as 1898, friendly nations were spying inside Canada. It demonstrates that, at a time when Canada lacked a Department of External Affairs and the United Kingdom looked after Canadian interests in other countries, Canada was so important to at least two nations that they were prepared to operate inside Canada without reference to Canadian law or legal niceties. It demonstrates the role of consulates in that disregard for Canadian law, a problem still of concern to the Canadian Security and Intelligence Service (CSIS). It is more difficult, however, to demonstrate that intelligence gathering seriously affected the outcome of the Spanish-American War. Also, while the experiences of 1898 may have affected subsequent intelligence gathering in the United States, there is little evidence that they did so in Canada or in Spain.

Contrary to what others have written, this chapter demonstrates that clever American counter-intelligence did not smash the Montreal spy ring of 1898. Rhodri Jeffreys-Jones and Norman Penlington had to write without benefit of Spanish sources, without which it was not possible to make the links between the Spanish spies expelled early in July 1898 and the rest of Spain's intelligence network. Phyllis Sherrin, faced with the same handicap, exaggerated the importance of Spain's spy in Victoria and failed to realize his subordination to superiors in Montreal. As late as 1989, Nathan Miller was to write, "The breakup of the Montreal spy ring was the most effective piece of American counter-intelligence of the war." The present writer has already discussed the spy ring, but not in the detail now available.

As Rhodri Jeffreys-Jones has explained, the United States spy system had two branches – foreign and domestic. In the realm of foreign intelligence, the United States Navy had its own spies abroad. A correspondent of the *New York World* watched as Spanish Admiral Pascual Cervera y Topete sailed with his fleet from the Portuguese-owned Cape Verde Islands towards the Caribbean. The United States had a spy at Cadiz itself, base of the Spanish navy. Since 1895 the Coast Guard had been on the lookout for filibusters offering illegal assistance to Cuban rebels. It was relatively simple to switch sides, and to adapt Coast Guard procedures and conditions to wartime conditions. Nor was American foreign intelligence limited to naval matters. American agents travelled behind Spanish lines in Cuba. The United States even had a spy, Domingo Villaverde, right in the palace of the Spanish Captain-General of Cuba; he operated the Havana end of the cable that linked Havana with Key West.

The Spanish government was just as active in the realm of foreign intelligence. The problems addressed in this chapter stemmed from Spain's relocation of officers from its Washington legation to Canada, where they worked alongside officials of the Spanish consulate-general in Montreal. At the outbreak of the war, moreover, Spain upgraded its consular posts in Halifax and Quebec City, key East Coast Canadian ports, with the appointments of Joaquín Torroja and Pedro Arias y Solís, previously consuls at Philadelphia and Tampa respectively. Spain also sent a young man, Angel Cabrejo, to Victoria, where he pretended to chaperone his sister, who pretended to be studying there. From Victoria he could easily monitor traffic on the Strait of Juan de Fuca, through which ships headed to and from the naval base at Puget Sound had to pass.

Thus Canada came to be the scene of the cut-and-thrust of espionage and counter-espionage between a former and a future world power. The State Department in Washington instructed consulates to be on the alert for anything unusual, and U.S. consulates in Halifax, Montreal, Vancouver, and Victoria sent numerous reports about suspicious people and events. For example, the U.S. consul in Victoria, Abraham Smith, quickly became aware of Cabrejo's presence and notified Washington accordingly.

Until the aftermath of World War II, most countries had legations – smallscale embassies – in foreign capitals. Only the largest nations thought that they could afford embassies, and Canada was not in that category. It was, however, common for foreign countries to have consulates in major cities where there were shared interests, usually economic or cultural. (Countries of the British Commonwealth did not count as "foreign," and Commonwealth governments called their legations/embassies in other Commonwealth capitals "high commissions" because the head of the high commission, the high commissioner, was accredited to the head of government, the prime minister, rather than to the head of state, the monarch, who was also monarch of Canada.) A really important consulate was called a consulate-general, and headed by a consul-general instead of a consul. A consulate with a minimum of consular work (provision of visas, helping citizens in distress, promotion of trade) might operate on a part-time basis. Such an operation would be called a vice-consulate, and headed by a vice-consul. Most vice-consuls were local businessmen for whom consular work was only a part-time activity.

For reasons we shall examine below, consulates were crucial to Spain's intelligence offensive. But they were also important to the United States. U.S. consulates were active on the intelligence front worldwide. From Gibraltar the U.S. consulate could monitor Spanish naval traffic headed in the direction of the Philippines, and in Hong Kong Americans and Spaniards – including people connected with their respective consulates – kept a wary eye on each other. U.S. consulates from St. Thomas in the Danish Virgin Islands to Veracruz in Mexico, as well as in Kingston, Ontario and Montreal, fed information to the U.S. Secret Service.

For it was the Secret Service that had assumed responsibility, during the Spanish-American War, for U.S. "domestic" surveillance. The Secret Service had thirty years of experience watching for smugglers of forged money. It received assistance from the post office, which intercepted suspicious correspondence, and from interested military personnel and private citizens. With their help, the Secret Service maintained surveillance over Spain and Spain's friends. To U.S. counter-intelligence ways of thought, Montreal and Toronto fell into the "domestic" category.

The Secret Service, headed by businessman/journalist John Elbert Wilkie, reported to the Treasury Department, the body directly concerned with counterfeit money. The Coast Guard also reported to the Treasury. There were legitimate concerns that information from Spanish spies would facilitate naval attacks on American cities and provide information about the United States Army, its capacity and its intentions, to Spanish officers. One New York detective agency warned Wilkie to "be on the lookout for Spanish spies disguised as priests." Mrs. Cora Hemer of Pittsburgh warned President McKinley, who forwarded the message to the Secret Service, about "Spaniards who are passing themselves as French and Italians." R.E. Logan, a military officer at Kansas City, Missouri, advised that Enrique Guerra, Spanish vice-consul in that city until the outbreak of war, had not gone to his reported destination in Mexico for the duration of the conflict, but to Tampa – point of embarkation for Cuba-bound U.S. troops. Some of the Secret Service discoveries were rather important: above all, a letter from a Spaniard in Houston to General Ramón Blanco, Spain's commander in Havana, offering to poison the water supply "and get two or three thousand of these despicable Americans out of the way in one night."

While these were matters of legitimate concern, other Secret Service activities were potentially a source of diplomatic embarrassment. For example, Wilkie received a warning from a post office official in Washington to keep one Mrs. George B. Bacon of Montreal under close surveillance, and the Secret Service intercepted Spanish consular mail from Jamaica and the Bahamas – yet there is no evidence that anyone approached the neutral governments concerned in order to request permission for these activities.

Canada as a whole proved attractive to the Spaniards for a variety of reasons. First, Canada offered direct cable service to Europe. Most cables south of the United States led to that country, the inviolability of whose cable system Luis Polo y Bernabé, the Spanish minister in the United States at the outbreak of hostilities, reportedly did not trust. Forced to leave Washington, Polo and his colleagues took an express train to Buffalo and crossed the border at Niagara Falls. Toronto's *Mail and Empire* reported that as soon as he found himself on Canadian soil, Count Polo "received and sent a large number of cable and telegraphic messages." One of Polo's concerns while in Ontario was the safety of Spanish subjects working in the cigar industry at Tampa, Florida. From Toronto, Polo advised Pío Guillón, the minister of state or foreign minister, that it was possible to communicate with Spanish authorities in Cuba through the Spanish consulate in Kingston, Jamaica: arrangements had been made for schooners to run from the north coast of Jamaica to Santiago de Cuba.

Also helpful was the fact that Canada appeared to have only minimal counter-intelligence to monitor the Spaniards and their activities, so that interference from the host government seemed unlikely. Until crises arising out of World War I forced a reassessment of the arrangement, Canada did not control its own foreign relations but left such matters to the United Kingdom. The British Empire was to speak with one voice, and if the United Kingdom went to war, all parts of the empire found themselves automatically at war against the common enemy. If the government at Westminster proclaimed neutrality, as Lord Salisbury's government did in 1898, the entire empire would be neutral. Foreign embassies and legations were across the Atlantic in London, and Canada had neither a diplomatic corps of its own nor a body to watch the diplomats, officials, and spies of others.

Foreign governments that wanted to send a message to the Canadian government in Ottawa were supposed to contact the Foreign Office in London, which then relayed the contents to the Colonial Office, which in turn told the Governor General in Ottawa, de jure an appointee of the Crown but de facto an appointee of the British government. Foreign countries, did, however, have consular posts on Canadian soil, and they could report to their respective embassies in London or directly to their own foreign offices. Spain had opened consular posts in Quebec City in 1865, Halifax in 1867, and Montreal in 1870, where officials could assist merchants with Spanish goods or sailors in distress. The presence of these posts meant that there was an infrastructure into which Polo and members of the legation staff could blend.

Montreal offered particular advantages. By 1898 Spain had a consulate-general in that city, led by Consul-General Eusebio Bonilla Martel. Toronto, by contrast, had only a Spanish vice-consulate headed by an Anglo-Canadian, and the staff from the Washington legation would have been highly conspicuous beside him. Moreover, Montreal was the hub of Canada's rail transportation network. Trains to New York, Halifax, and the Pacific coast radiated from what was then Canada's largest and most strategically located city. Also, from Montreal observers could monitor the movement of ships between the Great Lakes and the Atlantic Ocean, and in that city Spanish officials could make contact with decision-makers at several Canadian head offices. If Canada was the country from which to operate, Montreal had to be the centre of any Canadian operations.

On 6 May the legation staff – including First Secretary Juan Dubosc and Naval Attaché Ramón Carranza – took a train to Montreal. Once there, the legation staff occupied rooms 126 and 128 at the Windsor Hotel on Dominion Square, and proceeded to work in conjunction with Bonilla's consulate-general. From Montreal, Polo sent an agent to Washington to uncover what he could about a possible U.S. invasion of Cuba. On 20 May, his last full day in Montreal, Polo assigned specific intelligence (*vigilancia*) duties to members of his staff and provided a monthly budget for that purpose. Polo evidently made no attempt to establish direct contact with any of Spain's other Canadian consuls. Similarly, he avoided contact with both Canadian and British Columbian authorities. Consul-General Bonilla, however, was in touch with Angel Cabrejo in Victoria, as well as with Joaquín Torroja, the Spanish consul in Halifax.

On 21 May, Polo left Montreal for Spain (to throw journalists off the track). The same day, Bonilla received an additional £2,000 for intelligence and telegrams. Two days later, he and Dubosc began to send cable after cable to the Spanish minister of state. Their ciphered cables reported on the movements of U.S. warships in the Pacific and in the Caribbean, on U.S. troop movements, and on U.S. war plans. For example, on 26 May Bonilla reported rumours that the United States would not attack Havana before destroying the Spanish fleet. As early as 4 June, Dubosc was able to identify Puerto Rico as a target for invasion. Not a single cable bore Carranza's name, although he recruited spies who funnelled data to him. Aware of their high profile, the transplants from Washington hired spies whose background was not Spanish and whose surnames ended in consonants. One was George Downing, a former officer of the United States Navy. The name J. Henry Balfour appeared on a letter mailed to Carranza from Wyncote, Pennsylvania, which the Secret Service managed to intercept. Anxious for people with military experience to join the United States Army at Tampa and at San Francisco, Carranza managed to find Frank Arthur Mellor of Kingston, Ontario, who in turn recruited others. Carranza also hired Englishmen, presumably because they would not be as obvious as Spanish spies. These individuals enjoyed varying degrees of success.

The Secret Service was well aware of what Dubosc and Carranza were doing. While Carranza talked to Downing at the Windsor Hotel, a Secret Service agent in the next room listened and took notes. Downing was arrested in Washington and was found dead in his jail cell a few days later. The Secret Service intercepted a letter from a Spanish official in Madrid to Dubosc while Dubosc was still in Toronto. On 28 May one W.A. Wallace of Denver, Colorado, informed George D. Meikeljohn, the assistant secretary of war, that he had overheard a conversation in which Dubosc's name was mentioned. Secret Service files include even a 21 May newspaper report under a Montreal dateline saying that, although Polo was leaving for Spain, Dubosc was remaining to "direct Spain's spy system in America."

On 6 June Canada's major newspapers carried banner headlines about these activities. Americans had entered the house at 42 Tupper Street into which Dubosc and Carranza had moved, stolen a letter which Carranza had written to a cousin in Spain but had not yet mailed, and passed it along to their superiors in Washington. The letter purportedly contained a description of Carranza's espionage activities, details of U.S. naval dispositions, and a recommendation that the time was now ripe for the Cadiz squadron to bombard Boston, Portland, and Long Island. Washington officials translated Carranza's letter into English and released it to the newspapers, according to Carranza embellishing its contents in the process. Sir Julian Pauncefote, British Ambassador in Washington, saw what he thought was the original letter in the company of an embassy official well versed in Spanish, and he guaranteed the authenticity of the translation. Whether the published letter was a translation of the authentic original, however, remains in some doubt.

Repercussions of this exposé rebounded in Madrid, London, Washington, and Ottawa, but Dubosc, the anchorman at the communications desk, stalled for time. He hired a Montreal lawyer, H.C. St. Pierre, to argue his case with Canadian authorities. At a press conference on 9 June, Dubosc denied any wrongdoing at all. It was perfectly all right, he said, to provide "Spain with news and general information … published openly here in the newspapers." Of course, given the nature of Carranza's activities, Dubosc was not being entirely honest. Nevertheless, Dubosc threatened that any deportations of Spaniards arising from the incident would seriously damage British neutrality.

Despite Dubosc's warning, the Canadian government of Sir Wilfrid Laurier ordered both him and Carranza to leave Canada, but Dubosc remained in Montreal until 9 July. In the month that remained to him, he continued to inundate Madrid with cables. On 8 June, for example, he reported the American army's logistical problems in Tampa (the rallying point for troops prior to departure for Cuba) where soldiers were suffering heat prostration and mules were dying. The next day, while notifying Madrid of the plans of Admiral William T. Sampson and the "deplorable" state of the U.S. army, he said he was certain that the Canadian government "would expel us." "We are surrounded by American spies," commented Dubosc before returning to the subject of ship movements. Over the next month, Dubosc and Bonilla sent dozens of cables about U.S. ship and troop movements, the state of the U.S. army, and U.S. war plans.

By 21 June Dubosc had also established contacts within Montreal's business community to find ships that would take food and other necessities to Spanish forces in Cuba and Puerto Rico. The very day of his departure,

Dubosc was still active, advising Madrid about attempts to send food from Halifax to Spanish soldiers in Cuba and Puerto Rico, announcing the annexation of Hawaii by the United States and speculating about the Philippines. Furthermore, he made sure that Spanish clandestine operations would continue after his departure. They became the responsibility of the consul-general at Montreal and of the consuls at Halifax and Quebec City. The Spanish officials in these last two cities who would be assisting Bonilla were, as already noted, men of experience.

One can argue, of course, that the American agents who entered the Tupper Street household and stole the Carranza letter were more deserving of expulsion than the Spanish officials, who had broken no Canadian law. However, British policy at the time was to cultivate good relations with the United States, and the Laurier government was not inclined to rock the boat. Thus, despite Spanish protests, Colonial Secretary Joseph Chamberlain had instructed Laurier to expel Carranza and Dubosc, and it would have been contrary to both British policy and Laurier's own sentiments to prosecute any Americans. In British eyes, Dubosc "was using Canadian territory for the purpose of operations of a belligerent nature against the United States government." Rejecting the charge, Spanish authorities continued to protest the expulsions long after the war had ended.

Spanish operations in Montreal could, nevertheless, continue because, unlike Carranza and Dubosc, Consul-General Bonilla had a legitimate reason for being in Canada. Thanks to a "patriotic" employee of the Western Union Telegraph Company, the U.S. Secret Service managed to intercept ciphered telegrams that Bonilla had sent to Spain's agents in Vancouver and Victoria, Frank Mellor and Angel Cabrejo respectively. In the absence of the key, the telegrams were not useful to the American interceptors, who discussed Bonilla's role among themselves but decided not to raise the matter with the Canadian government. So Bonilla continued, without impediment, to cable Madrid about U.S. war plans and ship movements, and with news from the war zone as reported by American newspapers and other sources.

Within the confines of the possibilities open to it, the Spanish government made use of the intelligence it received from Montreal. Despite the fact that Canada still lacked the legal right to deal directly with foreign countries, Bonilla took it upon himself to protest to Ottawa about the permission that Canadian authorities had given the American cruiser, the *Gresham*, to sail out of Lake Ontario, through Canadian waters on the St. Lawrence River, towards the Atlantic Ocean. Spain's new minister of state, the Duke of Almodovar del Río, approved Bonilla's initiative, and instructed Spain's ambassador in London, the Count of Rascón, to do what he could to stop the *Gresham* from reaching international waters. Rascón protested that the *Gresham*'s passage would constitute "a clear violation of [Canadian] neutrality."

Alerted by the British consulate in Chicago that the *Gresham* and three sister ships were setting sail, Lord Salisbury had time to prepare for a confrontation with Spain. Salisbury told Spanish authorities that, before the outbreak of war, the government of Canada had promised the *Gresham's* commander that she would be allowed to set sail. Although the war had subsequently started, Canadian authorities believed that they should keep their promise. When Rascón persisted, Salisbury assured him that he had telegraphed Montreal but "had not yet received a categorical reply." Rascón finally had to settle for a request that Salisbury insist that the Canadian government act "in strict compliance with neutrality." Despite the outcome, the time and energy that the Duke of Almodovar del Río and the Count of Rascón gave to the *Gresham* affair provide impressive testimony to the effects of consular intelligence reports and initiatives.

Throughout the spring and summer, Bonilla continued to receive sums of money from Madrid with which to pay for *vigilancias*. The Spanish Foreign Office stated that the moneys were coming "to improve the situation of this Consulate General in the present circumstances" on the advice of the Spanish Minister in Washington (Polo), who, of course, was no longer there. Bonilla sent news of ship movements as well as of matters of public record, such as the contents of the Governor General's Speech from the Throne at the end of the 1898 parliamentary session. (In that speech, Lord Aberdeen – the Governor General – expressed his hearty approval at the improvement in relations between Canada and the United States.) In Polo's absence, Bonilla supervised Spain's consular employees across Canada, in Bermuda, and throughout the West Indies. In addition, he continued with normal consular duties, such as the repatriation of Spanish prisoners of war, and looked after the requirements of Spanish subjects throughout North America, with Austrian help where necessary. Once the fighting stopped, moreover, Bonilla fed Madrid rumours of U.S. plans for the peace talks.

On balance, it appears that the departures of Polo, Carranza, and Dubosc added stress to Bonilla's life, but that he managed to cover the gaps rather well. The same cannot be said of Dubosc and Carranza. Energetic, patriotic and competent, they nevertheless had to cope with too many American counter-spies in Montreal. The advantages of Montreal's accessibility to the United States, which were partially responsible for attracting the Spaniards to that city, could also work in the Americans' favour, and given the proximity of the United States to Montreal and the bias of the British and Canadian governments, the Spaniards could not win, no matter how accurate the information they managed to retrieve.

Yet, although it made sense to know what the enemy was doing and thinking, all the intelligence in the world could not have helped Spain to defeat the United States in 1898. Spain's was a lost cause, and its leaders knew it. Indeed, one can argue that the Spanish-American War, bloody and unpleasant for those who participated, was also a charade whose roots lay in the Spanish political situation. Spain's Liberal Prime Minister, Praxedes Sagasta, had assumed office on 4 October 1897 after the assassination of his Conservative predecessor, Antonio Cánovas del Castillo. For a generation the two men had headed coalitions that took turns being in and out of government. One of Sagasta's first steps upon regaining office in 1897 was the dismissal of General Valeriano Weyler y Nicolau, Captain-General of Cuba. As Captain-General, Weyler had directed the war against the Cuban insurgents, and his determined measures had proved grist for the mill of anti-Spanish propagandists inside the United States.

Spaniards who wanted Spain to keep its empire regarded Weyler as a hero, and on his return to the Spanish peninsula they gave him a hero's welcome. Sagasta's grant of autonomy (internal self-government) to Cuba and Puerto Rico early in 1898 reinforced the Prime Minister's soft image in the eyes of Weyler and his supporters, and Weyler was not reluctant to make speeches. Given the chauvinistic mood Weyler helped to engender, Sagasta had little choice but to fight the United States. Defeat at the hands of the North American giant after a gallant fight would be more honourable than Spanish withdrawal without an international war. Such "honour" might well allow the Sagasta government and the fragile monarchy to survive; Spanish withdrawal from Cuba without a war against the United States would probably be fatal to the Sagasta government and the dynasty. And Spaniards did fight gallantly — on land, at sea, and in the intelligence war. Lose they did, but the dynasty survived.

To a certain extent, it is true that Madrid contributed to its own defeat. For example, it was in vain that Admiral Patricio Montojo y Pasarón pleaded with his home government for equipment necessary to the defence of the Philippines. Segismundo Bermejo, the minister of the marine, told him to compensate for lack of weaponry with additional enthusiasm, but enthusiasm alone was no match for the U.S. fleet of Admiral George Dewey. Admiral Cervera, too, found fault with high officialdom — he was appalled at the lack of planning on Bermejo's part before he had to set sail for the Caribbean on a voyage that he considered utterly quixotic.

More seriously, though, geography, natural resources and people were on the side of the United States. For the Americans, Cuba was close to home, and their ships arrived in the battle zone ready for action. For the Spaniards, Cuba was a distant place, and their ships arrived in need of refurbishing. Coal — the fuel used by both navies — was readily available to the Americans but not to the Spaniards. The engines of two of Cervera's ships, the *Maria Teresa* and the *Cristobal Colón*, were in such need of fine tuning that they burned excessive quantities of coal — 900 tons of it between Cadiz and the Cape Verde Islands alone. In the Cape Verdes it proved to be impossible to buy more than 700 tons, for the prescient United States consul there had bought most of the available coal himself. Informed by Bermejo that there were quantities of coal on the Dutch West Indian island of Curaçao, Cervera headed there but managed to get only 400 tons. With his ships undermaintained and underfuelled, Cervera's ability to manoeuvre was limited, so he took shelter in the harbour of Santiago de Cuba. When a British vessel attempted to deliver coal to his fleet at that port, the U.S. navy captured her. Even had mobility not been a problem, the Spanish admiral would have found most Cuban harbours in the hands of insurgents and friendly to the Americans. Without effective naval power, Spain could not be a viable adversary of the United States.

Conclusions

Prime Minister Laurier was probably wise to expel Dubosc and Carranza, although it was quite partial of him to do so while the American burglars remained at large. Whatever the merits (or otherwise) of Spanish goals in the Spanish-American War − and the desirability of continued Spanish rule in Cuba was, at best, arguable − Spain could not win. There was no advantage to Canada in an association with the loser, especially when the adversary was the adjacent and powerful United States.

Probably because the war was militarily one-sided, decided by two quick U.S. naval victories off the Philippines and Cuba, neither Canada nor Spain absorbed serious lessons about intelligence gathering. Canada's knowledge of the art was to remain rudimentary for a long time. Decades later, the Canadian government still had to depend upon British and American sources to screen foreign diplomats or refugees entering Canada. In 1942, the Spanish government of Generalissimo Francisco Franco nominated Fernando de Kobbe Chinchilla as that country's consul to Vancouver. Before the Canadian government accepted him as persona grata, it asked the British and American governments whether to do so. Only after he had been at his post for several months did Ottawa discover that he might be a Japanese spy. When Soviet cipher clerk Igor Gouzenko defected from his legation in September 1945 with extensive documentation on an international spy ring, the Canadian government did not know what to do and had to seek advice from the British and Americans. As refugee claimants left Europe for Canada on the eve of World War II, Canadian authorities depended on the FBI and British security agencies to distinguish between genuine refugees and Communist, Nazi, and Fascist infiltrators. Because of this continuing Canadian dependence at the end of World War II, British and American intelligence agencies were able to debrief Nazi agents and then "approve" them as immigrants fit for residence in Canada. Nevertheless, economy has overridden need, and Canada has continued to let others gather most of its foreign intelligence.

2
Agent X and
the Boer War, 1900*

U ntil the 1931 Statute of Westminster, Canada was at war whenever
Great Britain was at war, and Great Britain's enemies instantly
became Canada's enemies. Even before Confederation, Irish-
American Fenians launched violent attacks against British North America,
and a force led by the Scottish-born Gilbert McMicken tried and failed to
cope with them. Irish hostility toward all things British, including the
Dominion of Canada, continued through the nineteenth century and in
1900 threatened Esquimalt and Victoria. This chapter will describe the threat
and the countermeasures to deal with that threat.

The Context

It was a Fenian bombing campaign of 1883 to 1885 in London that persuaded British authorities to increase spending on secret agents. Because Ireland
was part of the United Kingdom, the Home Office (not the Foreign Office)
financed secret agents inside the United States to monitor the activities of Irish-
Americans. Canada's rudimentary secret service, the Dominion Police, also
owed its origins in some measure to Irish-Americans. In 1868, when a Fenian
assassinated Thomas D'Arcy McGee, a Father of Confederation and a cabinet
minister, Prime Minister Sir John A. Macdonald took action. He asked
McMicken, like himself an immigrant from Scotland, to organize the
Dominion Police. Its immediate tasks were to monitor and infiltrate the Fenian
movement and to protect cabinet ministers, but, as time passed, it became
responsible for security on Parliament Hill and for most federal services east of
Lake Superior. In 1885 an Ottawa policeman, Colonel Arthur Percy Sherwood,
became head of the Dominion Police, a post he held for a generation.

The Dominion Police did not act alone. In 1873, the North-West
Mounted Police (NWMP) began to patrol the Prairies, and continued to do so
until they merged with the Dominion Police in 1920 to form the Royal
Canadian Mounted Police (RCMP). The NWMP also assumed responsibility for
law and order in the Yukon during the gold rush of 1898 and its aftermath.

---

* This chapter was co-authored by Michael D. Stevenson, who helped to research and write
it when he was a graduate student at Laurentian University.

In British Columbia, except in communities large enough to have their own police forces to handle local problems, the British Columbia Provincial Police enforced the law.

These forces did not send their police outside Canada, despite precedents for such action. Before Confederation, McMicken had led a secret service of some twenty to twenty-five men who entered Buffalo and Detroit. This happened during the American Civil War, after Confederates (Southerners) attacked St. Albans, Vermont from Lower Canada (now the province of Quebec). Such incidents had the potential to provoke hostilities between the United States (the North) and the British Empire, sovereign authority in Lower Canada. In that case Great Britain would have entered the war on the side of the Confederacy (the South). As such an eventuality was in the interest of neither Great Britain nor the United States, the mayors of Buffalo and Detroit did not object when McMicken's men searched for Confederates – and then Fenians – on their territory. The Civil War ended in 1865, and when McMicken headed the new secret service, the Dominion Police, in 1868, there was no such justification for sending officers onto American soil. On the contrary, the various Canadian police forces usually obtained whatever information they needed from American sources through the Pinkerton National Detective Agency.

Allan Pinkerton had moved to Chicago from Scotland in 1842 at the age of twenty-three. Eight years later Pinkerton founded his detective agency. Initially it spied on labour activists, and then it watched Confederates for the United States government (the North) during the Civil War. From the late nineteenth century, and well into the twentieth, the Pinkerton National Detective Agency worked in partnership with the Dominion Police, the British Columbia Provincial Police, and British consular officials across the United States. When the Dominion Police needed information from the other side of the border, Sherwood did not send one of his own men, but used Pinkerton.

Controversial as Great Britain's war in southern Africa proved, in Canada and in Britain, the government of Prime Minister Sir Wilfrid Laurier allowed the recruitment of some 7,000 young men to serve in Britain's forces. The war between the British Empire – including Canada – on the one hand, and the Orange Free State and the Transvaal, on the other, also affected the United States. Secretary of State John Hay and other influential people strongly favoured the British war effort. To them Great Britain was a benevolent, civilizing, and stabilizing force. In part because of their influence, the United States actually became the protector of British interests in the Orange Free State and the Transvaal during hostilities. Other Americans just as strongly disagreed. To them Great Britain – the enemy of 1776 and 1812 – was a greedy bully, a predator after the lands and wealth of Boers who had gone out of their way to be alone. Americans of Dutch, German, and Irish extraction were the most vocal admirers of the Boer republics. The Dutch at New York, distant relatives of the Boers, were descendants of colonists whom the English had conquered in 1664. Germany was beginning a naval armaments race against the United Kingdom, and the Irish resented centuries of British rule in their homeland. These three ethnic groups could exert considerable political pressure.

The war also represented opportunity to many Americans. It was an occasion for making weapons and selling them to belligerents. Armies needed food and beasts of burden, which American entrepreneurs could provide. The Spanish-American War of 1898 had come and gone with such rapidity that some individuals had experienced less military action than they had wanted or anticipated. For them, the war in southern Africa offered an exciting alternative to civilian life, and for some it mattered little on which side they fought. Given the values of the era, few in the United States – or Canada for that matter – thought of the war in terms of what would be best for the Black peoples of southern Africa.

Terrorism and Counter-Intelligence on the West Coast

From the standpoint of Canadian-American relations during the Boer War, the prospect of Irish-American terrorists attacking targets located in Canada was of primary importance. To some Irish-Americans, the people of the Boer republics appeared as potential allies. The greater the British military commitment against the Transvaal and the Orange Free State, the greater the chance that Ireland could free herself from Great Britain. Besides, many Irish thought that the Boers, as enemies of the hated British, deserved sympathy and humanitarian assistance. The Fenian spirit remained alive and well in both Ireland and America. The words of Irish-American Edward J. Bourke summarize a common attitude:

> The disasters to the British forces in South Africa should be a source of congratulation the world over, for has not that robber nation [Great Britain] been the curse of another people [the Irish] who, for seven hundred years, have been fighting their battles, to achieve the same ends that the Boers are now waging such unrelenting warfare against the pick-up of the British Army to obtain?
>
> Yes, the injury of England is of great moment to the Irish-born man, driven as he has been from the home of his kith and kin, and seeking an asylum here.

The men associated with Great Britain's consular network in the United States realized that Irish-American animosity posed a threat to British interests, and they monitored Irish-American activities closely. They followed newspaper reports of meetings, they hired detectives to follow particularly suspicious individuals, and they heeded information passed to them by friends of Great Britain, usually British expatriates who had moved to the United States. Others in the United States shared that awareness. Late in December 1899 the *Boston Herald* warned its Irish-American readers in an editorial entitled "It cannot be repeated" that most Americans would find a revival of Fenian attacks quite intolerable: "The Canadians are our friends; they are bound to us by ties of relationship, from the fact that hundreds of thousands of Canadian birth are living in the United States ... Besides this, we have trade connections that are ... of immense value." Attacks on Canada, said the *Boston Herald*, would harden American opinion and push the United States from its position of neutrality in the Boer–British war into closer partnership with Great Britain.

Like the editorial writer of the *Boston Herald*, British officialdom in the United States was not prepared to wait passively until trouble appeared. People in the consulates realized that Irish-Americans were listening to heady speeches by individuals such as Maud Gonne, "the Irish Joan of Arc." Famed for her beauty, Maud Gonne was a lover of the Irish nationalist playwright and poet William Butler Yeats. Later she married John MacBride, whose Anglophobia was so intense that he had volunteered for the Boer cause in order to have the pleasure of fighting the British. He lost his life in the Easter Rebellion of 1916, but Maud continued the fight, even after most of Ireland achieved Dominion status in 1922. Aware of fanatics like Maud Gonne, Sir Percy Anderson – British consul-general in New York – asked Pinkerton to act. Pinkerton was to monitor arms shipments to the Boers and recruitment to the Boer armies, investigate an alleged plot by Irish-American employees of a Chicago meat-packing plant to poison a shipment purchased by the British army, and watch the Irish-American community.

From the perspective of the 1990s, Canadian efforts to monitor Irish-American activities appear haphazard, to say the least. Arthur Percy Sherwood, head of the Dominion Police, maintained a subscription to the *New York Herald*, and depended upon casual contacts. Over the holiday season of 1899–1900, a long-lost friend in Chicago, one Peter Daly, wrote to Sherwood to offer information on Irish-American activities. When Sherwood returned to the office on 5 January after an absence of some days, he accepted Daly's offer and promised remuneration from a special fund that he had at his disposal. Nevertheless, Sherwood confided to Pinkerton, he had "some doubts as to his [Daly's] credibility."

One Irish-American scheme to attack Canada involved an attack on the British naval base at Esquimalt, certainly a plausible target. Alerted early in

January 1900 by Great Britain's vice-consul in Seattle, James Laidlaw — the British consul at Portland, Oregon — informed Lord Pauncefote, British ambassador in Washington, of a Spanish-American War veteran at Seattle by the name of Magee. A private on the battlefields of the Philippines, in Seattle Magee answered to "Captain." In that city close to Victoria and Esquimalt, where residents had raised funds to assist the Boers, Magee reportedly was "organizing a military company."

Laidlaw took the matter seriously enough to ask vice-consul Pelly in Seattle and others to maintain close surveillance. Laidlaw also cooperated with Clayton Pickersgill, British consul-general in San Francisco, who had superior resources for investigation. Pickersgill engaged the consulate-general's law firm, Cormac & Donohoe & Baum, which in turn employed an amateur detective identified only as Agent X. So mysterious was X that even Pickersgill did not learn for months that X was a woman.

In May 1900, F.S. Hussey, superintendent of the British Columbia Provincial Police, went to San Francisco on a fact-finding mission, became ill, and stayed there longer than he had intended. It is thanks largely to him that even the most meagre details about X are available. From hospital he wrote to his superior officer, "Special Agent X is a woman employed by Mr. Cormack. Mr. Pickersgill has only recently ascertained this fact. I shall call her before I leave this city." Cormac & Donohoe & Baum had written to Pickersgill carefully hiding X's gender:

We have employed "X" at the rate of $120.00 per month, that is to say, $4.00 a day. This appeared to us to be the most satisfactory arrangement as we required X to be constantly on the qui vive both day and night. In addition we paid X any extraordinary expenses incurred, such as travelling expenses outside San Francisco, and on one or two occasions we have authorized X to entertain Mr. and Mrs. Cnopius, Mrs. Dreffield, Mr. Van Baggan, etc., at luncheon and at theatre when we were informed by X that these social meetings would doubtless be productive of less guarded conversation, and hence we might obtain information of importance. We would add that X's opinion on this subject has been justified by the result. Our arrangement with X runs from month to month ... The Pinkerton people we have employed merely as and when required.

Much as Hussey admired X's efforts, he considered her "more or less a novice in detective work," totally dependent on instructions from the law firm. Pickersgill, thought Hussey, should have hired a professional detective agency, and while Hussey recuperated in a San Francisco hospital, the province of British Columbia did just that. The attorney general's office engaged the Pinkerton agency, which directed its observations of Irish-Americans who might attack targets inside Canada from its office at Portland, Oregon. This happened, however, *after* months of effort on the part of X, on whose credibility and credentials Pinkerton was to pass judgment.

In order to protect X from potentially dangerous terrorists, Cormac & Donohoe & Baum opened a post office box under an assumed name, where X could deposit her reports. With a willingness to take considerable risks in return for expenses plus $120 per month, X was able to win the confidence of potentially violent people and not arouse suspicion. She even became secretary of certain Irish secret societies. One person whom she befriended was a recent arrival from the Transvaal named L.K.P. Van Baggan. During his first year in San Francisco, Van Baggan had organized a chapter of Wilhelmina, a Dutch society, for which he worked full time. Wilhelmina members had raised more than $1,000, supposedly "for Red Cross purposes and hospital funds for the Boers," but they did not hurry to forward the money. The local Irish society, the Celtic Union, approached Wilhelmina with another suggestion: the money could be better spent "blowing up 'the works at Esquimalt.'" Van Baggan said that "there were plenty [of] volunteers who would be glad to go to make the attempt at Esquimalt." However, procedural differences intervened. "The Celtic Union wished a Transvaal man to do the work," said Van Baggan, "and the W.S. [Wilhelmina Society] were not organized for that sort of thing although they would be glad to see it accomplished."

While the Celtic Union and the Wilhelmina Society dithered, another mysterious San Franciscan, known only as JFM, wrote to Pickersgill with an offer to sell "the most valuable information that will save millions of dollars." Cormac & Donohoe & Baum sent an agent to meet JFM and "a detective to shadow him when he left the place of meeting." JFM explained that he was "inside of the pro-Boer movement and knew all about it." Friends of the Boers, he continued, had raised more than $1,100, but the money's Dutch and Irish trustees disagreed about its use. Some thought it should support "legitimate Red Cross purposes," but others wanted to finance "some overt act of violence, for example, the destruction of Government buildings in Canada." Although JFM said that he was revealing this information in order to save lives and property, Cormac & Donohoe & Baum suspected that his motive was revenge on associates whom he did not like. Later, on the basis of information supplied by Pinkerton, Cormac & Donohoe & Baum concluded that JFM was a Clann-na-Gael member named David Starr Jordan. At the time, the Clann-na-Gael was the most active Irish-American terrorist organization in the United States.

Little by little, JFM told his interrogator that a Dutchman named Van Der Line (or Van der Lyn or Van der Lie; JFM did not know for certain) and an Irish-American, Francis Scanlan, had left San Francisco the previous Sunday,

4 February 1900, for Seattle. From there they would cross to Victoria and arrange the destruction of "the Government buildings there," presumably meaning the recently opened and highly impressive provincial legislature. JFM gave physical descriptions of Netherlands-born Van Der Line, whose first name he did not know, and of the New York–born Francis Scanlan, both of whom he described as "dangerous." Both, said JFM, were "very generously provided with funds," a point confirmed by X, who said that they had the backing of the Celtic Union in Chicago, which had a bank account of $100,000. Moreover, said JFM, Van der Line and Scanlan had contact persons along their route and carried with them "all the appliances necessary for their purposes." In Seattle they would stay with a saloonkeeper named Gill, who had presided at a recent pro-Boer rally. Then, after "four or five days," they would proceed to Victoria, where they would arrange for "other parties" to set off the actual blast or blasts. Van der Line and Scanlan planned to be back in Seattle before the explosions, and from Seattle they would go to Chicago, an Irish-American stronghold. JFM promised to attend further meetings and to keep the consulate-general informed. Pickersgill immediately forwarded the information to the most senior naval officer at Esquimalt. The British embassy alerted the State Department to the potential danger, but an investigation by American authorities proved utterly fruitless. Superintendent Hussey was later to report, "I don't take much stock in the reports of JFM."

For their part, British Columbia authorities wasted no time. On 9 February 1900, the very day that Pickersgill contacted Esquimalt, Hussey took decisive action. He ordered his police in Victoria onto full alert, arranged cooperation with Victoria's municipal police force, ordered "close examination of passengers coming to Victoria by boat and otherwise," and, in partnership with the attorney general of British Columbia, engaged the Thiel Detective Agency to help. Thiel's Pacific coast superintendent, a man named Barnes, left at once for Seattle to be joined by "two of his best operatives," people stationed in Portland. The three hoped to locate and shadow the terrorists. Hussey also recommended that "two reliable and trustworthy watchmen" stand guard outside government offices in Victoria.

Meanwhile X continued to entertain her unsuspecting sources at restaurants and at a theatre, and to attend their meetings. On 15 February she reported that the Wilhelmina Society had given its funds to Dr. W.J. Leyds, a Transvaal agent in Brussels, and then dissolved itself. All Wilhemina Society members plus "many Irish" then formed the Transvaal Society, which began with a bank balance of some $3,000. Van Baggan would serve as corresponding secretary, L.C. Cnopius as vice-president, and one of the first decisions was "to send an ambulance corps to South Africa ... under the command of Van Baggan." Present at Transvaal Society gatherings was David Starr

Jordan, whom Cnopius thought "to be an agent of the Irish Societies to watch the Transvaal Society." A week later X reported that one of her sources had said that "the man of whom I made a report [presumably Van Baggan] had gone 'where there would be snow,' and," observed X, "he has not gone east."

Days later police arrested two suspicious men at the Esquimalt dockyard. JFM told Cormac & Donohoe & Baum that, according to his secret society contacts, the two were working for Van der Line and Scanlan. He also informed the firm that Scanlan had taken up residence in a "hamlet" one mile from Seattle, while Van der Line was fundraising in Spokane. By this time JFM was desperately frightened of being seen by the wrong people; he announced that he would sign any future correspondence with the code "100," less traceable than his initials. He confirmed that both men had been to British Columbia but had returned to the United States. Pickersgill relayed all this news to the superintendent of the British Columbia Provincial Police.

On 4 March, X reported additional hard news, along with some ominous threats. One man named Flannigan was an active Knight of the Red Branch who, apparently, immersed himself in causes like the Transvaal, leaving his wife alone with their eight small children. When X appeared on her doorstep, Mrs. Flannigan was so grateful for adult company that she talked and talked. Under the impression that X was either apolitical or shared her husband's politics, Mrs. Flannigan said that Van Baggan and Cnopius felt quite certain that they were under observation. They also suspected so strongly that Pickersgill was involved that Mrs. Flannigan had "heard more than one threat against him." Because of the consul-general's warnings, they were certain, British authorities had doubled the guard at Esquimalt and foiled the sabotage plan. Cnopius thought that the guards had arrested "the right men sent by the Hibernians." Unless those two men could be released in time to launch another attack within the next two weeks, continued X, another Knight of the Red Branch – a veteran of the Royal Navy who might or might not have worked at Esquimalt – would "make the attempt." If he were to fail, Pickersgill's life would be in serious danger and the Irish would try something else. What that would be X did not know; she was not certain whether the Irish themselves had decided. Funds were pouring into the Transvaal Society, reported X, $500 the previous week alone.

The next day X wrote another report about the anger against Pickersgill and warned him to be very careful. On 13 March she noted that the two men arrested in Victoria had been released, and that they then had "returned to San Francisco having learned a good amount which will be of use to the three who have been chosen to take their places." One of the three claimed to have a relative on Vancouver Island who would assist them. JFM had also heard of the second plot, and again Pickersgill forwarded the information to a grateful F.S. Hussey, superintendent of the Provincial Police in Victoria.

Throughout March 1900 the British Columbia Provincial Police and the senior naval officer in Esquimalt remained in constant contact with the British consulate-general in San Francisco which, in turn, passed messages back and forth. On 28 March, X reported that she had interviewed a fanatically anti-British Irish-American named Donovan the previous day. Donovan had spent four weeks in Esquimalt with every intention of "carrying the campaign into Canada." He told X that his father was an Irish Fenian whom the British had executed. After the execution, British authorities had confiscated the family's property. Nothing, thought Donovan, was "quite bad enough for anything English." Unable to remain in Ireland, he had moved to Syracuse, New York, and become an engineer.

Unfortunately, Donovan remains a thoroughly mysterious individual. He confided in X, but only up to a point. Even she did not know who he was. The most thorough description of him comes from Wellesley Moore, acting consul-general in San Francisco, whose source was X:

> Donovan is known to be a most dangerous character but it has been found impossible to ascertain anything about him. He does not keep his appointments, generally arriving at some unexpected time, and is extremely cautious having noticed that the house where "X" lives was being watched, thus frustrating all efforts to trace his movements.

It was Irish-Americans from Chicago, not San Francisco, who planned and financed the attack on Esquimalt, Donovan told X. In Portland, Oregon, Donovan and a man from Utica, New York, received instructions from a Chicago Irishman, then sailed for Esquimalt on what turned out to be a fruitless mission. Donovan blamed lack of time for this, saying that he needed two additional days. As it was, he managed to befriend naval employees at Esquimalt who, on one occasion, actually admitted him to the yard. "Then the guard was doubled and no stranger [was] allowed to even get in [sic] sight of the place." Fearing discovery, their sponsors ordered them to return to Portland. Donovan's colleague, but not Donovan, thereupon returned to New York state.

Donovan had other fascinating news. Currently, he told X, there were three Irish-American agents in Esquimalt, one an ex-employee at the dockyards who hoped shortly to get his job back. The second and third men had cover stories to justify their presence near the base; one was supposed to be a capitalist interested in mineral-rich land owned by the other.

Like so many others, Donovan made many threats against Pickersgill. He "has been watching the Consul-General," wrote X, and he was "a fanatic ... ready to throw away his life or anyone else's if he can accomplish anything."

He had no family, but lavish amounts of money supplied by the Chicago Irish. As far as he knew, the two men arrested to date were innocent.

Over the next few months, X managed to maintain Donovan's trust so well that on the afternoon of 20 June, Donovan appeared on the doorstep of X's suburban home near San Francisco with a beautiful woman. She had "large wide-open lustrous brown eyes," was "shapely" and had "naturally curly ... long red hair." X estimated her age at between twenty-five and thirty. She spoke with an Irish accent, and her clothes indicated that she was not American. She had very little luggage.

Donovan told X very little: "This lady is a friend. She will stay here all night. She has been on a long journey. You will ask her no questions, nor will she ask you any." He then gave X five dollars to cover her expenses and left. The next day, a few hours after the woman's departure, Donovan reappeared to enquire whether she had gone. When she had the opportunity, X studied photographs of Maud Gonne to determine whether she had unwittingly played host to Ireland's famous female liberator. She had not. The visit, bizarre in many ways, seems no more than Irish punctilio. To bachelor Donovan, it seemed inappropriate that a woman should stay with him.

The Threat to Ontario

Meanwhile, frustrated in Esquimalt and Victoria, the terrorists turned east. On 21 April 1900 three of them tried to dynamite a lock on the Welland Canal, a critical transportation artery that bypassed Niagara Falls and allowed ships to travel between Lake Erie and Lake Ontario. According to Toronto's *Globe* of 23 April, two men – later identified as John Nolan of Philadelphia and John Walsh of Washington, D.C. – stepped off the 6:20 p.m. train at Thorold, Ontario, each carrying a small briefcase. Nobody thought anything unusual as they "walked a short distance up the railway track and then made for the canal bank, which they followed until they arrived at lock twenty-four." Nolan and Walsh disappeared behind a building where they prepared the fuses. One of them headed for the upper gate, one for the lower. The *Globe* continued:

> Nothing was thought of their action at the time. The man at the lower gate quickly tied the valise to a rope, and setting fire to the fuse, lowered it down about eight or ten feet against the side of the lock gate. He then walked quickly away, passing his companion on the way to the road, and calling to him to hurry up and drop it, which his companion did. At this time the first explosion occurred smashing the iron work of the gate to pieces and blowing a hole in the woodwork.

Two or three minutes later, the second charge exploded, doing similar damage to the upper gate.

Fortunately for the canal and the surrounding area, the gates held. The body of water between locks twenty-four and twenty-five, according to the *Globe,* was almost a mile in length and could have caused extensive damage. As it was, the explosions broke windows throughout the area, and people in both St. Catharines and Port Dalhousie claimed to have heard the blasts. Nolan and Walsh ran away, but they did not remain free for long. Witnesses in Thorold provided a description, and police throughout the area went on alert. Within hours, some officers hid themselves while Nolan and Walsh approached, then jumped and overpowered them. Each terrorist had a loaded revolver in his pocket at the time. Because Nolan and Walsh had been in the area of the Welland Canal for a week, long enough to arouse suspicion and attract police attention, the police knew that they had a companion. When they located him, he claimed to be a German named Karl Dullman. Dullman, however, turned out to be Luke Dillon, an Irish émigré.

Sherwood worked with Pinkerton to find the evidence necessary for a conviction and with another New York detective, R.J. Bryan, to determine the real identity of Karl Dullman. A court convicted the three and on 25 May sent them to Kingston Penitentiary. On 4 July Sherwood sent a confidential warning to the warden at Kingston that, according to the British consul in Chicago, their friends might blow up the penitentiary so that they could escape. After his release in 1916, Dillon worked for the Irish Republican Army until his death in 1929.

Back in San Francisco, Donovan had returned, and X warned that Esquimalt was still not out of danger. X described Donovan as "a very dangerous man, a fanatic ... ready to attempt anything ordered by the head of the society in Chicago." Donovan's own trip to Chicago had been a relatively harmless affair, only to report on developments (or lack of them) with regard to Vancouver Island. From Chicago he had gone to Seattle, where one of three conspirators gave an optimistic progress report on the plot to blast Esquimalt. British naval authorities there, thought the conspirator, were relaxing and becoming complacent, and the plotters knew exactly where to place their dynamite for maximum impact. Donovan was certain that the Chicago group behind the Esquimalt conspiracies was also responsible for the attack on the Welland Canal. Aware too that Pinkerton's detectives were keeping him under surveillance, Donovan carried a gun for his own protection.

The Return of Agent X

Incredibly, the British embassy in Washington did not care to spend funds on intelligence, and Pickersgill had some difficulties in persuading Pauncefote to pick up the tab. There was no money to pay X, and the consulate-general in San Francisco had to forego her services. For over seven weeks, from 27 April to 19 June, she filed no reports. During that interval

Pickersgill, the target of Irish-American threats, became ill and died, and X on her own initiative surfaced with two items of devastating news.

First, Donovan had told X that he and men under his command had poisoned Pickersgill. Without relaying that particular rumour, Cormac & Donohoe & Baum then spoke to Pickersgill's doctor. The doctor attributed Pickersgill's illness entirely to typhoid fever and emphatically denied that there was any reason "to believe that any poison or other deleterious drug or substance had at any time been administered to him with criminal intent." For their part, Cormac & Donohoe & Baum concluded that Donovan had lied to X. "It was doubtless the idle boast of a depraved man," they wrote.

Also, on the afternoon of 19 June Donovan told X of plans to dynamite the Lachine Canal at Montreal and the Sault Ste. Marie Canal on the Canadian side of the St. Mary's River, which links Lake Superior with Lake Huron. Lachine would be first, he said, and three men had already gone to Montreal to do the job. The men slated for Sault Ste. Marie had already been chosen. Donovan claimed personally to be "making charts of the different canals and locks on the Great Lakes."

The Dominion Police took these threats seriously. On 11 July 1900, Sherwood defended his force's expanded estimates in a letter to a government auditor. He explained that he needed $26,000 to hire men to guard Canada's most strategic canals: twenty-one at Welland, five at Sault Ste. Marie, sixteen at Lachine and four at Soulanges (both near Montreal), and sixteen at Cornwall. He also needed $5,000, he said, "to be exempted from ordinary audit and publication." When the auditor questioned the $5,000, Sherwood answered sarcastically that it was a matter of "common sense."

> We cannot expect information from the right sources unless in position to assure persons possessing it that their connection can never be known. If further outrages are intended ... we must not be hindered from coping with the miscreants for want of a little money, and latitude in the manner of spending it. These precautions were taken years ago by Sir John A. Macdonald when I first entered the service, only the amount then was considerably larger.

Terrorist plots against Canadian targets appear to have stopped about the middle of 1900, presumably because British intelligence was adequate and authorities north of the border really were on guard. On 14 July 1900 Cormac & Donohoe & Baum told Wellesley Moore, the acting consul-general in San Francisco during Pickersgill's illness and after his death, that Donovan had "no suspicion whatever of Agent X." On the contrary, he constantly pressured X also to join a secret terrorist society dedicated to the liberation of Ireland. X resisted the invitation, and with good reason. Such groups were invariably more vindictive to traitors whom they discovered within their ranks than to outsiders. In the light of X's relationship with Donovan, it is probable that if there were anything further to report, X would have done so. After 1990, X disappears from the records.

Conclusions

Certain members of the Irish-American community, as the Welland Canal explosions indicate, did pose a threat to the safety of Canadians and Canadian property during the Boer War. Given the recent history of Anglo-Irish relations, this was understandable and hardly surprising. However, as the rumours surrounding the death of Clayton Pickersgill indicate, there was also talk without action. There appears to have been action at Esquimalt, and without intelligence and counteraction, the consequences would probably have been more serious than they were. Whether there were real threats against Kingston Penitentiary and canals near Montreal and Sault Ste. Marie is not clear, but Canadian authorities were wise, especially after Welland, to take precautions.

Canada's intelligence gathering beyond its borders remained rudimentary, dependent on British consular officials who had many other concerns, and on a private foreign detective agency, Pinkerton. It was understandable that the government of a sheltered country, remote from the world's trouble spots, would not feel a need to spend heavily on intelligence gathering until there was convincing evidence of danger. Even if all the rumours had proven reliable and all alleged Irish-American schemes had come to fruition, they would have been costly in terms of lives and property but no threat to the survival of Canada itself. In modern military jargon, the damage and loss of life would have been "tolerable." Also, it was understandable that neither the British nor the American government would invest very much in the security of Canadians, Canadian property, and other targets inside Canada. When informed, the governments of British Columbia and of Canada did respond with appropriate concern. The government of British Columbia hired professional detective agencies, rather than the more economical Agent X, and the Dominion Police acted with relative vigour, at least *after* the explosions on the Welland Canal.

Yet, given the vulnerability of Canadians along the border and the fact that any loss of life would have been heart-rending, the Canadian and British Columbian governments did demonstrate a degree of nonchalance during the early months of the Boer War. They were fortunate to have friends who would provide *any* information, and they came to realize that the security of people and property on their territory was their own responsibility. That so much information came at so little cost to Canadians was fortunate, but not something on which subsequent generations, or even the current one, could continue to rely.

3
Terrorist Threats and Conspiracies during World War I*

Aprominent Canadian historian recently – and correctly – asserted that, with exceptions, the Canadian state had almost no security and intelligence capacity in (or before) 1914. Nevertheless, there were exceptions. This chapter reviews the exceptions and demonstrates the amateurish performance of those charged with responsibility for Canadian intelligence during World War I. It does, however, give higher marks to the Dominion Police than to other British and Canadian intelligence officials.

From the Boer War to World War I
It was 1903, and Franz Bopp, consul-general of Imperial Germany at Montreal, was concerned. Rumours were circulating about an anarchist plot against Franz Joseph II, the elderly emperor of the Austro-Hungarian Empire. Bopp had good reasons for taking the threat seriously, and he sought the cooperation of Canadian authorities. Anarchists had killed the French president in 1894, the Spanish prime minister in 1897, Empress Elizabeth of Austria in 1898, King Humbert of Italy in 1900, and President McKinley in 1901. The intended assassin was supposed to be an Italian named Virgilio Fava, who had left Buffalo for Montreal one week earlier. His host in Montreal would be somebody named Qintavalli. Fava's reason for travelling to Vienna via Montreal was also plausible. After an anarchist had assassinated President McKinley in 1901, the United States Secret Service had kept U.S. ports under tight surveillance, and anarchists expected fewer obstacles if they sailed from a Canadian city. The Dominion Police came to Bopp's assistance.

In order to locate Qintavalli and Fava, Sherwood engaged Silas H. Carpenter, a Montreal detective. Sherwood and Carpenter also cooperated with members of Montreal's Italian community, as well as with Bopp. Bopp became impatient with the lack of progress, but Sherwood explained that a leader of Montreal's Italian community had said that "most of their people change their name when moving from one place to another." He also assured Bopp that Canadian intelligence work was moving faster than it would have fifteen years earlier. When Bopp lamented the time needed for

*The author is grateful to Paul Derro and Earl Reid, graduate students at Laurentian University, for assistance with the research for this chapter.

letters to travel between Montreal and Ottawa, Sherwood said that in an emergency, officials would call each other on the telephone. Sherwood also authorized Bopp to deal directly with Carpenter, although he asked Carpenter to keep him informed of such dealings. The trail of paper disappears at this point, leaving one to assume that nobody ever found Qintavalli and Fava.

Another better-known event of 1903, the Alaska boundary dispute between Canada and the United States, appears to have had little impact upon the Dominion Police and Canadian intelligence. The influx of gold miners to the Yukon from 1898 had made settlement of the border a matter of considerable importance. The Canadian and American governments disagreed as to where it should fall, and the United States secretary of war, Elihu Root, actually sent troops to Alaska to enforce American claims. Evidently nobody seriously expected war, and the Dominion Police were not looking to see where the United States Army might be gathering. This was hardly surprising. In December 1895, when war between the British Empire and the United States had seemed a somewhat greater possibility, the Dominion Police had taken no action. At that time, the administration of President Grover Cleveland had been backing Venezuela in a boundary dispute with British Guiana, and the Anglo-American tension had continued until all parties agreed to submit the dispute to arbitration.

On Britain's part, British intelligence failures during the Boer War led to reforms that British analyst Christopher Andrew terms "modest." Until 1907, the chief targets of British intelligence lay in South Africa, France, and Russia. Few considered dangers from Germany or the United States. The Entente Cordiale of 1904 between Great Britain and France produced a change in attitude, and gradually the energies previously directed against France turned against Germany. Andrew dates the founding of the Secret Service Bureau (later the SIS and MI6) from October 1909, but says that until the outbreak of World War I, its foreign section served the Admiralty ahead of the Foreign Office. What limited resources were available focused on Germany, not on North American targets. The Home Office, however, maintained agents in North America to monitor Irish-American activities.

Along with Irish-Americans, British concern began to focus on Sikhs. In 1907, a new period of Sikh unrest began in India, and as Sikhs had been migrating to British Columbia since 1905, it seemed wise to maintain some sort of surveillance. The Sikh population in British Columbia peaked at some 4,000 around 1907; because of people who returned to India and others who emigrated to the United States, the population fell to roughly 2,000 by 1914. Most were men, initially driven to Canada by poverty and overpopulation in the Punjab. Their hope was to earn money to support their families still in India. As the years passed, the hostility they encountered in British

Columbia radicalized most of them. Moreover, authorities in both Great Britain and India knew that Irish-Americans were willing to make common cause with the Sikhs in a united effort against the British Empire. Indeed, some Sikhs were holding talks with the Clann-na-Gael.

In 1905, Home Office agents had instructions to report to the India Office as well as the Home Office if they found anything of interest. In 1910, the Indian government sent an agent of its own to the United States and Canada, but withdrew him in 1911. However, because Sikhs were more numerous on the Pacific coast than elsewhere in North America, and because the Pacific coast lay thousands of kilometres from Washington and Ottawa, intelligence operations there assumed a life of their own.

Both Canada's Governor General, Earl Grey, and Prime Minister Sir Wilfrid Laurier came to see Sikhs as a threat to the British Empire. Lobbying them was an individual named William Hopkinson. Son of a British soldier and an Indian mother, Hopkinson had been born in Delhi in 1880. Anxious to deny his Asian roots, he endeavoured to be more British than the British. He had served with the Indian police in the Punjab and Calcutta, rising to the level of sub-inspector. Hopkinson spoke Punjabi and other Indian languages fluently. In 1908 he had arrived in Vancouver, and in short order he had persuaded a correspondent from The Times of London to write a story about Sikh nationalists on the Pacific coast. The article, published 22 May 1908, said that Sikhs in Vancouver and Seattle were raising funds and circulating information about how to build bombs, all in order to support rebels in India. William Lyon Mackenzie King, then deputy minister of labour, was preparing a royal commission report on Asian migration, and he interviewed Hopkinson that spring. His report included the information provided by Hopkinson. On a trip to Ottawa, Hopkinson met Earl Grey and Laurier, then found employment as an immigration officer in Vancouver. Earl Grey found Hopkinson highly credible and sought to utilize his services.

Later an officer of the Dominion Police, Hopkinson established ties with the British consulate-general in San Francisco, as well as American police forces and immigration offices. For a while in 1913–14, Hopkinson received supplemental income from India's department of criminal intelligence. In the course of his investigations, Hopkinson spent time in the United States, from San Francisco to New York. One of the results was the arrest in the United States of Har Dayal, a charismatic Sikh activist; Hopkinson had persuaded the appropriate Americans that Dayal constituted a security risk. There Hopkinson also managed, among other achievements, to delay for years U.S. citizenship for another Sikh, Taraknath Das, the editor of a Vancouver-based newspaper that relocated in Seattle in an effort to escape Hopkinson's harassment. Hopkinson observed that Sikhs who had contacts with Indian revolutionaries had learned how to handle explosives, and he created a network of informers among Sikhs and others to monitor Sikh activities. Unaware that he was receiving money from non-Canadian sources, those Americans who were aware of Hopkinson thought of him as an ally against undesirables rather than an agent of British imperialism.

Visible minorities from any part of Asia were not welcome in pre–World War I British Columbia. Some British Columbians feared the precedent. If a few hundred Asians could migrate, hundreds of millions more might follow. The world was not tolerant in 1914. While no Western country actually killed people for their religious beliefs, few welcomed cultural or religious diversity, let alone differences in skin colour and styles of clothing. On all counts, Sikhs made themselves unpopular. The desire to escape Punjabi poverty was, however, greater than the fear of British Columbian intolerance, and in the spring of 1914, a shipload of Sikhs sailed to Vancouver and forced the issue. Their ship, the Komagata Maru, arrived 23 May 1914, but she never received permission to land or unload, and was held offshore without food or water for two months.

Before the Komagata Maru returned to Asia with all her passengers (two months to the day later), Hopkinson made frequent visits. Aboard ship, he acted as an interpreter and collected intelligence. Not surprisingly given his high profile, Hopkinson had become controversial: Canadian Sikhs began to feel that he knew too much about them. Meanwhile, the fate of the Komagata Maru angered Vancouver's Sikh community. Canadian immigration officers at the United States border south of Vancouver found one returnee from the United States, Mewa Singh, trying to smuggle two revolvers into Canada. Bodies of Sikhs who had collaborated with Hopkinson began to appear. A priest, Bhag Singh, tried to kill Hopkinson's friend Bela Singh with a sword, but Bela Singh shot the priest dead. Bela Singh had to face trial, and Hopkinson was to testify on his behalf – but on his way to the courthouse, he was shot and killed by Mewa Singh. Hopkinson's immediate successor, A.L. Jolliffe, limited his intelligence work to Canada, in part because by the second half of 1914 the British government did not want to antagonize Americans by conducting potentially controversial operations inside the United States.

German Intelligence and Terrorist Activity in Canada

Well before hostilities began, the German consulate-general in Montreal reported to Berlin on political and naval developments inside Canada. In 1912, one official travelled as far as Vancouver Island so that he might write a credible report on the expansion of Esquimalt's naval facilities. The naval attaché in Washington and a German consular official in Sydney, Australia, also provided data on Canada's political and military situation. Similarly, off-shore British officials collected information of interest to Canada. Early in

August 1914, the governor of Newfoundland and the British consul in Saint-Pierre reported the whereabouts of German warships near Canadian waters. St. John's, Newfoundland – not then a part of Canada – became the Royal Navy's intelligence centre for the western North Atlantic.

The German navy made its own observations. The naval attaché in Washington kept the Kaiser up to date on the state of public opinion in the United States, and the navy had contingency plans for war in North American waters. As early as 1907, on orders of the German Admiralty, ships of the German navy visited Canadian waters. First, the *Bremen* explored and reported on the defenses of Halifax and Quebec City. Then in 1912, the *Victoria Louise* visited Halifax, where her captain grasped every opportunity to learn about Canadian naval policy.

Good detective work, vigilance, and luck restricted the damage inflicted by Germans and German-Americans, but British intelligence efforts were not totally successful. It is probably unreasonable to expect that they could have been. Good British work and clumsiness on the part of too many Germans revealed that there were conspiracies involving no less a personality than Franz von Papen. (At the time von Papen was military attaché at the German embassy in Washington; years later, he would be the second-last chancellor of Weimar Germany.) Other conspirators included Arthur von Zimmermann at the Foreign Office in Berlin and Count Johann-Heinrich von Bernstorff, German ambassador to the United States. One recent author has tabulated four efforts at violence (in Montreal, Saint John, Sault Ste. Marie, and Cornwall) in 1914, five in 1915 (one in New Brunswick, two in the Windsor-Walkerville area of Ontario, one in Manitoba, and one in Vancouver). On the other hand, some alleged conspiracies did not exist, and innocent people suffered embarrassment and inconvenience.

Right at the beginning of hostilities, British technicians cut the cable between Germany and the United States. Henceforth, messages had to pass through British territory, and Britons eavesdropped. On 16 January 1915, Berlin instructed von Bernstorff to recruit Irish-Americans for sabotage and destruction. The British knew that. They also knew that for decades before 1914, German immigrants had been moving to the United States by the tens of thousands each year. Nobody could know how many harboured pro-German sympathies.

One suspicious person, Emil Wilhelm Lang, was both a German subject and a draftsman with a phenomenal memory. The neutral United States government became aware of his case in April 1915 when it was representing German interests throughout the British Empire, including Canada. On behalf of the German consulate in Philadelphia, the United States consulate in Sault Ste. Marie, Ontario located Lang in a Canadian prison. Before his arrest, Lang had "made plans of both the Canadian and American Locks, the

International Bridge, other bridges and terminals of the C[anadian] P[acific] Railway, the Algoma Central Railway, and bridges, etc. of the railways on the American side." Canadian officials told the United States consulate that Lang had posted his drawings from New York and sent them to the German government. Iron ore from Minnesota, vital to the steel industry, passed through the locks at Sault Ste. Marie, and a significant explosion would certainly have hurt the Allied war effort and any American preparations for possible military intervention. Lang's arrest followed the dispatch of his drawings, and a terrorist with skills in engineering might well have taken advantage of this security breach.

The Albert Kaltschmidt case demonstrates a clear instance of knowledge about a terrorist that reached Canadian and British sources too late to be useful. On the morning of 21 June 1915, a terrorist bombed Walkerville's Peabody Plant, which had contracts to provide the British Army with almost $1 million worth of uniforms, gloves, and clothing. The same day, good luck saved the Windsor Armories when a time bomb failed to work properly. Had it gone off, said Windsor's *Evening Record*, it would have devastated a number of nearby buildings. Within the week, investigators found twenty sticks of dynamite near a building of the Gramm Motor Truck Company, which had been selling trucks to the British government; forty sticks near a boarding house for Ford workers; and thirty-six sticks outside the Invincible Machine Company, shortly to become a munitions factory. A former watchman at this last site, William Lefler, confessed and then implicated others, including his former boss, Albert Kaltschmidt.

At the outbreak of war, Lefler worked at the Tate Electrical Company, where Kaltschmidt was manager. Businessmen from Toronto then bought it, changed the name, dismissed Kaltschmidt, and launched its transformation into the Invincible Machine Company. Kaltschmidt found a new job with Kresge's in Detroit and moved across the river, dogged by a reputation as a friend of Imperial Germany. Encouraged by the German embassy in Washington and motivated by revenge, German nationalism, or a combination of the two, Kaltschmidt then asked Lefler to take action on his behalf. According to Lefler, Kaltschmidt advanced $25 for planting the explosives and promised $200 more upon the successful completion of his work. For his efforts, Lefler received a ten-year sentence in Kingston Penitentiary, and British officials expended considerable energy in a vain attempt to extradite Kaltschmidt. Count von Bernstorff himself placed $10,000 in Chicago banks to cover Kaltschmidt's expenses in the event that American authorities arrested him.

The Lang and Kaltschmidt cases were, however, only the tip of the iceberg. Even in 1915, British and American authorities began to discover a genuine German conspiracy of sabotage inside the United States, but they did not know that Ambassador von Bernstorff himself was involved.

Gradually they learned that some of his subordinates were. German documents released after World War II reveal that von Papen actually recruited Germans in Chicago, St. Paul, Seattle, and Detroit. Armed and organized, these paramilitaries prepared to attack Canadian targets. German documents also reveal that Kaltschmidt was another of von Papen's recruits.

Following the outbreak of war, von Papen opened a second office in New York, where one Horst von der Goltz visited him. In September 1914, von der Goltz persuaded von Papen to dynamite the Welland Canal. Von der Goltz recruited other New York Germans who were willing to disrupt that important Canadian traffic artery, including Krupp's agent in New York, Captain Hans Tauscher. Factories owned by the Krupp family were the single most important supplier of weapons to the German army. Tauscher managed to convince the Dupont company that he needed dynamite in order to blast tree stumps on his New Jersey farm, and he gave the dynamite to von der Goltz. Von der Goltz and his accomplices, among them Friedrich Busse of New York, caught a train to Buffalo, with the dynamite packed in their suitcases. Secret Service agents who had followed them did not stop them, but security on the Welland Canal was intense, and they did not ignite the dynamite. (The British consul-general in New York, Sir Courtney Bennett, had warned that the Welland Canal was a target for German terrorists, and Canadian authorities had taken steps to protect it.) Later Busse was to testify that von Papen had paid their expenses.

In October 1914, von der Goltz returned temporarily to Germany. On the return trip to the United States, he stopped in England to report on German air raids against that country, and the British arrested him. American authorities in turn extradited him from the United Kingdom, and back in the United States, he sang. Von der Goltz and others went to jail, although Tauscher did not because he supposedly had not known how they planned to use the dynamite.

Late in 1914, after Japan had entered the war on the side of its British ally and seized China's Shantung Peninsula from Germany, the German government feared that Japan might send forces via the Pacific Ocean and Canada to Europe. On 12 December 1914, the German Foreign Office instructed von Bernstorff to disrupt Canada's railways so that this could not happen. On 3 January 1915, Arthur Zimmermann, still an undersecretary at the Foreign Office on Berlin's Wilhelmstrasse, told von Bernstorff that the German General Staff wanted the embassy "to destroy the Canadian Pacific in several places for the purpose of causing a lengthy interruption of traffic." The Foreign Office suggested that Bernstorff recruit Irish terrorists, as they would have readier access than Germans to Canada. The embassy, however, launched its first attack against a border point – the CPR bridge across the St. Croix River at Vanceboro, Maine. This, of course, *was* accessible to Germans.

The Wilhelmstrasse telegrams ordered von Bernstorff to give von Papen the necessary funds to disrupt the CPR.

To this end, von Papen summoned Werner von Horn, a German reserve officer, from Guatemala. Von Papen wrote von Horn a cheque for $700, drawn on the Riggs National Bank in Washington, D.C. In return, von Horn was to blow up the bridge at Vanceboro. As the St. Lawrence River was frozen at the time, Saint John, New Brunswick, was a vital Canadian port, and the CPR provided the shortest link between Saint John and Montreal. The British embassy in Washington warned the Governor General in Ottawa, but the warning arrived too late to be useful. Fortunately, von Horn's bomb, placed at the New Brunswick end of the bridge, did little damage, and when authorities in Maine arrested him, von Horn said that "an Irishman" whom he did not know had met him near the scene of the action and handed him the explosives.

Canadian authorities demanded von Horn's extradition. Von Bernstorff, frantic lest von Horn reveal the role of the embassy in the attack, sought and received Zimmermann's permission to fight extradition on the grounds that von Horn had committed an act of war, not a crime. This proved successful. Von Horn admitted guilt and went quietly to penitentiary in Atlanta. Not until von Papen carelessly allowed British officers to capture his chequebook with the stub for von Horn's cheque did the Allies have hard evidence of the embassy's involvement. After the U.S. entered the war, Canadian efforts at extradition proved successful; convicted in Fredericton, von Horn served time at Dorchester Penitentiary in New Brunswick.

Paul Koenig, another of von Papen's agents, had an alcoholic relative, George Fuchs, who lived in Niagara Falls, New York. Eager to attempt yet another attack on the Welland Canal, in September 1915 Koenig recruited Fuchs for $18 per week to monitor canal traffic and find possible weak spots in the security system. Then Fuchs moved to New York and quarrelled with the fastidious and sober Koenig over a bill worth less than three dollars. Questioned by New York police, Fuchs proved garrulous and spoke of Koenig. Police invaded Koenig's room and discovered that the obsessive-compulsive Koenig had maintained voluminous records of his own and related activities. The documentary evidence thus provided helped to convict Werner von Horn and persuaded the Wilson administration to declare von Papen persona non grata.

There might well have been other attacks. Reinhard R. Doerries, a German historian, says that Ambassador von Bernstorff successfully opposed a planned attack against British Columbia by German reservists in the state of Washington. Von Papen, Doerries continues, "began to organize groups of fifty to one hundred reservists in several cities such as Chicago, St. Paul, Seattle, and Detroit, to be used as shock troops against Canada." Bad weather foiled a bridge bombing near Megantic, Quebec, and yet another attack against the CPR — between Andover and Perth — failed.

Von Papen then sailed for Europe via Falmouth in England; because of his diplomatic status, the British government had agreed to let him pass through England on his way to a neutral country, from which he would travel to Germany. The safe-conduct guarantee, however, did not extend to his luggage, which British officers examined with interest. Among their finds were the chequebooks with evidence of payments to von der Goltz for his attack on the Welland Canal and to von Horn for his effort at the Vanceboro bridge. In April 1916, American authorities arrested von Papen's deputy and successor, Wolf von Igel, for his role in von der Goltz's Welland Canal plans.

Sikh Challenges

Throughout that period of World War I when the British Empire was at war and the United States was neutral (1914–17), British and Canadian intelligence agencies cooperated against Sikhs living in North America, Irish-Americans, and agents of Imperial Germany. Against the Sikhs they scored considerable success. The Sikhs, a challenge to British authority in India, might, they feared, help the Germans. Irish terrorists, who hated the British and worked with Germans, were another threat, but they appear to have attempted amazingly few attacks on Canadian targets.

Before his unceremonious departure from the United States, von Papen also tried to recruit Sikhs as German agents. On 27 December 1914, another cable from Zimmermann to von Bernstorff told the ambassador to provide financial assistance to Sikh revolutionaries at the University of California's Berkeley campus, where Har Dayal was a teacher. In the nick of time to avoid deportation from the United States, Dayal went to Berlin. In 1915, von Papen tried to recruit Indians living in Vancouver to dynamite CPR bridges and tunnels in British Columbia, but he failed.

Unknown to Canadian authorities, the German consulate-general in San Francisco had established ties with Taraknath Das, another Sikh whom Hopkinson had suspected. The Canadians did not realize that by mid-1915 Germans were providing Sikh residents of North America with money to provoke a revolt in India. From 1916 to 1918, Britain's India Office engaged an agent, Robert Nathan, to monitor the Sikhs. A civil servant, Nathan had lived in India for twenty-six years. In Vancouver he worked for the British Intelligence Agency, MI5 (Military Intelligence 5) and had access to information on Sikhs that the British consulate-general in San Francisco had been collecting since Hopkinson's trip there in 1911. For reasons of political expediency, Nathan kept a much lower profile than Hopkinson had inside the United States, although he did assist American authorities in finding evidence against Sikhs. The idea of a British agent on American soil might have been politically sensitive in 1916. From Vancouver Nathan communicated with London through the office of the governor general. By 1916, telegraph offices in Vancouver were sending copies of every telegram received or sent by an Indian to British authorities in London, and this practice continued until December 1919, when wartime censorship laws expired.

Nathan cooperated with Malcolm R.J. Reid of the immigration department in Vancouver. Among Reid's sources were reports from Andrew Carnegie Ross, British consul-general in San Francisco, and Indian newspapers confiscated by the Canadian post office. Some of Hopkinson's sources continued to appear in person at the immigration office in Vancouver, and Reid travelled the entire length of the Pacific coast, from the Canadian border to the Mexican one. In 1918, the North-West Mounted Police (by then the Royal North-West Mounted Police) assumed the security responsibilities of the Dominion Police in the Canadian West, but the Mounted Police did not want to employ Reid. Surveillance of the Sikhs diminished as, once again, the threat appeared to be on the wane.

Meanwhile, however, two Sikhs — Balwant Singh (who had been a priest in the Sikh temple in Vancouver) and Harnam Singh (owner of a grocery store in Victoria) had died on the gallows in British India after returning there and facing prosecution by the government. Balwant Singh had been found guilty of "waging war," and Harnam Singh had a track record of working with bombs and other explosives. Significant evidence against them came from people who had reported to Hopkinson and Reid on their activities in Canada and the United States. After April 1917, the work of Hopkinson, Nathan and Reid led to convictions of Sikhs, including Taraknath Das, inside the United States. One of the most Anglophobic Sikhs, Har Dayal, was safe in Germany, but Franz Bopp, the German consul-general at San Francisco (the same individual who had once sought help from Canadian authorities in Montreal against anarchist terrorists), faced considerable embarrassment because of his encouragement of Sikh nationalists.

Canadian and British Counter-Measures

With the outbreak of war in 1914, the Dominion Police assumed responsibility for the protection of Canada against terrorists. Once again it engaged the Pinkerton National Detective Agency to do its groundwork inside the United States. It was important, thought Sherwood and Colonel (later Major-General) Willoughby Gwatkin, chief of the army's general staff, that Canadians should not waste too much time and energy on matters of home defence when there was a war to be won in Europe. At the same time, Canadians ought to be prepared for real dangers.

There was some cause for concern. According to the census of 1910, residents of the United States born in Ireland numbered 4,504,360. Some of these were Orange Protestant Irish, but there were other Americans not included in that figure who had a parent or grandparent from Ireland and who shared the Green prejudices and values. German archival materials captured after the defeat of Nazi Germany revealed the extent of Irish-American collaboration with Germans in the early years of the twentieth century. One Irish-American organization with a military wing, the Ancient Order of Hibernians, had had a pact with the German-American National Alliance since 1907, and it, in turn, kept in touch with the German embassy in Washington. The Clann-na-Gael, founded in 1867, survived the Boer War and remained active. The principal grievance – British occupation of Ireland – remained a reality, and in 1916 the Irish Republican Brotherhood took advantage of Great Britain's prolonged difficulties and launched the Easter Rebellion of 1916.

British and Canadian authorities were concerned about possible terrorist attacks that might be launched against Canadian or British targets from bases in the United States. German-Americans had obvious reasons to take action, and Anglo-Irish relations were steadily deteriorating. As the Easter Rebellion erupted, they became particularly tense. As in the Boer War, British consular officials across the United States monitored Irish-Americans very closely. Volumes of Foreign Office correspondence are replete with reports of Irish-American rallies, Irish-American opinion, and attempts on the part of Irish-Americans to influence American opinion. British officials monitored the newspapers closely, but they also received mail from concerned private citizens who did not like what the Irish-Americans appeared to be doing.

To some extent, the British relied on their own resources for Irish-American control, but, as they were operating in the United States – a friendly foreign country whose British policy under Woodrow Wilson was one of benevolent neutrality – they also cooperated with Americans, at least after Robert Lansing replaced Bryan as Secretary of State in 1915. In May 1917 one Daniel Callaghan informed F.P. Leay, British consul-general in Boston, of "a scheme for the destruction of British vessels in port at Boston, etc." Leay in turn reported the matter to Cecil Arthur Spring Rice, British ambassador in the United States, and Spring Rice told Leay to notify the local police about any such threats.

However, British authorities did more than depend on the local police. For some years the Home Office maintained an agent named Armstrong in New York. Armstrong was to observe the Clann-na-Gael, and since success – not to mention his personal survival – depended on absolute secrecy, not even the Foreign Office or the British embassy in Washington was supposed to know about him. Indeed, so secretive was his work that the present author could find nothing about him in the records of the Home Office.

After the 1916 Easter Rebellion, Armstrong's effectiveness declined. On 10 June 1916 an editorial in the *Gaelic-American*, the Clann-na-Gael newspaper published in New York, denounced Armstrong as an "agent provocateur." "There is plenty of material for a very sensational exposé," it said.

> There are hundreds of this scoundrel's letters which he fondly hoped had been destroyed, and unimpeachable documentary evidence to prove that the Brit. Govt. is responsible for him – that he is its agent."

Lord Hardinge, undersecretary at the Foreign Office, explained to Spring Rice that sensitive papers had indeed fallen into the hands of the Clann-na-Gael. While those papers did not actually lead Clann-na-Gael members to find and kill Armstrong, they revealed enough to make the Clann-na-Gael very cautious and more difficult to monitor.

The next round of excitement followed the execution of Sir Roger Casement, a leading member of the Irish Republican Brotherhood. Sir Roger was an Ulster Protestant, not a Roman Catholic, whom the Crown had knighted for services rendered at British consular posts in Africa and South America. Nevertheless, he became a staunch Irish nationalist and, after the outbreak of war, he travelled to Germany. He wanted to persuade Irish prisoners of war in German camps to defect from the British Army and fight alongside the Central Powers' armies. On the eve of the Easter Rebellion, he returned to Ireland in a German submarine with warnings that German military assistance to the forthcoming rebellion would be inadequate and that the rebellion should not proceed as scheduled. British authorities captured him, convicted him of treason, and executed him. Americans had lobbied extensively to save the lives of Casement and other nationalists, and when they failed, the British embassy reported a state of high tension throughout the United States. That British actions in Ireland would have repercussions in North America was evident from a report filed by Spring Rice:

> Naval attaché states extreme Irish organization is much strengthened and embittered and has received unexpected additions from moderates. Murphy of N[ew] Y[ork] has joined. This means violent action in congress and elsewhere, pressure on the governments, and crimes here and in Canada.

However, in retrospect Canadian officials did exaggerate dangers from across the U.S. border. Most of the roughly 8,500 aliens whom Canadian authorities interned without a hearing were not spies, saboteurs, or terrorists. The Dominion Police penetrated German-American and Irish-American groups and found little evidence of plots against Canadian targets. Many former residents of the German and Austro-Hungarian empires who lived in the United States had left Europe to escape that continent's storms, not to carry them across the Atlantic. The politically active could return to their homelands and enlist there. Too many imaginations did run wild on the flimsiest evidence. Nevertheless, German officials were involved in conspiracies, American authorities were indifferent, and there were actual terrorist attacks. Without vigilance, there might well have been others.

Concerns of the U.S. State Department

Channels of communication between Washington and Ottawa were circuitous, for Canadian and American cabinet ministers did not communicate directly with each other at that particular stage of Canada's constitutional development. The U.S. secretary of state would express his problem to the British embassy in Washington, and the embassy would forward the matter, usually to the Governor General but occasionally to the prime minister. The Canadian cabinet, in turn, would ask the Governor General to express its feelings to the British embassy in Washington which would then forward them to the State Department.

As long as William Jennings Bryan was secretary of state (to mid-1915), the United States government was somewhat nonchalant about such matters and reluctant to cooperate. British consular officials did not display formidable talent in matters of intelligence gathering, and while those British officials concerned themselves with unsubstantiated rumours, friends of Germany slipped across the border and did their work.

Bryan's primary concern was maintenance of United States neutrality. To that end, Bryan corresponded at length about armed Canadian soldiers who he alleged made repeated visits, wearing their uniforms, to the streets of Detroit. He even threatened to intern such individuals. When the Canadian government of Prime Minister Sir Robert Borden requested specific information about these soldiers, Bryan replied: "It is presumed that the Canadian army officers in the neighboring part of Canada know where their men have crossed into United States territory." Ottawa said that it would do its best to prevent any recurrences, but suggested that the entire controversy might have arisen from a misunderstanding. Either residents of Detroit who had joined the Canadian army had decided to desert and go home in full uniform, or the complainants could not distinguish between Canadian and American uniforms.

Despite the Vanceboro explosion, Bryan was so determined to preserve all appearances of his country's neutrality that he rejected a request to place guards at the American ends of international bridges. He refused on somewhat dubious constitutional grounds, given that an international bridge is by definition partly in a second country. The American end of an international bridge, he explained, was inside a state, and under the constitution, each state was responsible for law and order within its boundaries. Only if a state could not cope with a particular situation and called upon the federal government for assistance could Washington become involved. That scenario, thought Bryan, was unlikely as long as the United States remained neutral. (In all fairness to Bryan, he was unaware at the time of von Papen's role in the Vanceboro bridge bombing.)

Even when Robert Lansing succeeded Bryan, terrorism was not always the priority that it might have been. Despite the war, the secretary of state, the State Department, the British embassy in Washington and appropriate Canadian officials could find time and energy for the case of George M. Ball, a United States citizen convicted of murder in Swift Current, Saskatchewan on 15 October 1915 and sentenced to death. Because of an appeal from Secretary Lansing, Canadian authorities first postponed Ball's execution by a month (to 7 February 1916) and then commuted his sentence to life imprisonment. Correspondence on his case fills almost forty pages of diplomatic files. In normal times Ball's case might have been an admirable example of compassion at the State Department, but in 1915–16 it diverted considerable energy from issues such as terrorism that seemed more important to many Canadians.

British and Canadian Mistakes

Even after von Papen returned to Germany, Canadian concern over German-sponsored terrorism and espionage continued. Canadian authorities interned one Kurt Thaden of Calgary as a security risk, and Mrs. Thaden made frequent visits to the United States consulate in Calgary to request assistance. The United States consul in that city, Samuel C. Reat, wrote to the German consul in Chicago about Mrs. Thaden, but a communication of November 1915 went by mistake to Horace Nugent, the British consul-general in Chicago. Nugent forwarded its contents to his superiors at the British embassy in Washington, who in turn told the Governor General, the Duke of Connaught and Strathearn. The Canadian government then ordered an investigation by the Royal North-West Mounted Police (RNWMP). The RNWMP selected Commander Fitzpatrick Joseph Horrigan of its "E" Division for the task, although, on an earlier occasion, Consul Reat had found Horrigan such a nuisance that he had lodged a formal complaint against him. After the report had been made, the Governor General wrote

> You will notice on page 2 of [Horrigan's] report that Mr. Reat has been transferred to India. This would seem to be worthy of more than passing interest as experience gained of him in Calgary was such as to give the impression that he was pro-German, rather than neutral, and his opportunity for making mischief in India would probably be greater than it was in Calgary.

There is nothing in either British or American documentation to warrant such distrust of Reat; American documentation makes it clear that the Governor General's opinion was little more than the product of a tense era. For five years before his appointment to Calgary, Reat had been U.S. consul in Japanese-occupied Taiwan, until health problems had forced him to move to a cooler, drier environment. Thinking himself fully recovered after a year in Calgary, Reat applied for a transfer back to Asia, on which he considered himself an expert. When he left for Rangoon late in 1915, prominent American and Canadian residents of Calgary, including the mayor and members of Parliament, praised him for services rendered. Unfortunately for Reat, Rangoon and even Guatemala City proved more than his constitution could tolerate, and in 1918, he returned to Calgary as consul. If there had been serious grounds for suspicion that Reat had been partial toward Imperial Germany, it is unlikely that Canadian authorities would have found him persona grata.

Indeed, Reat's correspondence indicates total surprise when in Rangoon he learned that he had been accused of having "pronounced pro-German tendencies." The reasons for this he could only guess at, and he made a wrong guess. Shortly before his departure from Calgary, he remembered, he had made "adverse reports regarding the Detention camps at Lethbridge and Banff." Moreover, as consul in Calgary, Reat had realized the importance of both impartiality and the appearance of impartiality. On one occasion, Reat had reprimanded his subordinate in Lethbridge, consular agent George S. Montgomery, for not maintaining the appearance of strict neutrality. Montgomery had allowed one German to use his office as a mail depot: the man's mail would arrive at the U.S. consular agency, and Montgomery would deliver it to him unopened. Only after one batch included "a German newspaper from New York which had been prohibited by the Government of Canada from circulation," did Montgomery refuse to accept any further mail on behalf of Germans. "It seems as though we did enough without their taking advantage of us and making it risky for us to do them a favor," he wrote to Reat. Reat replied like a stern parent to an errant child. "It would be necessary," he warned, "for you to exercise every precaution in allowing German citizens to use your office as a medium for correspondence. I would not permit it at all."

Reat's correspondence in connection with the Thaden case indicates little more than normal human concern for people in distress. At any rate, Canadian authorities rejected Thaden's pleas for release on grounds of health, and American authorities – both at the consulate after Reat's departure and at the State Department in Washington – appeared satisfied with the Canadian action.

Meanwhile, imaginations ran wild, and on the flimsiest of what passed for evidence, British officials involved Canadian and American cabinet ministers and police in endless hours of unnecessary work. The worst offender by far was Sir Courtney Bennett, British consul-general in New York. The fruits of Sir Courtney's vivid imagination, his ability to write, and his total lack of judgment would provide a highly entertaining chapter in themselves. Given the numbers of warnings he passed on, the odds were that once in a while he would be right, and in the case of the Welland Canal, reported above, he was. Unfortunately, Bennett also reported a series of German-American conspiracies centring on Buffalo, where large numbers of well-trained, highly equipped Germans were supposedly gathering for an invasion of Canada. His numbers changed, but by March 1915 they had reached 80,000. A few weeks earlier, Prime Minister Sir Robert Borden had asked the commissioner of the Dominion Police Force, Colonel Sherwood, for a report on these invasion threats. Sherwood turned to one of his intelligence agents in New York, and the agent was brutal. "It is to be regretted," he said, "that we are even forced to investigate such rumours as these, that are to us ridiculous in the extreme." The agent had absolute confidence in his Buffalo sources, two "highly reputable business men ... [who] belong to all the German societies and are in [a] position to be in touch with everything that is doing in Buffalo in German circles." These men denied that there were any new German organizations in Buffalo, any Germans drilling, or any possibility of Germans drilling either in Buffalo or in Niagara Falls, New York.

Sir Courtney was not at all embarrassed by his lack of credibility. He thought that he was right and that everyone else – including the Canadian government – was out of step. Early in 1915 he warned of a Germanophile American judge named Seager at Yonkers, New York, and of dangerous Germans at the Eggers Square Hotel in that community. The Dominion Police investigated, presumably through Pinkerton, and concluded: "[T]here does not appear to be much foundation for the consul-general's apprehensions." When Spring Rice informed Sir Courtney of the police report, the consul-general stormed

I am inclined to believe that the enquiries made by the Canadian Authorities at Yonkers and at Buffalo have been very casual and that either wilfully or through incapacity, the Canadian Government has received information which is not by any means in strict accordance with the facts."

On another occasion, Bennett warned of a dangerous German named Henry Muck. Vague as Bennett's information was, Spring Rice dutifully forwarded it to the State Department, which asked the Attorney General's office for an investigation. On 19 June 1915 Lansing quoted what Bennett had written. Later, however, Lansing had to tell the British embassy that the Attorney General's department found it quite impossible to investigate "a German named Henry Muck [who] has lately been in Boston and is now somewhere in the State of Maine."

British, Canadian, or American officials disproved most of Bennett's conspiracies. Internal evidence condemns others. As the Niagara tourist season began in 1915, Bennett received an anonymous letter which he took seriously. The writer claimed to have taken a cruise through the Niagara gorge and noticed a fellow passenger who, instead of watching the scenery, appeared to be reading the New York Times. When the writer looked more closely, he observed "several columns placed in German type." He spoke to the reader and immediately won his confidence by telling him of his Hungarian birth. There and then, with other passengers presumably within earshot, the reader told the Hungarian expatriate about "tons of explosives secretly transported into Canada and distributed to persons who are members of secret organizations."

However, Bennett was not alone. In January 1915 one S.R. Bradbury told C. White Mortimer, British consul in Los Angeles, of German-Irish plots against Canada. These involved the burning of grain elevators at Fort William and Port Arthur (now Thunder Bay), the placing of time bombs aboard troop ships at Halifax and Saint John, an attack on Manitoba, the destruction of property belonging to the Canadian-owned Grand Trunk Railway at Portland, Maine, plus the destruction of bridges and buildings at Kingston, Montreal, and Quebec City. The State Department launched an investigation and concluded "that Bradbury ... probably invented the story and put it into the form of a letter to the Consul." Spring Rice accepted the State Department's conclusions and forwarded them to the Governor General in Ottawa.

As the war continued, concern increased. Clive Bayley replaced Sir Courtney Bennett in New York, but people were jumping to conclusions more than ever, and innocent people suffered inconvenience or loss of reputation. On 29 January 1917 F.P. Leay, British consul-general in Boston, notified the embassy in Washington that the Countess Dekomiss, who would be taking the train to Montreal, was reportedly a German spy. The embassy contacted the Governor General, by this time the Duke of Devonshire, who told the Prime Minister's Office, who told Joseph Pope (undersecretary of state for external affairs), who ordered a police investigation. The police located one Mildred Dora Kormiss at the Ritz-Carlton Hotel in Montreal, "where she and her effects were searched ... without any incriminating evidence." Mrs. Kormiss was a divorcée, previously married to one David S. Kormiss and before that to Count Gerrard of Paris. She had come to Canada as a visitor to meet an ex-Norwegian named Jenessen, a former resident of Hawkesbury, Ontario who was then living in New York. Despite the lack of evidence, Pope reported, "Both of these people were ordered out of the country and escorted to the boundary last night."

Perhaps even more amazing was the case of a Buffalo man, George W. Krenz. Krenz was a traveller for Campbell's Soups, with customers on both sides of the border. C.W. Brown, assistant general manager of the Chevrolet Motor Company in Flint, Michigan, rented a car driven by one J.W. Collins, who had once been a friend of Krenz's. Collins told Brown that Krenz's work for Campbell's Soups was a cover to let him spy for the German government and gather "information regarding camps, munitions factories, bridges, etc. in Canada with a view to destroying them." Brown repeated what he had heard to an Anglican clergyman named McIntosh at Fort Erie, who in turn told John J. McLaren, a lieutenant-colonel at St. Catharines, Ontario. On the basis of this fifth-hand information, the department of external affairs launched an investigation and wrote a report, which failed to find any wrongdoing on the part of Krenz.

The State Department's Sense of Perspective

American State Department officials responsible for matters relating to Canada appear to have exhibited more restraint than did their British counterparts. They were aware of the links between Irish rebels and the German government. They were aware of an authentic Irish terrorist who lived in the United States, John Devoy. Unlike Consul Reat, Mrs. Kormiss, and George Krenz, John Devoy really was worth watching. It was he who had founded the Clann-na-Gael newspaper, the *Gaelic-American*. He was one of the conduits whereby Clann-na-Gael money and policies travelled to the Irish Republican Brotherhood. He collaborated with Ambassador Bernstorff in efforts to help Sir Roger Casement recruit an Irish brigade. Quite understandably, the U.S. consulate at Cornwall monitored the arrest of Fred Guvrick, who was mistakenly suspected of arson in connection with the burning of the Parliament Buildings in Ottawa. Guvrick was travelling from Ottawa to Tupper Lake, New York, at the time of his arrest, and any error in this affair was a Canadian one, not an American. Equally understandably, the U.S. consulate at Calgary monitored the case of Albert Schopper, an American of German extraction suspected of flight to Canada in order to avoid the draft. The U.S. consulate-general in militarily sensitive Halifax asked the U.S. justice department to investigate two suspicious people who might have been Americans, A.M. Mealy and Dr. C.H. Johnson, but it does not appear to have jumped to any conclusions about them. Mealy and Johnson had no visible means of employment but were "well supplied with funds." When the U.S. consulate in Port of Spain, Trinidad, reported the case of two young men of military age, Harry B. Weber and Erwin W. Weber, who had arrived from Canada without any passports, the War Department quickly cleared them as reliable people. And when the U.S. consulate in Toronto reported hearsay information on a German doctor in Nova Scotia whose home was a possible supply station for German submarines, the State Department simply told the consul, Chester W. Martin, "to communicate this information to the Canadian authorities, if you have not already done so." It would appear that, under the circumstances, the State Department employees exhibited an appropriate degree of caution and vigilance without the paranoia of Sir Courtney Bennett.

Conclusions

On balance, British and Canadian efforts at intelligence gathering during World War I appear to have been only partially successful. Terrorists failed to disrupt the Welland Canal, at least in part because of Canadian and British vigilance. The search through von Papen's luggage and subsequent arrests may well have prevented some violence. Other German plots failed because they were unrealistic or badly organized. On the other hand, British and Canadian intelligence failed to prevent explosions along the Maine–New Brunswick border and in the area around Windsor, Ontario. Authorities dealt with Lang too late to stop his sending secrets to Germany. Colonel Sherwood displayed some sense of perspective, but – as Reat, Mrs. Kormiss and George Krenz discovered – too many imaginations ran wild and caused inconvenience, even embarrassment, to innocent citizens. Perhaps it is not surprising. One does not expect to find people – even American, Canadian, or British citizens – at their best in time of war.

4

American Surveillance of
Canadian Communists, 1921–33

"Soviets secretly paid Canada's Communists $2 million"

Long before the *Toronto Star* splashed that banner headline of 14 March 1992 across its front page, Canadians were well aware of Soviet interest in Canada. That the KGB should have sent such a sum of money between 1978 and 1989 was no new phenomenon. Long before Soviet cipher clerk Igor Gouzenko defected in 1945 and revived anti-Soviet feeling, Soviet authorities had been providing Canadian Communists with advice, money, and moral support. To many Communists, including Canadian ones, loyalty to the Soviet Union took priority over loyalty to their own supposedly reactionary countries.

The RCMP has long been vigilant with regard to Canadian Communists. Indeed, major reasons for the reorganization of the Royal North-West Mounted Police and the Dominion Police into the RCMP included fear of Communism after the Winnipeg general strike of 1919 and a perceived need to cope with the menace on a nationwide basis. The RCMP was watching Communists even before twenty-two Communists met at Guelph, Ontario in 1921. Czechoslovakian-born John Leopold, an undercover RCMP officer, served under the alias Jack Esselwein as a labour organizer in Regina, Winnipeg, and Toronto. As such, Leopold participated in Communist activities from 1920 to 1928. From the floor of the House of Commons Winnipeg's socialist member of Parliament, J.S. Woodsworth, charged on 4 April 1922 that the once-admirable crime-fighting Mounted Police had become "a secret service department ... acting as spies, as agents provocateurs [against] the labour ... movement."

Now, however, additional documentation from the National Archives of the United States as well as recent books published in both the United Kingdom and the United States illustrate the role of American authorities in the surveillance of Canadian Communists. This chapter examines the work of American officials in this regard.

The Birth of Communism in Canada

In March 1919, Communists meeting in Moscow formed the so-called Third International (also known as the Communist International or Comintern), committed to the "liberation" of the entire world. (The First International had died in 1872 with the defeat of the Paris Commune. The Second disintegrated on the outbreak of World War I.) Lenin indicated support for propaganda, infiltration, and even terrorism to achieve the goals of world revolution, and the Communist Party of the Soviet Union provided money, advisers, and literature.

Across the world, Communists spied for the Soviet Union and assisted the Soviet Union's foreign policy goals. The three neighbouring republics of Lithuania, Latvia, and Estonia were early centres of Soviet activity outside Soviet boundaries, and Canada was not immune. The Comintern sought unity among Communist revolutionaries in both the United States and Canada, and it was to discuss unity that those twenty-two Canadian Communists, who came from Manitoba and points east, met in Guelph in the spring of 1921. Attending the Guelph meeting was Comintern agent Caleb Harrison, a U.S. citizen, who operated under the alias "Atwood." He contributed $3,000 of Soviet origin and "generally supervised the convention." Participants included Matthew Popowich (also spelled Popovitch) and John Navisisky of Winnipeg's Ukrainian Labour Temple; John Ahlqvist (also spelled Ahlquist) and John Latva of the Canadian Finnish Organization; Jack MacDonald, born in Scotland; Tom Bell, born in Ireland; and Florence Custance and William Moriarty, born in England.

Ian Angus, historian of the Communist Party of Canada (cpc) during the 1920s, found that most early Canadian Communists were unassimilated immigrants (presumably defined as people whose mother tongue was usually a language other than English or French, and who carried a disproportionate amount of political and cultural baggage from their country of origin), and their leaders were labour organizers. Among the original leaders, the only one born in Canada was Malcolm Bruce, from Prince Edward Island. Finns and Ukrainians were particularly numerous, although the party did organize a series of miners' strikes led by people with British surnames. In Quebec, whatever support there was for left-wing radicalism came from the Anglophone and Jewish communities.

The Workers Party of Canada held its founding convention in Toronto on 17–20 February 1922; in April 1924, it was renamed the Communist Party of Canada (cpc). Forty-three delegates went to Toronto from various points in Ontario, sixteen from the West, five from Quebec. The Workers Party of Canada claimed 4,800 members, of whom 2,200 belonged to the Finnish

Socialist Federation. Among the members were others of Eastern European extraction. The party declared

> Recognizing that the Communist International is the only real cen-
> tre of world revolutionary activities, the Workers Party will strive to
> rally the workers under the banner of the Third International.

According to Angus, the number of dues-paying members was 2,876 by 1929, but had fallen to 1,386 in 1931.

Reactions to the Spread of Communism

The Canadian, British, and American governments were duly concerned about the spread of Communism. So shocked had they been when in March 1918 the Bolshevik government made a separate peace with Germany at Brest-Litovsk and withdrew from World War I that all three countries were among those sending forces to overthrow Russia's Communist revolutionar-ies. Communists' militant atheism alarmed some religious believers, and politicians in Ottawa, London, and Washington blamed Communists for labour unrest and political extremism. There was also a fear that from its base in Russia, Communism would engulf the world, and rhetoric from Moscow did not lessen such fears.

In the aftermath of World War I, the Canadian and British governments employed fewer police and intelligence-gathering officials. A society at peace need not normally invest in intelligence gathering at wartime levels. Until 12 December 1918 the Dominion Police had been responsible for security matters right across Canada, but as of that date, the Borden government restricted their mandate to the area east of Fort William and Port Arthur. In comparison with the Royal North-West Mounted Police, the Dominion Police suffered from serious disadvantages. The former had 2,500 officers, the Dominion Police a mere 140. The Mounted Police carried arms and underwent a form of military training. To some extent, the Dominion Police were little more than an administrative office that delegated tasks to others. In 1920, the Dominion Police and the Royal North-West Mounted Police merged to become the Royal Canadian Mounted Police. In turn, the RCMP became smaller. In 1920 it had only 1,680 officers, though by 1926 it had grown to 1,963. Across the Atlantic, MI5 had 800 agents in 1918, only 13 by 1930. Nevertheless, the infrastructures remained in existence, often more effective than they had been because of consolidation and such technologi-cal developments as finger-printing. Canada depended almost entirely upon the United Kingdom for foreign intelligence.

Although the United States was self-reliant, the same pattern prevailed there. Between 1918 and 1922, the United States Army slashed its staff at the Military Intelligence Division from 1,441 to 90. The Office of Naval

Intelligence declined from just short of 1,000 to 42. In 1927, the State Department eliminated its U-1 Bureau for gathering intelligence. To a considerable degree, then, the Secretary of State depended upon what consular officials and diplomats could tell him, and as the United States lacked a legation in Ottawa until the end of the decade, consular posts were very important.

In all three countries, security organizations did monitor the background and the ongoing activities of both civil servants and people in the private sector. The U.S. State Department depended heavily upon a vigilant consular network to monitor Communist activities in Canada and elsewhere around the world. On 3 March 1923 the British Colonial Office forwarded intelligence from Scotland Yard of Soviet intentions to promote revolution in Canada. While Prime Minister Mackenzie King did not see fit to include the matter in his diary, American consular officials were certainly interested in Communist plans for Canada. In 1923 the U.S. State Department communicated with Mackenzie King about a message from Moscow to the Workers Party of America. Moscow told American Communists how to organize a Communist revolution in the United States and expressed hope for its success. American authorities feared that what Communists were planning for the United States they might also plan for Canada. This appears to be the first occasion when Washington alerted Ottawa to the Communist threat.

The First Crisis

On 16 March 1921, the Soviet Union and the United Kingdom had signed an accord known as the Anglo-Soviet Trade Agreement. Canada formally adhered to it on 3 July 1922, and the first Soviet trade delegation arrived in Montreal in March 1924.

The Soviets' baggage caused problems. An official with the Canadian Pacific Railway told T.A. Low, federal minister of trade and commerce, that the Soviets were sending twenty cases of literature to the trade commission that their envoys were establishing at 212 Drummond Street in Montreal. Article V of the Anglo-Soviet Trade Agreement guaranteed exemption from customs examination, but Low thought the quantity of literature excessive, and a series of "accidents" occurred. Mail from Moscow inaccurately addressed to the trade commissioners found its way to CPR offices where it was opened, read, and resealed, supposedly in an attempt to find the correct address. Some of the books were antireligious, others Russian classics or standard reference works. Some urged workers to rebel and establish Soviet-style regimes in their own countries. Soviet officials protested the violation of Article V.

O.D. Skelton, the undersecretary of state for external affairs, and industrialist F.H. Clergue, who hoped for lucrative trade agreements with the USSR, persuaded Mackenzie King not to worry excessively. Skelton, a former professor at Queen's University, said that most of the literature in question was already available in university and public libraries. He agreed that the trade commission needed a library of its own, and he thought that since there were only single copies of the offending material, they could not be distributed for propaganda purposes.

At that time, Canadian and U.S. authorities were sharing so little security information that Washington learned of the Soviet literature controversy only through reports published in the *Montreal Star* and the *Montreal Gazette*. Albert Halstead, U.S. consul-general in Montreal, read those accounts and warned the State Department that a Communist presence in Montreal ought to be a matter of concern to Americans.

> The delegation came to Canada with diplomatic passports and a number of trunks. The Canadian officials have stated that in view of the fact that the delegation had diplomatic passports it was impossible for them to examine its luggage. Previous experiences with Soviet delegations indicate the probability that the delegation brought with it propaganda papers. It is but forty-five miles from Montreal to the American line. Telephonic communications with any American City can be obtained between [sic] fifteen minutes and an hour ... That communication is not censored, nor is telegraphic communication, which can be had as readily to any part of the United States as it can between any two cities in the United States. It is nearer to New York from Montreal than it is to Chicago from New York, and the distance from Montreal to Chicago is practically the same as from New York to Chicago. It is very easy for any individual to come from the United States to see Russian delegates even if the latter, because of passport and border regulations, cannot enter the United States except surreptitiously. That they might improperly have visaed passports issued by other countries is amongst the possibilities.

Leland Harrison at the State Department then ordered John Foster, U.S. consul-general in Ottawa, to keep him posted about anything he heard on the subject.

In reply, Foster soft-pedalled any need for concern. According to his informants, half the shipment was "entirely unobjectionable," and included pamphlets readily available elsewhere. The Canadian government, said Foster, had engaged a civil servant from the Kerensky era "to make a careful examination of all this shipment." The Canadian government, fully aware of the dangers of imported Communist propaganda, was quite capable of containing the menace, he thought.

Despite the literature issue and a subsequent controversy over alleged forgeries of Canadian money by the Soviet government, the trade commission survived until 1927. Then, in May of that year, Scotland Yard raided ARCOS (the All-Russian Co-operative Society) and seized files that confirmed that Soviet sources were financing labour unrest in Great Britain. Moreover, Czarist codebreakers who had defected to the British cryptographic service were monitoring Soviet activities. Citing evidence of "military espionage" against the United States, the United Kingdom, and the Dominions, the British government of Stanley Baldwin severed diplomatic relations. Mackenzie King agreed with Baldwin's actions, and followed suit. The Soviet diplomats, he said, had abused Canadian hospitality and engaged in "espionage" and the distribution of "subversive propaganda."

Thus, in the matter of the trade commission and subversive literature, Canadian and American authorities thought along similar lines and, without consulting each other, reached similar conclusions.

Assistance from Third Parties

Besides the consular officials, the U.S. State Department did have a listening post at Riga. Located just beyond the Soviet border, the Latvian capital was useful as a place in which to intercept mail between Canadian and Soviet Communists, especially as the United States lacked diplomatic ties with the Soviet Union itself. In March 1922, the office of the commissioner of the United States in Riga intercepted a letter sent from the Central Executive Committee of the Communist Party of Canada to the Women's Secretariat of the Central Executive Committee of the Communist International. The following month, it was able to examine a confidential report on the finances of the CPC. In 1925, the United States legation in Riga noted the forwarding of $5,000 from Soviet sources to striking miners in Nova Scotia.

Non-American sources within Canada also proved useful. In 1929, Wesley Frost, who had succeeded Halstead as United States consul-general in Montreal, received clippings from the Croatian-language newspaper *Radnik*, published in Chicago. The consul-general in Montreal from the Kingdom of the Serbs, Croats, and Slovenes (later Yugoslavia), Captain A.S. Seferovitch, warned Frost that *Radnik* was "virtually a Soviet-Bolshevik organ." Seferovitch told Frost that *Radnik* had readers in the Hamilton area, where it was "causing serious labor unrest." Within days, Canada Customs banned the import of *Radnik*, and the U.S. State Department asked Frost to thank Seferovitch for his "interest ... in this matter." In the aftermath of the Soviet literature controversy, the Canadian government appears to have been more than willing to restrict Communist activities once it became aware of them, even if doing so threatened the free exchange of ideas in a democracy. The *Radnik* affair is the second documented case of Canadian-American cooperation in the fight against Communism.

Canadian Sources for American Communist-Watchers

For most of the 1920s, U.S. consular officials based in Canada continued to monitor Communist activities within Canada. On 21 December 1921, the U.S. consul-general in Winnipeg, Joseph Brittain, sent to the Secretary of State a copy of *Manifesto No. 1* issued by the Workers' Alliance of Winnipeg, a Communist group that claimed 2,000 members. At the same time, he forwarded a Workers' Alliance resolution of 19 November 1921 "on solidarity with the Third (Communist) International." The resolution called for "the abolition of Capitalism and the establishment of Communism." Fred C. Slater, U.S. consul in Fort William and Port Arthur (now Thunder Bay), forwarded to the State Department information about Communists in Canada's Ukrainian community. Francis R. Stewart, U.S. consul in Niagara Falls, Ontario, reported on the activities within his consular district of Communist activist and orator Oscar Ryan, a long-time collaborator and admirer of long-time party leader Tim Buck. Consular officials depended heavily upon what they read in Canadian newspapers. Once the United States opened a legation in Ottawa, American diplomats appear to have made greater use of Canadian-government printed matter than had their consular predecessors.

The U.S. consul in North Bay, William E. Chapman, went a step further. Using a mutual friend, Chapman engaged a clergyman, the Rev. Edwin Kyllonen of Kirkland Lake and Sudbury, to help him monitor Northern Ontario's Red Finns. Chapman took this action after the *Ottawa Journal* reported the arrest of nine Sudbury men on 15 April 1931, "following Communist demonstrations, in which a crowd of 3,000 took part." A policeman, Patrick Poland, suffered an eye injury during the violence. Chapman also noted a radio report of "a similar disturbance" in Timmins. Later that year, Chapman identified a Communist spokesman who had appeared before the town council of Timmins to demand relief for the unemployed, "a man who calls himself Amos T. Hill who appears to be a so-called 'Red Finn' of another name." Chapman's suspicions were well founded. Born as Armas Tuomar Myllymaki in Finland in 1897 (where *maki* meant hill), Hill had moved to Canada before World War I and to Sudbury before 1921. In the nickel community, Hill was an active pro-Soviet Communist. The State Department commended Chapman for his report and asked him to monitor Communist newspapers, visits of Canadian Communists to Russia and Russian Communists to Canada, and "documentary material that may be found by the police authorities in the possession of communists under arrest."

Chapman continued to report – about Red Finn Alfred Hautamaki and about Soviet influence on Canadian Communists as reported in Toronto's *Mail and Empire* – before he recruited Kyllonen. Hautamaki, described as "a prominent Finnish Communist," was president of the Lumberworkers Union. Born in Finland, he had moved as a child to the United States before moving to Northern Ontario as an adult in 1920. In 1927 he visited the Soviet Union. Chapman and Kyllonen agreed that Kyllonen would not sign letters that he wrote to Chapman in case "his letters and other papers sent to this office should fall into the hands of communists before reaching the Consulate." Kyllonen proved to be a treasure-house of information about the Red Finns of Northern Ontario, including John Ahlqvist, editor of the Sudbury-based Finnish Communist newspaper, *Vapaus* (Liberty). Kyllonen even translated sections of *Vapaus* for the consulate. Kyllonen also sent the consulate a list of "Active Finnish Communists in Canada."

Canadian police departments also kept the consuls informed. On 11 November 1931, Wesley Frost, the U.S. consul-general in Montreal, reported a conversation with the commanding officer of the RCMP in Montreal and one of his subordinates. They gave a full and frank account of Communism in the Province of Quebec, whose importance – given the influence of the Roman Catholic Church – they tended to minimize. Back in North Bay, Chapman was able to borrow five Communist posters from police in Kirkland Lake. His agreement with the mining community's men in blue was that while he might ship the materials to the American capital for study and photographing, the State Department would return them.

These talks with Kyllonen and individual Canadian police appear to have been unnecessarily provocative. Most influential Canadians of the period were militantly anti-Communist and prepared, without much outside prodding, to take drastic action to curtail Communists and alleged Communists. In 1929, Aaroo Vaaro, editor of *Vapaus*, was imprisoned because he had published material that was "seditious, immoral, anti-Christian, anti-British." Evidence from the RCMP undercover officer Esselwein/Leopold put eight leading Communists behind bars in 1931: they were amazed to see their former comrade appear in RCMP uniform to testify against them. Also in 1931, Sudbury's city council urged the federal government "to deport all undesirables and Communists." Other communities agreed. In 1932, Canadians roared with approval as Prime Minister R.B. Bennett allowed ships of the Royal Canadian Navy to go to El Salvador, where a supposedly Communist rebellion was taking place. Unnecessary as it was for American officials to spy in Canada in order to protect their country's interests, their actions aroused little controversy. Few Canadians were aware of what the consuls were doing, and most who were aware were in full accord. Moreover, in collecting information without regard to Canadian authorities, Americans were following a tradition begun during their Civil War and continued during the Spanish-American War.

Conclusions

In the years between the end of World War I and Hitler's accession to power, American surveillance of Canadian Communists took many forms: reading newspapers and official publications of the Canadian government, working with third parties, working with the Canadian government, and working with individual Canadians. However, attitudes among peer groups on both sides of the border were so obviously similar that there was no need for underhanded American espionage on Canadian soil. John Foster, the consul-general in Ottawa, realized this, but not all his associates, as the Kyllonen case demonstrates, agreed.

Cooperation was not yet the hallmark of Canadian-American relations that it would become. In every way, Canada's ties with the United Kingdom remained stronger than those with the United States, and this, in the eyes of some American officials, made Canada a legitimate target for surveillance. Nevertheless, the first steps toward Canadian-American intelligence cooperation were being taken. The 1923 warning about Moscow's message to the Workers Party of America and the *Radnik* affair six years later illustrate the U.S. State Department's willingness to forward information to Ottawa as well as Ottawa's willingness to act on it. The U.S. consulate-general in Montreal and the consulate in North Bay worked with uniformed police. However, a deeper, more consistent, less haphazard arrangement for sharing information remained in the future.

5

Nazi German Consular Posts as Sources of Information, 1933–39

More than thirty years ago, Canadian political scientist James Eayrs speculated that Erich Windels, Germany's consul-general in Ottawa, duly reported the Liberal government's support for British appeasement policies. Eayrs was correct, and what he said of Windels was also true of Ludwig Kempff, Germany's long-serving consul-general in Montreal, and of Windels' assistant, Hans Ulrich Granow. Kempff, Windels, and Granow were very interested in Canadian foreign relations, for those relations would indicate the extent, if any, of Canadian support for Great Britain in any Anglo-German war. Canada, then as now, was the senior and most powerful Dominion.

The information that these men and their colleagues forwarded to Berlin fell into three categories: clippings from newspapers and other reports of political developments that were not confidential, surveillance of dissident Germans in Canada, and contacts with people on the lunatic fringe of the Canadian right wing. Only the second and third categories could have been at all controversial, and only the second was in any way significant. Other writers – principally Lita-Rose Betcherman, Jonathan F. Wagner, and Martin Robin – have shown that bigotry had roots in Canada as well, and that Canadian right-wingers neither needed nor received much support from Germany's consular posts or from Nazi officials, some of whom were operating in Canada before 1933. This chapter demonstrates that most of the information that the consular officials forwarded was of a nature such that a host government might reasonably have expected foreign envoys to forward it. Given the nature of the Hitler regime, Mackenzie King's government should not have permitted the expansion of the consular network – beyond Montreal and Winnipeg to Ottawa, Toronto, and Vancouver – that took place between 1936 and 1939. At the time, Canadian authorities – like authorities in most other countries – simply could not imagine the wickedness and sinister intentions of the Hitler regime, and they agreed to what seemed to be a routine expansion in the interests of greater efficiency. The expansion appears to have generated little if any controversy at the time.

That Nazi Germany's consular appointees to Canada proved less than full-blown spies is compatible with the findings of an American author, Michael Geyer. In 1986 he wrote

> The [German] Foreign Office dominated the diplomatic network. Until 1938, when Joaquim von Ribbentrop took over, its procedures for intelligence-gathering remained virtually unchanged. If anything, the prevalent view in the Foreign Office from 1933 to 1938 was that, now that the republic had disappeared and a career diplomat, Konstantin von Neurath was in control, it could revert to its old professional ways. Though not without commotion, the civil servants in the Foreign Office succeeded in heading off challenges from organs of the National Socialist Party. Personnel changes were rare in the diplomatic missions and only somewhat more frequent in the consular service. Harmony was furthered by mutual understanding that espionage was to be kept strictly separate from the diplomatic and attaché services.

Wagner agrees. Because of his racial theories, Hitler underestimated the strength of the United States. A country with so many Jews and Afro-Americans, reasoned the Führer, simply had to be weak, and because of its size and racial mixture, Canada had to be even weaker. Hence, the officials who represented Nazi Germany in Canada were largely on their own, said Wagner, left to guess what Hitler would want.

The Personalities

The German representative who served longest in Canada was Ludwig Kempff, a trained lawyer who was consul-general in Montreal from 1921 to 1937. His correspondence at the Auswärtiges Amt (Foreign Office) archives in Bonn is extensive, and not until 24 September 1935 does he appear to have concluded a letter with the words "Heil Hitler!" Wagner portrays Kempff as a bureaucrat who obeyed a government about which he had serious doubts, but there is room for argument on that score. Robin says that "Kempff saw the light in 1933 and became a loyal servant of the New Germany." This seems a reasonable assessment. After 1933, Kempff seems rarely if ever to have travelled farther than Ottawa, although his area of jurisdiction included Ontario, Quebec, the Maritime provinces, and Newfoundland (which at that time was not part of Canada). In 1937, he died suddenly – though of natural causes – in Montreal.

Erich Windels, a career diplomat, arrived in Ottawa in 1936 and remained until Canada and Germany severed diplomatic relations in September 1939. Then he served as consul-general in Philadelphia until President Roosevelt ordered the closure of all German consular posts in the United States over the summer of 1941. His deputy at the consulate-general in Ottawa was Hans Ulrich Granow, whom Wagner categorizes as another career diplomat.

Heinrich Seelheim, German consul in Winnipeg from 1930 to 1937, had a Ph.D. in geography. He had entered the foreign service in 1920, served as secretary at the German legation in Rio de Janeiro from 1921 to 1923, and then returned to head office in Berlin. Seelheim's area of jurisdiction included the four western provinces, and, younger than Kempff by twelve years, he did travel as far as Vancouver. Seelheim was a Social Democrat when he arrived in Canada; unlike Kempff, he formally joined the Nazi party in 1934, although he rarely wrote "Heil Hitler!" Germans in his territory were more recent arrivals and, on the whole, less assimilated to Canadian ways than those in Kempff's. His anti-Semitic views and strong defence of the Hitler regime received extensive coverage in Vancouver newspapers when he visited that city early in 1935. Seelheim told one group of Vancouverites, for example, of a Jewish factory-owner who, prior to 1933, used to rape his female employees and then dismiss them if they became pregnant. After the Nazis came to power, the women beat the man up. He deserved his fate, said Seelheim, but incidents such as this were being misinterpreted by well-meaning foreigners.

When Seelheim won promotion to the consulate-general in Yokohama and left Winnipeg late in 1937, Berlin replaced him with Wilhelm Rodde, who had been a Nazi since 1932. Wagner thinks that Rodde lacked either the "intelligence and sensitivity of Kempff [or the] charm of Seelheim." Robin's comments on Rodde are equally uncomplimentary. Rodde's consulate employed five people.

Kempff's successor in Montreal was Henry Eckner. Although only a consul, not a consul-general like Kempff and Windels, Eckner headed a staff of ten. Robin, whose sources are purely Canadian, says that the RCMP found most of his actions compatible with normal consular behaviour. Available documentary evidence has little to incriminate either William Henry Mahler, a naturalized British subject born in Germany, who became vice-consul in Vancouver, or Karl Gustav Knopp, an ideological Nazi who resided in Canada before his appointment as Germany's honourary consul in Toronto.

Newspaper Clippings and Nonconfidential Political Developments

Both Kempff and Seelheim wrote extensive reports on the Canadian political situation, federally and provincially. These reports were idiosyncratic only inasmuch as they devoted abnormal attention to Fascists and Jews. At the time of Quebec's 1933 provincial election, Kempff reported at length on J.A. Chalifoux. Chalifoux was president of La Fédération des clubs ouvriers de la province de Québec, which shared many Fascist values, but he was not formally a candidate in any provincial constitutency. Kempff also wrote at length about Adrian Arcand's Fascist movement in Quebec. Arcand, born in Quebec City in 1899, was an effective orator and newspaper editor who made no secret of his admiration for Adolf Hitler and his anti-Semitism. The banner of his Parti national social chrétien, founded in 1934, featured a swastika with maple leaves and a beaver. In reporting results of the 1935 election, Kempff noted that Communists had lost even in such heavily Jewish ridings as Toronto's Spadina and Montreal's Cartier.

For years Kempff had been monitoring the activities of Senator Raoul Dandurand, one-time Canadian delegate to the League of Nations, and from 1930 Liberal leader in the Senate. "It is well known," said Kempff, "that Dandurand has been one of the most anti-German of Canadians." He had supported France's occupation of Germany's Ruhr valley (1923) and in the Senate promoted the French line, even using the word "Hun." At the time, said Kempff, he had complained personally to Mackenzie King, who spoke to Dandurand. For a time Dandurand softened his anti-German rhetoric, and indeed for a short time became friendly.

Kempff's interest in Canadian foreign relations was ongoing. From 1921, when he arrived in Canada, Kempff monitored Canada's moves toward autonomy, away from a unified foreign policy for the entire British Empire. Kempff dutifully recorded a mid-June 1935 ceremony on an island in Lake Champlain to commemorate the Rush-Bagot Accord of 1817, which ended the Great Lakes naval arms race between Britain and the United States. Kempff noted the concerns expressed in the House of Commons when some members thought Italy's consul-general in Ottawa was promoting Fascism among Canadians of Italian extraction. Kempff reported denunciations of Italy and Germany at the 1935 convention of the Trades and Labour Congress, which met in Halifax: his information came from the Montreal Gazette. He reported at length on parliamentary speeches of Prime Minister Bennett about Canadian-Japanese relations. He wrote biographical sketches on Vincent Massey, newly appointed Canadian high commissioner in the United Kingdom, and of members of the newly elected Liberal cabinet. This was normal procedure for representatives of any government. In June 1936 Kempff reported at length on a House of Commons debate on the Ethiopian crisis and enclosed the Hansard version of the prime minister's speech. When Mackenzie King addressed the League of Nations later that same year, Kempff provided Berlin with a copy of his speech.

Kempff and his staff also monitored the coverage of Germany in Canadian newspapers. In the summer of 1933, they were pleased by a series of articles written by Erland Echlin, a freelance journalist who spent the warm months of that year in Europe and sold his work to Toronto's Globe and the Montreal Gazette.

Echlin's thirteen articles, all but one of which appeared on the *Globe's* front page, were full of praise for Hitler and the Nazis. Echlin described Hitler's popularity as manifested in both large demonstrations and small groups of childen. "The children of Germany are his children," said the column of 19 August. "In them and in music he has the relaxation which is not found in what most men call the amenities of life − golf, bridge, or comfortable talk."

Echlin admired Hitler's record of achievement since his assumption of power at the end of January. The Nazis had eliminated unemployment and removed aggressive beggars from the streets of Berlin. They presented a pleasant alternative to the Weimar Republic, whose ineffective and petty politicians had "deliberately impoverished" the German people. Repeatedly Echlin noted that Hitler had preserved Germany from Bolshevism, which he regarded as the ultimate horror. By ordering twenty-eight Protestant bodies to merge into one, Hitler had strengthened the church and thus had "really saved all religion in Germany, Catholic and Protestant alike, from the atheism of the Bolsheviks."

"Tales" of outrages against Jews resembled "the rumour of Mark Twain's death, an exaggeration; to put it more plainly, imaginative lies." In Echlin's words, "Far more Nazis have been killed in their rise to power than Jews since." He quoted a Canadian rabbi named Eisendrath, whom he met in Berlin, as saying that, despite his obvious Jewishness, everyone had treated him "with the greatest kindness."

From Geneva more than a month later the *Globe* published a letter from Eisendrath. Echlin, he charged, had quoted him out of context. Germans still treated foreigners politely, but their treatment of German Jews was another matter, and Echlin had chosen to ignore what the rabbi had said about that. The same day the *Globe* editorialized that there might have been "a misunderstanding" between the reporter and the rabbi.

After the appearance of eight articles, Echlin ran low on funds. Goebbels' Ministry of Public Enlightenment and Propaganda agreed to provide 500 Reichmarks so that he could prolong his stay in Germany. Some days later, Hitler granted Echlin an exclusive interview. Echlin found Hitler's voice "moderate" and "kindly" and said bluntly, "He stands for peace." If other great powers would accept an arms control agreement, Hitler would as well. However, "if other countries are to be armed to the teeth, then Germany must, in all fairness, be allowed to arm sufficiently to defend her frontier."

The significance of Echlin's articles is difficult to measure. Official German correspondence about Echlin and the *Globe* fell into the hands of American forces at the end of World War II. In a confidential memorandum, the Ministry of Enlightenment and Propaganda found the articles of "great importance in view of the fact that the Canadian public has been exceptionally thoroughly permeated by hostile propaganda." On 22 August, Harry W. Anderson, the Globe's managing editor, congratulated Echlin for writing so "efficiently and entertainingly." The articles, wrote Anderson, had "been so good." (A copy of Anderson's letter to Echlin was found among the captured German papers.) On 29 July, the Globe carried a letter to the editor from Edwin Poppe of Toronto, who compared Echlin's "seriousness" and "fairness" to the "onesided sensational newspaper reports" of other journalists. Joshua D. Smith of Beamsville telegraphed the German consulate-general in Montreal to report that Echlin had created a "very favorable impression ... in [the] Niagara District." The truth was so incredible that Canadians believed the words of an apologist.

What Kempff and Seelheim reported came from Canadian newspapers and was not at all secret. The same is true of their colleagues, Windels and Granow. When Windels and Granow opened the consulate-general in Ottawa, they covered Canadian foreign relations. Among the documents that survive is a 1937 report by Granow on the League of Nations Society in Canada. When Mackenzie King announced that Senator Dandurand would again head Canada's delegation to the League of Nations Assembly in 1937, Granow submitted a revised version of Kempff's 1935 letter which described Dandurand as one of the most anti-German people in Canada. Windels wrote a lengthy report on Canadian reaction to Germany's forcible annexation of Austria (the Anschluss) in late winter 1938. Press coverage was extensive, said Windels, as the crisis was unfolding. However, after a review of questions from opposition members of Parliament and the prime minister's reply, Windels observed: "In the face of the latest developments in Europe, the Canadian government is at pains to exercise the strictest neutrality and reserve." In other words, as Hitler invaded and annexed Austria, he would have nothing to fear from Canada. Unfortunately, the German holdings of correspondence on the Munich crisis seem to have been lost, but undoubtedly they would have been similar.

The information that Kempff, Seelheim, Windels, and Granow sent to Berlin was potentially valuable to German authorities as they planned their foreign relations and sought to help Germans in Canada. It is not possible, however, on the basis of the documentary evidence, to accuse any of these individuals of espionage. What they reported was available to anyone who read newspapers or followed debates in the House of Commons.

From his base in Montreal, Kempff monitored the local press for signs of anti-Semitism in Canada. While his fascination with the subject reflects badly on Kempff and the government that he served, it does not appear to have done any harm. Kempff was reporting facts, albeit unpleasant ones, that were hardly secret. In one of the earliest of such developments, one can argue that

Kempff was simply notifying his government of Canadian reaction to one of his government's policies. That reaction might conceivably have affected such matters of substance as bilateral Canadian-German trade or Canadian foreign policy. If Germany disliked the consequences of its anti-Semitic policies, news of the consequences might have led to a change in those policies.

Montreal was a centre of Jewish settlement in Canada, and on 26 March 1933, a crowd protested Germany's ill-treatment of Jews: the German government's boycott of Jewish businesses; mass dismissals of Jewish doctors, professors, and other professional people; the slandering of Jewish writers, artists, and scientists; and the German government's promotion of anti-Semitic propaganda. Kempff notified Berlin of the demonstration, and of similar demonstrations by Christians and Jews in Montreal, in Ontario, and in Prairie cities On 8 April, Kempff forwarded to his government a letter of protest written by J. Graner, campaign chairman of the Ontario Protest Committee. Graner had presented Kempff with a copy of a resolution, adopted by "mass meetings of Jews and non-Jews" at Massey Hall and the Bay Street synagogue on 2 April. The purpose of the meeting was to protest "against the persecution to which the Jews in Germany are being subjected." Similar meetings, Kempff reported, took place the same day in several Ontario cities, from Belleville to Windsor, from Welland–St. Catharines–Niagara Falls (a joint meeting) to Kirkland Lake and Timmins.

Kempff also forwarded coverage of an early April rally in Montreal on behalf of German Jews. In its issue of 7 April, the Montreal Gazette estimated the number of participants at 10,000. It was obvious and appropriate, Kempff thought, that Berlin ought to know what its Jewish policies were doing to Germany's image. Some prominent people participated in the April rally: Senator Raoul Dandurand, who had headed the Canadian delegation at the League of Nations in 1924 and served as chair of the League Assembly in 1925; Montreal mayor Fernand Rinfret; the Hon. Honoré Mercier, Quebec's minister of lands and forests; four members of the federal House of Commons (including Mayor Rinfret); and a rabbi and Christian clergy from the Montreal area. Participants called upon the Canadian government to take "such appropriate action as may be required."

Kempff also noted the depth of anti-Semitism among French Canadians. From the 21 April issues of the Montreal Gazette and of the Montreal French-language daily La Patrie, he was able to describe a counter-rally. On 20 April, a largely French-Canadian crowd heard orators denounce "the nefarious power of Jewry in Montreal" and accuse Jews of sympathy for Communism. André Laurendeau, later editor of Le Devoir and co-chair of a royal commission, blamed "deplorable party politics" for French-Canadian participation at a Jewish rally. According to the Montreal Gazette, Laurendeau said, "There are 80,000 Jews in Montreal ... and they vote 110 per cent strong ... Jewry ...

embodied the masters of the metropolis [Montreal], the Jews having the financial power to contribute the electoral funds – providing the politicians are at their service." Laurendeau thought it ridiculous to criticize the German boycott of Jewish suppliers and merchants. When Liberals won elections in Canada, they boycotted Conservatives, and vice versa, he argued. La Patrie said that Laurendeau expressed doubt whether the alleged atrocities against Jews were really happening.

Through the pages of Le Devoir Senator Dandurand replied: "Hitler was already condemned by all people of conscience." Later in 1933 Kempff notified Berlin that Fascist, anti-Semitic French Canadians had founded a weekly newspaper, Le Patriote. Its 26 October 1933 issue included a swastika on its masthead. That same issue published a report about a meeting of 20 October at which Adrian Arcand had delivered a speech. One of the ideologues behind Le Patriote, Joseph Menard, also spoke; he had been involved in anti-Semitic activities for three years.

Kempff also wrote a report on Fascism in Ontario. Again, he learned by reading the newspapers of the founding of the National State Party of Canada at a convention in Toronto during the month of July. On a Toronto beach a scrawled "Hail [sic] Hitler!" appeared. People with leather jackets, oilskins, and sweaters carried a huge swastika on the beach; others wore buttons with swastikas.

For his part, Windels followed a Sunday afternoon CBC talk show, "Review of the News," which featured such commentators as Halifax Professor H.L. Stewart and George Ferguson, editor of the Winnipeg Free Press. Windels had a good understanding of the Broadcasting Act which regulated the CBC's arms-length relationship with the Canadian government. There is no evidence that Windels had any impact on what the CBC broadcast. From Montreal, Kempff's successor Eckner wrote to Windels about unfavourable publicity arising from such 1938 developments as the Austrian Anschluss and the Munich crisis. He clipped a Montreal Gazette article about support from the Trades and Labour Congress for a boycott of German goods.

Arguably Kempff and Seelheim, Windels, Granow, and Eckner were loyal civil servants doing their job. They relayed to Berlin news that might have shaped subsequent German foreign policy, trade policy, or policies toward Jews. From a Canadian standpoint, this was a two-edged sword. If Germans were unaware of the anger or unhappiness of Canadians about certain policies, they certainly would not feel any pressure to change those policies. On the other hand, his awareness of those policies prompted Granow to appeal to German Canadians to protest a Jewish boycott of German goods and to go out of their way to buy German coal in order to offset any such boycott.

Surveillance of Anti-Nazi Germans

The consuls' second type of activity had greater potential for damage. In November and December 1933, both Kempff and Seelheim reported the activities of one Dr. C.R. Hennings, fluent in English as well as German, who was touring Canada on an anti-Nazi crusade. Early in 1934 Kempff read in the *Montreal Star* a statement by a refugee scientist, Eugene Eigel. Eigel said that he could not return to Germany as he had publicly disagreed with "some of Hitler's policies." Eigel knew that any German who expressed disapproval of Nazis or Nazi policies at a public forum ran some risks. Someone might act as an informer, and in Montreal that person was Kempff. Kempff read Montreal's newspapers assiduously, and he had other sources as well. He then notified Berlin, which could take whatever reprisals it chose against the speakers, if they returned, or their families, if they did not.

This practice continued. In March 1935, Seelheim reported that a former member of the Reichstag, Toni Sender, was on an anti-German propaganda tour of Canada. He had spoken three times in two days, said Seelheim, once at the Communist-Socialist-Jewish Winnipeg Conference against War and Fascism. In December of the same year, Kempff wrote to Berlin about a political dissident who had delivered lectures in Montreal's American Presbyterian Church and to the Montreal Women's Club. Gerhard Seeger had been a Social Democrat in the Reichstag, and the theme of his addresses was "Hitler, a Menace to Civilization." After a list of Nazi infringements on decency, Seeger suggested, in good English, that the 1936 Olympics might take place more appropriately in Czechoslovakia than in Berlin. Kempff did not indicate his source, except to say that it was "reliable."

In the same report, Kempff discussed Emil Ludwig, another dissident but a less effective communicator. His English was not as good, his voice did not carry, and he repeatedly made uncomplimentary remarks about monarchs as though he were speaking in the United States. Ludwig spoke at "His Majesty's Theatre" before an audience that had bought tickets for admission; Kempff read about his address in the *Montreal Herald*. From the *Montreal Gazette*, but under an Ottawa dateline, Kempff learned that Ludwig had repeated his speech in the Canadian capital, where the Governor General, Lord Tweedsmuir, had received him.

In 1936, a Sudbury resident named Adam Sharrer went to Germany for the Berlin Olympics. Authorities there arrested and jailed him because of what another Adam Sharrer, a German subject, had written in an anti-Nazi German-language Canadian newspaper. Presumably one of Hitler's agents in Canada, perhaps someone at one of the consulates, had studied Canada's German-language press and forwarded the Sharrer article to the appropriate Nazis. Sudbury's Adam Sharrer did not regain his freedom until he could prove that this was a case of mistaken identity.

Obviously Kempff and Seelheim did not intimidate all dissidents. However, they must have caused some to think carefully before speaking and, human nature being what it is, they must have scared some into silence. Many Germans who visited Montreal or Winnipeg undoubtedly did not know Kempff and Seelheim, even by name, but they knew that the system of which these officials were part could well be maintaining some form of surveillance.

The Canadian government, by contrast, appears to have been remarkably unconcerned. It might have known that Kempff and Seelheim had easier access to local newspapers than to distant ones. Even if it could not have known the size of their newspaper budget, it must have known that there were limits in terms of time, energy, and money to what any one individual could read. However, if anti-Hitler Germans made speeches to Canadian audiences, and surely such speeches were desirable in terms of public awareness, the risk to the speakers should have been kept to a minimum. The expansion of Germany's consular network from two posts to five could hardly have been helpful to anyone but Nazis and their friends.

The Canadian Right Wing

Reports on Canada's right-wing extremists, based on newspaper accounts and personal contacts with some of them, were most unlikely to persuade Berlin to support them actively, or to take them seriously in any way.

In great detail, Kempff narrated the story of the brown shirts and Montreal's Dominion Day parade of 1 July 1933. He had heard a rumour that local brown shirts would participate in the parade as it passed through Montreal's streets; about the same time, the *Toronto Star* said that there were some 80,000 Fascists in Quebec. A *Montreal Gazette* article of 10 June said that Fascists of La Fédération des clubs ouvriers de la province de Québec thought that they based their ideology on encyclicals of Popes Pius IX (1846–78) and Leo XIII (1878–1903).

On 19 June, a Dutchman named Booy, who wore a brown shirt and a National Socialist–style cap, went to Kempff to discuss the parade. Booy placed before Kempff a copy of the Fédération's constitution, which did indeed state that it sought to pursue the political doctrines of Popes Pius IX and Leo XIII. Booy wanted money so that immigrant workers could have a float in the parade. Two other consulates had each contributed a dollar, said Booy, and he wondered whether Kempff could match them.

Eventually Kempff did. However, first he quizzed Booy about the Fédération, and said that he could not contribute to any political organization. Booy responded that the cause he represented was nonpolitical. Supporters simply opposed Jews, Communists, and trusts. The Fédération, said Booy, had written to Mussolini and to Hitler to ask about their programs. Kempff then slipped Booy a dollar of his own and stated that this was a personal, not an official, contribution.

Some days later, Kempff read in a newspaper that the City of Montreal had refused permission for the parade. It would have to take place in other communities of Greater Montreal, and there would be floats to honour Christopher Columbus, Sieur de Maisonneuve (the founder of Montreal), Sir Wilfrid Laurier (at that point the only French-Canadian prime minister of Canada), and Mussolini. On 28 June, the Metropolitan Commission of Montreal declared that it was inappropriate for a Fascist political organization like the Fédération to take part in the parade. Only religious and patriotic groups ought to do so.

On 30 June, the Montreal Gazette reported that the Fédération's president, J.A. Chalifoux, was determined that there would be a parade from Lafontaine Park to Boulevard Pie IX after all. He did not see how the authorities could stop him and his people. They would fly the Union Jack.

The afternoon of 1 July, Kempff went to the parade route to watch. There was no parade, but he saw a man in a brown shirt riding on a motorcycle. Behind him was a car carrying four more men wearing brown shirts. They were headed in the direction of Pie IX. Kempff asked the brown shirts in the car whether the parade would take place. They replied in the negative but said that members of the Fédération would assemble in Belmont Park. When Kempff went there, there were only a few people, including a handful of brown shirts. As he was leaving, Kempff saw a brown shirt sitting on a so-called float. He asked about the parade, and the brown shirt said that it would take place the following Saturday (8 July), and that the float had simply not been ready in time.

The episode, trivial in itself, demonstrates several points. Fascism in Quebec began and continued quite independently of the German consulate-general in Montreal. Kempff was little more than a bystander. As a cautious lawyer and experienced official, Kempff was not inclined to interfere openly in the politics of a country other than his own. Nevertheless, he was willing to give moral support to a Fascist cause. Finally, the experience was hardly likely to bolster his confidence in local Fascists. Nor could he have been favourably impressed when the events planned for 8 July also failed to materialize.

Kempff continued to follow the Fédération and other right-wing Canadian bodies. A Fédération rally planned for 13 August finally took place on 20 August. There President Chalifoux denounced the Liberal and Conservative parties and predicted that Fascists would win the next election. Just as technology was modernizing, said Chalifoux, so must political systems. None of the current officeholders, he thought, could cope with the unemployment situation, and the Fédération then nominated candidates for the forthcoming provincial election.

Kempff's experiences parallel those of his colleague, Seelheim, and his successor, Eckner. Eckner told Germany's ambassador in Washington that Arcand had visited him. The initiative had been Arcand's, not Eckner's, and Arcand's purpose was to obtain Nazi propaganda which he might publish without any reference to point of origin. From Winnipeg, Seelheim also reported on the progress of Canadian Fascism. Like Kempff, he was cautious, and like Kempff, he gave moral support to the cause. Like Kempff, Seelheim was more an observer than a participant. He left organization of right-wing movements to others.

In western Canada, the first Fascist organization operated from Winnipeg. Early in November 1933, Seelheim reported that the Canadian Nationalist Party had been getting off the ground over the previous four months, and, according to its secretary, it had attracted some 1,000 members. Some of these were German Canadians. The president, William Whittaker, and the secretary, one H. Parker – obviously not of German origin – had recently visited Seelheim, but Seelheim thought that German subjects like himself should not belong to Canadian parties. Whittaker, a former police officer in India, and Parker reluctantly had to agree.

Winnipeg lacked, said Seelheim, a National Socialist organization, but there were possibilities. Based in New York was a group called *Freunde des neuen Deutschlands* (Friends of the New Germany). From a source in the RCMP Seelheim had learned that its Detroit branch would shortly be active in Canada. For his part, Seelheim warned people from the Detroit branch that the RCMP would be suspicious of any connection between the *Freunde des neuen Deutschlands* and Canadian nationalists or Fascists. From Detroit a spokesman answered reassuringly that his group had no links with Canadian Fascists. Hans Strauss, a Detroit Nazi, did come to Canada, and federal MP Samuel Jacobs, a key organizer of the April rally in Montreal, blew the whistle. Jacobs notified the RCMP and the Canadian government. Evidently neither lifted a finger. The *Freunde des neuen Deutschlands* organized branches in Toronto, Kitchener, St. Catharines, Montreal, Winnipeg, and Vancouver. Fortunately, through ineptitude on the part of the organizers, these efforts failed before spring 1934.

Winnipeg's Canadian Nationalist Party still worked underground most of the time, said Seelheim, although it had its own newspaper, the *Canadian Nationalist*. Seelheim said that a Winnipeg committee of Jewish rights activists and a Jewish leader were at pains to find out where the paper was printed and who was putting it out. Seelheim predicted that it would soon have a circulation of 6,000.

Of greater potential danger than Canadian Fascists or the *Freunde des neuen Deutschlands* might have been the Deutscher Bund Canada. This was a pro-Nazi organization aimed at ethnic Germans in Canada, not at French-Canadians or Anglophones. It sought only the deeply committed whose bloodlines were pure, and it had branches from Quebec to the Pacific coast. Saskatchewan alone had more than forty branches in 1939, but the actual memberships were small. Late in 1934, the Deutscher Bund's first year, Kempff estimated that membership totalled 1,120; its maximum (in 1937–38) has been estimated at 2,000. The Montreal branch had 170 members, Regina's 60. Of those 2,000, fewer than 5 percent were members of the Nazi party. Similarly, most of Canada's 88 Nazis of 1937 did not belong to the Bund. Kempff found the Bund and its people objectionable, a threat to his own authority. Yet, in his legalistic way, Kempff approached a Montreal law firm in 1934 to help the Bund establish itself in full accord with Canadian law.

In brief, German officials in Canada did have contacts with Canadian hate-mongers across the country, but the influence of these extremists was limited, and the contacts with German consular staffs appear to have been minimal.

Conclusions

Much of what the consuls did was routine and nonprovocative, the sort of work that representatives of a normal government would have done. Kempff wrote a letter of introduction to the German Foreign Office for Murray Chipman, who went to Germany and described conditions there for the *Financial Post*. He wrote about German immigrants to Canada who were suffering from unemployment. Seelheim presented the case of Paul Otto, an impoverished farmer from drought-ridden Saskatchewan. There is an entire file on Germans deported from Canada, both before and after the advent of Nazi government. However, thanks to Kempff and Seelheim, Berlin knew that there were Canadians who shared Nazi values in Quebec, Ontario, and Manitoba. Berlin was also aware of German dissidents who visited Canada to alert people to the Nazi menace.

Nasty as some of the information that Germany's consular officials forwarded to Berlin was, most of it hardly qualified as "espionage." There appear to have been no secret agents in the Canadian cabinet or in any other centre of power and authority. Similarly, with the outbreak of war in September 1939, German intelligence on Canada seems to have remained minimal. Maintenance of Canadian neutrality in any Anglo-German war had been a goal of German foreign policy, and when Canada declared war on 12 September 1939, that effort had obviously failed. So minimal did Canada's military power appear that monitoring it was not a high priority. Erich Windels left Ottawa and became consul-general in Philadelphia. Little documentation on that post is available at Auswärtiges Amt for 1939–41. However, if surveillance of Canada had been one of his tasks, surely Boston, Chicago, or New York would have been a more useful location than Philadelphia for a man of Windels' experience. How many ties has Philadelphia, even today, with Canada?

The intelligence that the Abwehr, Nazi Germany's foreign espionage authority, gathered on Canada appears to have been collected in a most haphazard way. On 29 June 1940, Hans Borchers, Germany's consul-general in New York, reported a discussion with the president of Montreal's Chamber of Commerce about Canada's attitude toward Germany and the war effort. Writer David Kahn says that Windels and the other German consuls across the United States "clipped newspapers and bought maps," but this was hardly espionage. The Abwehr hired a Panamanian named Julio to monitor ships as they passed though the Panama Canal, and Julio reported vessels coming from Canada. On 29 August 1940, the Japanese military attaché in Bern, Switzerland, said that on a recent trip to Vichy he had heard that Canada was sending copious supplies to the United Kingdom. Such scattered reports were of marginal utility compared with what Eduard Hempel, minister at Germany's legation in Dublin, was able to write about Luftwaffe damage and the sailing of British ships during the Battle of Britain.

Of course, sources other than diplomatic ones could supply information, but these nondiplomatic sources seem, like Julio, to have operated outside Canada. The German navy seized the coding instructions from the Royal Canadian Navy's destroyer *Athabaska*, which it sank off the coast of Brittany, although it could make little use of them. As Canadian rearmament was late, there was initially little to spy on, and by 1944, when the Canadian army had become formidable, radio reconnaissance allowed eavesdropping on Canada from a distance. Nevertheless, a German spy named Janowski arrived at the Gaspé Peninsula in November 1942, and quickly aroused suspicion by trying to spend obsolete currency. A sharp operator, he convinced Cliff Harvison – later head of the RCMP – that he might serve as a double agent, and he misled Harvison completely. Janowski lied to Harvison so convincingly that Harvison rushed his findings to MI5 in London. More experienced than Harvison in such matters, MI5 officials rejected most of Janowski's statements as disinformation. German spies landed from submarines in the United States as late as December 1944; others arrived via Lisbon, South America, and then Mexico – finally wading or swimming across the less-than-formidable Rio Grande. Others entered Canada but made little impression.

Perhaps Nazi Germany's greatest espionage achievement of the war inside what is now Canada was the erection of a weather station on the Labrador coast in 1943. Canadian authorities became aware of it only in 1981 when a member of the submarine crew that had installed it wrote to the Department of National Defence to inquire about its fate. Labrador, however, did not become a part of Canada until 1949. Within Canada itself, the RCMP's Operation Watchdog eavesdropped on a radio transmitter in Hamburg, but netted few significant results.

James Eayrs' suspicions were justified, but the information that Windels (and his predecessors and colleagues) forwarded was available to anyone who might have been reading any major Canadian newspaper or listening to the radio. However, the expansion of Germany's consular network between 1936 and 1939 and the acceptance of a genuine Nazi, Wilhelm Rodde, as persona grata, should not have happened. The larger the number of consular employees and the more widespread the consular network, the larger the number of newspapers those consular posts could monitor. Expansion allowed more extensive surveillance of dissidents, not simply of those who expounded close to Montreal or Winnipeg.

Canada had no foreign intelligence organization to scrutinize incoming officials such as Rodde, and Ottawa either failed to ask the British government the right questions or the British erred. Awareness of the Hitler menace came late. In May 1938, R.B. Bennett, then leader of the opposition, spoke in the House of Commons about a plan for a German development scheme on Anticosti Island. Suspicion intensified after the Munich crisis of autumn 1938 and Germany's subsequent annexation of part of Czechoslovakia in violation of the Munich agreement. Kempff, who was never a card-carrying Nazi, and Seelheim, who was a Social Democrat when he arrived in Canada, never openly exceeded the limits of Canadian tolerance. Kempff's low profile certainly helped him. Neither Kempff nor Seelheim (nor their successors) initiated Fascist movements within Canada, and their support was limited. Windels and Granow also appear to have been circumspect. German activity in Canada was usually quiet, and Canadian authorities were unaware of much that was happening.

They were also indifferent. Neither the government of R.B. Bennett nor the government of Mackenzie King demonstrated deep concern for German Jews. Somebody with the RCMP actually informed Seelheim about the *Freunde des neuen Deutschlands*. The views that Seelheim expressed during his Vancouver trip almost two years later might have alerted more sensitive authorities, but, in the words of James Eayrs in another context, it was "a low, dishonest decade." The values of Germany's government were fairly clear by 1936, and Seelheim's views went on record. It is at least arguable that Mackenzie King's government, which permitted the consulates to proliferate, is more deserving of criticism than the consular officials themselves, who did largely what they were paid to do.

Happily, little harm seems to have resulted from the delays. Few were converted by Axis-organized propaganda; support at the ballot box for right-wing causes was minimal. German sources captured at the end of World War II revealed only 250 Nazis in Canada by 1939.

6

The Futility of the Dupuy Missions: Vichy-France and Canada, 1940–42[*]

"RCMP spied on French diplomats after October 1970 crisis: report"

This headline in the *Montreal Gazette* of 23 May 1992 repeated a news item from Radio Canada of the previous day: during the 1970s, the RCMP – then Canada's spy service – had supposedly tapped the phone lines of French officials in Ottawa, Quebec City, and perhaps elsewhere. Worried about possible French support for Quebec separatists, the federal government had asked the RCMP to maintain surveillance of French diplomats. The RCMP had then allegedly installed listening devices around the French embassy, examined the embassy's garbage, and intercepted messages between the embassy and the Quai d'Orsay.

A cynic might well say, "Plus ça change, plus c'est la même chose." A historian might see obvious parallels with the early 1940s, when France had another government that Canadian authorities did not trust. After the fall of France in June 1940, Canada and South Africa maintained diplomatic relations with Vichy France, in part because some Allied leaders, notably Churchill, believed that a Canadian presence in Vichy could be useful for gathering intelligence about the activities of the French government there. By contrast, as early as 12 November 1940 CCF member of Parliament M.J. Coldwell said on the floor of the House of Commons that relations between Canada and Vichy constituted a risk. Termination of the risk, he argued, would be "a precaution which we owe to the people of Canada." Privately the Canadian government recognized the merits of his argument and took precautions of a different nature. It could only speculate on the extent of the risks. Now, with the assistance of recently declassified French documents, this chapter offers support to Coldwell's impression that the costs and risks of the relationship, which were considerable, outweighed any benefits to the Allied cause. In the end, not much damage was done, but the expense and energy diverted to guarantee that no damage was done were considerable.

---

* The author wishes to thank Gordon Dutrisac for his insights on this chapter.

For many years, information has been available on this subject; immediately after World War II, William Langer wrote an apologia of U.S.–Vichy relations. Then Paul Baudouin – first foreign minister of the collaborationist Vichy regime – wrote his memoirs and noted the activities of Canadian diplomat Pierre Dupuy. In 1949, Prince Xavier de Bourbon reviewed Dupuy's role as a diplomat in building bridges between Pétain's France and Churchill's United Kingdom. Thirty years later and armed with voluminous British documentation, R.T. Thomas examined the diplomatic significance of Dupuy's trips to Vichy. The same year, F.H. Hinsley and his colleagues discussed British electronic eavesdropping in Vichy-controlled France and London–Vichy relations in the immediate aftermath of the fall of France.

Canadians too have published information on their relations with France. Before the war ended, the *Canada in World Affairs* series discussed Canada's relationship with Vichy France, including the visits of Pierre Dupuy. Dupuy's reports on his trips to Vichy (France's provisional capital after the Franco-German armistice) appear in volume VIII of *Documents on Canadian External Relations*, published in 1976. Captured German material has also been available for a long time. When Paul Couture delivered a paper to the Canadian Historical Association in 1978, he had access to copies of the mail of French officials which Canadian authorities had intercepted. These intercepts are available at the National Archives of Canada. Couture's 1971 doctoral thesis, based largely on Canadian sources, demonstrates the relevance of the Ottawa–Vichy relationship to anglophone–francophone politics within Canada. Now, however, with the declassification of French documents, additional insights are available.

The Context

When Philippe Pétain replaced Paul Reynaud as prime minister of France on 16 June 1940, three Commonwealth allies had representatives at Bordeaux, France's provisional capital before the armistice: the United Kingdom, Canada, and South Africa. Pétain's foreign minister, Paul Baudouin, informed them of the French government's intention to withdraw at once from the war effort against Germany, an intention which the British, Canadian, and South African governments found quite unacceptable. France still had one of the world's most powerful navies and one of the world's largest overseas empires. Legally Algeria was still part of Metropolitan France. Given the non-European resources at its disposal, the French government could have retreated to North Africa and, with the support of the navy and any soldiers and air force personnel who might have been evacuated, continued the struggle from there. Instead of that, Pétain and his associates chose to capitulate.

Immediately the three Commonwealth diplomats still at Bordeaux – Sir Ronald Campbell from the United Kingdom, Georges Vanier from Canada, and Colin Bain-Marais from South Africa – set sail for England, their subordinates having left earlier. Neither the Germans, when they arrived, nor their French collaborators would have any Commonwealth diplomats to capture or hold as hostages.

The terms of the Franco-German armistice were appalling, and British reaction was hostile. France would surrender Alsace-Lorraine to Germany and allow German forces to occupy 60 percent of France, including the city of Paris. Although Germany would continue to hold French prisoners of war, Pétain agreed to repatriate German POWs, who could then fight again. Pétain also agreed to recall ships of the French navy to bases in European France. Churchill simply could not allow France's formidable fleet to fall into German hands, and to prevent that, on 3–4 July British forces overran any French ships then in British ports, then bombarded the French fleet at Mersel-Kebir, near Oran, Algeria. Baudouin's response was to sever diplomatic relations between the United Kingdom and France, while the French air force bombed Gibraltar.

Nevertheless, Churchill wished to maintain some links with Vichy France, if only to know what was happening there. To that end, he asked Canada and South Africa, the only remaining allies that had had diplomatic relations of their own with France, not to cut their ties with Pétain's government. In order to oblige, Canada and South Africa would have to pay a price. If their diplomats were to have access to Vichy-controlled France, Canada and South Africa must continue to host French diplomats and consular officials on their territory. Ottawa and Pretoria agreed to do so.

Early in 1942, South Africa cut its ties with Vichy but, at the request of the United States government, Canada did not. Secretary of State Cordell Hull wanted to minimize French-German collusion and to promote Allied interests. In order to do that he needed intelligence, and he felt that the State Department could gather intelligence more effectively if the United States was not the only Ally to have diplomatic relations with Vichy. In order that the Americans could continue to operate in unoccupied France, he thought, Canada too must host Vichy's diplomats.

There is little need to dwell on the relationship between South Africa and Vichy. Neither Bain-Marais nor any other South African official ever went to Vichy, Pétain's capital, because Prime Minister Jan Christian Smuts insisted on a guarantee that Pétain refused to deliver: that Pétain would maintain his seat of government in a part of France that German forces had not occupied (Pétain hoped to return to Paris). Inside South Africa, Maurice Simonin, minister at France's legation in Pretoria, and Pierre Armand, French consul in Cape Town, carefully monitored the South African political scene, including the National Party's opposition to Smuts' war policies, and Free French activity (defection of sailors and purchases of equipment within South Africa to be taken overland to Free French areas of equatorial Africa controlled by General Charles de Gaulle and his followers). It is obvious that authorities in Vichy did not hang on every word of Simonin and Armand. On 16 May 1941, for example, Simonin forwarded a warning from Smuts. If French-German cooperation were to become any closer, the South African prime minister said, his country would have no choice but to sever diplomatic relations with Vichy. Barely three weeks later, Vichyite forces fired at Anglo-Gaullists as they captured Syria. What Simonin and Armand did paralleled the actions of Vichy representatives in Canada.

The Players and the Dangers

When the French National Assembly met at Vichy on 9–10 July 1940 and voted the Third Republic into oblivion, transferring authoritarian power into the hands of the 84-year-old Pétain and his associates, the Vichy government inherited the Third Republic's diplomatic corps and consular officials. In Canada, these included René Ristelhueber, minister at France's legation in Ottawa; Henri Coursier, consul-general in Montreal; Henri Bonnafous, consul in Quebec City; Henri Bougeral, consul in Winnipeg; Fernand Gallat, consul in Vancouver; Auguste Tambon, consular-agent in Halifax; Rochereau de la Sablière, consular-agent in Toronto; and Canadians who served as consular-agents in Calgary, Edmonton, Regina, Saskatoon, and Saint John. Late in 1941 Jean Ricard replaced Bonnafous in Quebec City.

The fact that these people stayed at their posts was cause for concern. French diplomats around the world – Ambassador Charles Corbin in London, Minister Raymond Brugère in Yugoslavia, and Vice-Consul Paul Pazéry in Philadelphia – resigned in disgust and dismay, unable to defend the Pétain regime, its actions, and its policies. Others of dubious reliability from the standpoint of the Vichy government lost their jobs in purges orchestrated by Foreign Minister Baudouin. Further resignations, including those of François Charles-Roux at Vichy's Foreign Office and Roger Triau at the vice-consulate in New York, followed when arch-collaborationist Pierre Laval replaced Paul Baudouin as foreign minister on 27 October 1940. Ristelhueber and the consuls in Canada, however, remained at their posts, evidently willing to serve the Vichy regime and trusted by it. What sensitive information might they forward to Vichy, and from there what might reach the German enemy?

These were justifiable concerns. David Kahn, an authority on German espionage during World War II, has written: "Vichy France's Admiral Darlan offered the German navy information on British naval dispositions; the Führer was pleased to accept." German sources show that information forwarded from Ottawa to Vichy did reach German authorities. In August 1940, a German official in Bern wrote a report about Canada based on information from the Japanese military attaché in the Swiss capital. The Japanese had heard the news while visiting Vichy. In 1942, the German embassy in Rome forwarded more Canadian information, received via France, to the Foreign Office in Berlin. In all probability, these were not the only two such occasions.

Admittedly historian Robert O. Paxton – who studied both French and German records – repeatedly makes clear that Pétain and his associates were far more interested in collaboration with Hitler than Hitler was in collaboration with Vichy France. Paxton is convinced that Hitler did not ask the French to spy for him. Hitler placed the sensitivities of his Italian ally ahead of those of the defeated French, and French and Italian ambitions were often in conflict. Hitler wanted the French to keep out of the way while he clobbered his enemies; he did not regard them as partners or potential equals. On 2 May 1942 Hitler declared: "France declared war on us, so she must bear the consequences."

Professor John W.M. Chapman, who has examined German, Italian, and Japanese archives, provides circumstantial evidence that supports Paxton's hypothesis. In a recent article, Chapman shows that there was active intelligence sharing among the three principal Axis partners – but only to a degree. The three Axis belligerents did not fully trust each other. Given the limitations on intelligence sharing among partners at war, it is most unlikely that any one of them would have relied on a defeated enemy to any significant extent.

At the time, however, Canadian authorities could not have known that. Also, Ristelhueber was a bureaucrat, not a hero. There seem to have been no limits to what he would do to keep his job, no task too distasteful for his conscience, no particular loyalty to any master or ideology. He completely misled Prime Minister Mackenzie King, who considered him "very loyal in all his relationships." For almost two years, Ristelhueber also managed to persuade King that Pétain was a patriot making the best of a bad situation. Ristelhueber was an intellectual who had already authored a book about French traditions in the Middle East. Once he lost his position as France's minister to Canada he became a professor at the University of Montreal, where he wrote four books in four years. Yet on 25 November 1940 Ristelhueber wrote to Fernand Gallat, French consul in Vancouver, about two Vichy laws that affected civil servants. That of 17 July limited employment to children of a French father. That of 3 October denied employment to Jews, regardless of nationality. Ristelhueber wanted to know whether anyone at the Vancouver consulate was ineligible for employment under either of these rules. Gallat replied that everyone at his consulate was French, even under this restricted definition. That was not good enough for Ristelhueber. One week before Christmas he wrote Gallat again to insist that Gallat answer both questions. Was anyone at his consulate Jewish? On Christmas Eve, Gallat replied that nobody at his consulate had any Jewish blood.

In 1942, despite his best efforts, Ristelhueber's career as a French diplomat ended. When Pétain ordered French troops to fire upon American forces landing in North Africa, first the United States and then Canada severed diplomatic relations with the Vichy regime. The new French government at Algiers headed by Admiral François Darlan managed to contact Ristelhueber on 16 November, and the next day Ristelhueber indicated his willingness to work for Algiers rather than for Vichy. When a young man assassinated Darlan on Christmas Eve, Ristelhueber sent Algiers his regrets about the loss of a "great patriot." Through contemporaries and historians, Darlan has enjoyed a reputation as an arch-collaborator who switched sides at a most opportune moment. An opportunist himself, Ristelhueber wrote to Darlan's more principled successor, General Henri Giraud, asking for instructions and offering to serve, but neither Giraud nor his successor, Charles de Gaulle, was interested.

Ristelhueber's subordinates included men of questionable values. Despite his enthusiasm for Vichy's cause until Canada closed Vichy's consulates and its legation, Henri Bougeral, ex-consul at Winnipeg, then went to work for the Gaullists as head of their legation in San José, Costa Rica. Like Darlan and Ristelhueber, Bougeral appears to have been an opportunist. Potentially more dangerous was France's consular-agent in Toronto, evidently a true believer. As late as June 1942, twenty months after Pétain had issued a public appeal for collaboration with Hitler's Germany, and many months after Pétain had ordered his forces to fire on the British in Gibraltar (July 1940), on British and Gaullist forces in Dakar (September 1940), and on British and Gaullist forces in Syria (early summer 1941), Rochereau de la Sablière heaped praise upon Vichy's leaders. As he lost his position as France's consular-agent in Toronto, de la Sablière referred to Pétain as "our incomparable and so indispensable Marshal, standard-bearer of the moral and spiritual values which we must defend." Given the character of these men, it is quite possible that had their government asked them to do so, they would have spied for Germany. Given the track record of the Pétain government, it is not impossible that it would have given such orders had Hitler decided to exploit his French connection.

Canadian Envoys in Vichy and Vichy-controlled Territory

Pétain and his associates at Vichy in unoccupied France were the winners of the intelligence battles in 1940–42. Their officials remained at their posts across Canada and South Africa on an ongoing basis, and they reported to Vichy. By contrast, a lone and rather junior Canadian diplomat made three trips to Vichy over a period of slightly more than two years, while another resided briefly in Saint-Pierre and Miquelon.

Within Canada itself, a return to France by Canada's pre-armistice minister in Paris, Georges Vanier, would have been highly controversial. To avoid such controversy among Canadians, the Canadian government transferred responsibility onto his erstwhile first secretary, Pierre Dupuy. Vanier returned to Canada, and the Department of External Affairs elevated Dupuy to the rank of chargé d'affaires. Dupuy would reside in London but make periodic visits to France. (He could do this with a minimum of controversy, as he was also accredited to the London-based Dutch and Belgian governments-in-exile.) As far as Churchill was concerned, "Dupuy was [the] only means of contact that he, Churchill, had with Vichy." The United States, neutral until December 1941, had an embassy in Vichy and consular posts throughout France and North Africa, but Churchill could not be certain that Washington was forwarding all the information that he wanted.

There are several factors to remember when evaluating Dupuy's reports. First, there were limits to what any one individual could learn during visits to a police state, especially one as vulnerable to Nazi pressure as Vichy France. German ambassador Otto Abetz once sneered that the Wehrmacht could overrun all of France within thirty hours. Dupuy was aware that Hitler could reduce food rations to French prisoners of war or provoke troubles anywhere in France in order to justify reprisals. Pétain once said that the POWs were hostages. Moreover, Dupuy's reports were not exhaustive. He knew more than he included in them. Decades after the events in question, historian Raymond Tournoux interviewed Dupuy at considerable length, and Dupuy told him that when he went to Vichy he was on loan to the British government; he did not really travel there as a Canadian agent. Much of what he learned he reported directly to Churchill, some to Mackenzie King. Some he included in other reports.

Dupuy first went to Vichy in November and December 1940. Lord Halifax, the British foreign secretary, wanted him to answer three questions. What possibility was there that Pétain's France might ally itself with Nazi Germany against the United Kingdom? Could the French fleet at Toulon fall into German hands? Were the Pétainistes likely to try to retake those French possessions in sub-Saharan Africa that had aligned with Charles de Gaulle's rival government in London?

Unable to disclose his real reasons for going to Vichy, Dupuy offered a plausible agenda. He wanted to discuss the repatriation of Canadian civilians trapped in German-occupied France in exchange for German civilians interned in Canada. He also wanted to discuss financial concerns of those Canadians in France. Some faced destitution as they could not withdraw their own money from French bank accounts. The minister of finance expressed surprise and offered to let them spend what was theirs without restriction inside France and to make special arrangements for their trip home. As a gesture of good will, Vichy instructed French customs officials not to apply the rules very strictly as Canadians and their possessions departed.

However, there were several clues to what Dupuy might be doing. As early as 6 August 1940 Ristelhueber told Vichy that the British government approved of the ongoing relationship between Canada and Vichy, and he clipped a statement of the prime minister's, delivered that same day to the House of Commons, to that effect. On 27 December 1940, in connection with Dupuy's first visit to Pétain's capital, Ristelhueber wrote to Foreign Minister Pierre-Étienne Flandin. Ristelhueber noted reports in the *Winnipeg Free Press* and the *Financial Post* that Ottawa would not be communicating with Vichy without British consent. On 8 September 1941, Ristelhueber reported that one of Mackenzie King's first statements after returning to Canada from talks with Churchill was an assertion that Canada was maintaining its ties with Vichy at the request of the British prime minister. Early in 1942 Ristelhueber said that King had repeated that statement on the floor of the House of Commons. No official in Vichy appears to have given the matter much thought, perhaps because by that time Dupuy had stopped going to Vichy.

Even in May 1942, after South Africa had cut its ties to Vichy and when Canada was ordering the closure of Vichy's consular posts, Ristelhueber seemed to miss the significance of the clues. He reported a statement of Mackenzie King that after consultations with Washington and London, the Canadian government had decided to maintain its relations with Vichy "for the moment." There were important reasons for this which he could not reveal, said the prime minister. In a letter to Pierre Laval (one of Vichy's most powerful officials, executed after the Liberation for collaboration with the Nazis), Ristelhueber speculated on what the undisclosed reasons might be. He failed to suggest the real one – the State Department's belief that Canada's links with Vichy rendered American links with Vichy somewhat more respectable and less suspicious than they would otherwise have been. Ristelhueber guessed that King thought the ties with Vichy important for the maintenance of national unity within Canada. Finally, in August 1942 King replied to a question from CCF leader M.J. Coldwell with a statement that had been more accurate a year earlier than it was by then. When Coldwell questioned the value of the ties with Vichy, King said that it might be advantageous to be in a position to send someone to Vichy for up-to-date information. As King had little intention of sending Dupuy back to Vichy at that time, such a statement would not have interfered with his work. However, it did deflect French attention from the real reason for the ongoing Ottawa–Vichy relationship.

When gathering information, Dupuy took advantage of the many contacts he had at Vichy. Both among refugees from occupied France and among members of the Pétain government, he had friends whom he had known as first secretary in the Canadian legation in Paris. With help from the former director of the Maison des étudiants canadiens at Paris, one Firmin Roz, a personal friend of Pétain's, Dupuy arranged an interview with Pétain himself.

Dupuy's first report, dated Christmas Day 1940, said that Marshal Pétain was "still … hoping for a British victory." (The U.S. chargé d'affaires in Vichy had voiced a similar message the previous month.) French historian Robert Frank, however, with access to the available documentary evidence, has concluded that Pétain was playing games with Great Britain and with Anglophiles. He wanted to give the impression of sympathy, but his loyalty lay with the Axis.

Pétain and Admiral François Darlan, commander-in-chief of the French naval forces, guaranteed to Dupuy's satisfaction that Germans or Italians could not possibly seize the French fleet. Before they could do that, either the ships could escape from their base at Toulon, or, in a worst-case scenario, "be scuttled there in a few moments." One may well question whether the assurance had any validity. British forces had easily captured French ships in British ports in July 1940, and Vichy's agents in Tunisia were to allow Germans to capture fifteen warships and nine submarines at the French naval base at Bizerte. These were subsequently used against the Allies. When in November 1942 German forces were approaching the naval base at Toulon and Darlan ordered the fleet to sail to North Africa, local officers procrastinated so long that they had to scuttle their ships to prevent a German takeover. Obviously Darlan's control of the fleet was limited.

With regard to the third question, the Vichy authorities told Dupuy that de Gaulle should be fighting Italians, not other French people. While they promised not to use the navy to regain the Black African colonies, they refused to rule out an overland invasion. Churchill himself rejected Dupuy's advice arising from this particular matter – that he tell the Gaullists to fight Italians instead of Vichyite Frenchmen.

The tone of Dupuy's report was optimistic. Dupuy said that Pétain had received him "like a son." (The U.S. chargé d'affaires had heard that Pétain found Dupuy "nice but ingratiating.") Dupuy also reported that, with the exception of Laval, the French were doing the best they could to salvage what remained of their country. (Laval, Pétain's second foreign minister, was mistrusted even by his colleagues and had close connections with the Germans. Pétain had dismissed Laval on 13 December 1940 and ordered his arrest, but reinstated him in 1942.) Further, Dupuy found the people as a whole "very pro-British." (American officials in France agreed that the French people as a whole were highly sympathetic to the British cause, even if the value of widespread but passive support was quite another matter.) The Vichy government had sent 400,000 men to North Africa who, perhaps some day, might be useful to the Allied war effort, reported Dupuy. He did not foresee that less than two years later Pétain would order those troops to fire on Great Britain's American allies.

During the first half of 1941, Dupuy made two additional trips to Vichy. They were of limited utility. On his second visit (late winter 1941), Dupuy found evidence of rising differences between the Pétain government and its German master. Yet, historians have found that France had entered a new period of collaboration with Germany when, under German pressure, Vichy's third foreign minister, Pierre-Étienne Flandin, left office and Admiral Darlan succeeded him.

Dupuy was unjustifiably optimistic. He reported without reservation, "The Marshal [Pétain] assured me that Laval would never return to Government while he was there." Thirteen months later, on 18 April 1942, that assurance proved worthless. Dupuy said that French officials considered Admiral Darlan "anti-German," and he commented: "I found in French military circles a greater desire to collaborate with us." Within weeks, French forces were shooting at British forces in Syria. Dupuy reported that "thousands" of French servicemen were being sent to North Africa where, implicitly, they might eventually assist the Allied cause. Some of these undoubtedly remained to fire at American forces the following year. Assurances from Marshal Pétain, Admiral Darlan, and General Charles Huntziger — whose task it had been to sign Hitler's armistice terms on behalf of the Pétain government — that Vichy France would not cede French colonies, fleet, or bases to the Germans made Dupuy "happy." Whether these men could deliver on their assurances was another matter. Dupuy said, "This time I think the French have come a step nearer to us." As evidence, he cited efforts to cooperate in the exchange of information and assistance to escaped prisoners of war and to British civilians caught in Vichy France.

Dupuy's third and final report, on the basis of a late summer visit, sounded a pessimistic note but was not without hopefulness. Doubtful about Darlan personally, Dupuy nevertheless found "the great majority of the administration," the army, and 90 percent of the civil servants to be supporters of the Allies. Although Darlan had replaced Foreign Office employees who were openly favourable to the Allies, their successors were "no less favourable to us but more cautious in expressing their views." Even within the navy, whose top officer was Darlan, Dupuy found Darlan's influence less than it might appear. Many did not like their commander-in-chief, thought Dupuy, and Admiral Paul Auphand, the recently appointed inspector of the fleet, certainly disagreed with his superior. To avoid embarrassment to Auphand, who might some day be useful to the Allies, Dupuy warned, "His name should never be mentioned over the radio or in the press." (Professor William Langer, one of the first historians to have access to classified State Department documents and captured enemy archives, agrees that Auphand was hostile to the Axis.)

Dupuy blamed Darlan for Pétain's unwillingness to meet with him during the third visit, but he found virtue, perhaps too much virtue, in certain others. Intermediaries assured him that Pétain was giving Germany the minimum of collaboration necessary to gain the maximum amount of time. Darlan was the real villain, and his chief opponent within the military was General Maxime Weygand. In Dupuy's words, Weygand had become "the centre of resistance to Germany." Germany's difficulties in the Soviet Union were affecting its credibility within France, but some of the French suspected that German forces might occupy Spain and Portugal "within the next few months." Even supporters of the Free French, according to Dupuy, thought General Charles de Gaulle "unnecessarily provocative." Although few would disagree with this assessment of de Gaulle, Weygand was a rather weak reed on which to base Allied hopes.

While in France, Pierre Dupuy was not allowed to use the cipher, and this was a serious matter. Diplomats depend on ciphers for sending messages that might fall into the wrong hands or otherwise be intercepted. A cipher is usually a system of numbers, jumbled in such a way as to be intelligible to cipher clerks at the sending and receiving ends who have the key. As a substitution of, say, 1 for "A" and 2 for "B" would be too obvious, cipher clerks usually have complicated systems which they change frequently. An observer would not be able to make sense of the message, although he would know that it must hold some importance to be worth putting into cipher.

A cipher would have been particularly useful for Dupuy. Tournoux says that when Dupuy made his 1940 visit, various police forces – including the Gestapo – trailed him and spied on him from the moment of his arrival at Lisbon. On his second trip, both the French navy, controlled by the Anglophobic Darlan, and the Gestapo kept him under surveillance. Friendly French police gave Dupuy the names of two Nazi agents in charge of watching him and warned him to inspect his room every time he returned to it. This was just as well, says Tournoux, for he was carrying several important papers, and on one occasion, he did find a microphone under his bed.

Dupuy's third visit to Vichy turned out to be his last. Important people in Canada and South Africa questioned the utility of the third visit, or, for that matter, of any subsequent visits. Norman Robertson, Canadian undersecretary of state for external affairs, wrote: "Dupuy's sources of information are drying up." Despite what Dupuy was about to report, Robertson thought that very few people sympathetic to the Allies had significant positions in Vichy. As far as Robertson was concerned, Vichy's legation in Ottawa, whose existence helped make Dupuy's visits possible, was not in Canada's interests. Robertson and Pearson both thought that Dupuy tended to err on the side of optimism, as did even Churchill. Although Churchill insisted that Dupuy "gave much information which is most helpful," he tried to check Dupuy's "facts" independently.

Actually, Dupuy was not the only Canadian official on French territory in 1941. From 9 August 1941, career diplomat Christopher Eberts, whose rank was vice-consul, served as acting consul on the islands of Saint-Pierre and Miquelon. S.T. Wood, commissioner of the RCMP, had suggested that radio stations in Saint-Pierre and Miquelon were transmitting information about "our convoys and shipping ... The despatch of code cablegrams and telegrams, communications with vessels at sea and their remarkable knowledge of nautical problems, make it obvious that certain residents of St. Pierre et Miquelon are fully qualified to carry on espionage and sabotage along such lines." Wood urged that Canada "take over the control of the Islands."

One must remember that World War II predated the era of satellites that enable meteorologists to see at a glance what weather conditions are like worldwide. Forecasters depended upon surface reports from upwind, and given that neither side wanted to provide useful information about winds, tides, or storms to the enemy navy, weather reports were classified information. Radio St. Pierre was not brazenly issuing weather forecasts, but nobody could be certain that it was not sending coded messages. A certain tune or type of music, or a certain combination of words, could conceivably have meant one kind of weather, while variations might have meant other types of weather. Understandably, those responsible for the safety of the Royal Canadian Navy preferred to take no chances, and the islands that France had salvaged from her eighteenth-century North American empire had become a challenge.

Instead of a military invasion, the Canadian government responded by opening a consulate there. Eberts' task was to write reports "from time to time, on questions of trade, communications, navigation and shipping, and other subjects that may be of interest to the Canadian government." (Ristelhueber thought that he knew the reasons why the Canadian government was opening a consulate in Saint-Pierre: "to watch [the] situation there and assess the needs of a population which depends entirely on Canada for its imports.") Once he was in Saint-Pierre, Eberts issued a detailed report on its communications facilities. He had to admit: "There does not seem to be any means of finding out what material is contained in the messages sent from the [radio] station in Saint Pierre to France ... The only solution would be to have the station monitored here." Eberts also had some good news. U.S. authorities had refused to permit the sale of a short-wave transmitter to Francis Leroux, "an ardent pro-Vichy radio merchant in Saint Pierre." Maurice Pasquet, the U.S. consul in Saint-Pierre, agreed with the embargo. Intelligence problems in Saint-Pierre and Miquelon resolved themselves when the Free French captured the islands on Christmas Eve, 1941.

Vichy's Officials in Canada

The presence of Vichy's representatives in Canada was controversial, and Canadian authorities believed that it necessitated various measures of damage control. These took three forms, all of them effective to a limited extent. An obvious first step was interception of mail en route to or from France's legation in Ottawa and the consular posts across the country. This was happening at a time when such resources and expertise were badly needed on other activities. Second, Canada entered the fields of cryptography and electronic surveillance. While electronic surveillance of the Vichyite diplomats appears to have been limited to eavesdropping on their telephone calls, it soon developed into interception of ciphered cables among enemy diplomats, particularly around the Pacific Ocean. (There will be more on this subject in the next chapter.) Third, Canadian authorities asked Ristelhueber to be careful about what he and his consular subordinates reported.

In order that Ristelhueber would not notice, Canadian postal censors had tried to process his mail – read and record it – quickly. However, they were not fast enough, and he complained of delays in his mail. In order to avoid interference from Canadian postal censors, Ristelhueber consistently sent messages via courier to the French consulate-general in New York, which then sent them by cable to Vichy or by an even more secure route. Ristelhueber's pouch often travelled from New York to Lisbon, thence to the French embassy in Madrid. A courier would continue with the correspondence as far as Port Bou, on the French-Spanish border. Canadian postal censors suspected that something of this nature was happening, but they could do little. Indeed, when the Canadian government closed Vichy's consulates on 1 June 1942 and Henri Bougeral in Winnipeg lost his position as consul, Ristelhueber appointed him as the legation's courier. The Department of External Affairs was aware only that Bougeral had found some form of employment at the legation.

If war-weary Canadians hoped that Ristelhueber would forward their concerns to Vichy, they did so in vain. Little of what he wrote was written to persuade authorities at Vichy to modify their policies. Perhaps it did not matter. Except during Dupuy's first visit, Pétain and other members of his government appear to have been indifferent to what Canadians might have been thinking. When Pétain's forces fired upon British troops at Dakar, Ristelhueber reported Mackenzie King relatively indifferent. (In this case, there was some substance to what Ristelhueber said. The prime minister mentioned Dakar in his diary, but he did not criticize Pétain's forces for firing at the British troops. He did think the British attack on Dakar a highly provocative action and recorded that he personally had opposed it.) On 24 October 1940 Hitler and Pétain met at Montoire. The Quebec City daily Le Soleil was so disgusted that it suggested the time might have come to terminate Canada's relations with Vichy. Ristelhueber did not warn Vichy that Pétain's collaborationist policies were increasing the possibility of a diplomatic rupture. He simply labelled Le Soleil's stand "sad and surprising." As time passed and Canadian newspapers became increasingly hostile toward Vichy, Ristelhueber tried to change the newspaper coverage, not Vichy's actions or policies. On 29 June 1941, particularly incensed about negative publicity concerning the consulate-general in Montreal by that city's Le Jour, Ristelhueber complained to justice minister Ernest Lapointe. According to the French diplomat, Lapointe promised to speak to the prime minister. Finally, when the Canadian government ordered the closure of Vichy's consular posts across Canada in the spring of 1942, Ristelhueber dismissed the process as a charade. In order to maintain the legation, Ristelhueber wrote to Laval, Mackenzie King had to do something to placate his critics. For that reason, he had shut down the consulates.

Nevertheless, Ristelhueber's correspondence, intercepted or otherwise, offers no evidence that he deliberately forwarded information that might have been useful to the Germans. On 28 August 1940 Ristelhueber told the French consul-general in New York about rumours of the pending destroyers-for-bases deal; Ristelhueber thought that sixty such destroyers would be involved when, in fact, there were only fifty. On 28 September, the Foreign Office in Vichy asked Tambon in Halifax to indicate whether certain ships, not all of them French, had been unloaded. Ristelhueber noted Georges Vanier's appointment to the Permanent Joint Board on Defence. These matters might have been more sensitive than they turned out to be, but all quickly became matters of public knowledge or proved of little consequence.

Ristelhueber's reports contain little about matters that would not have been of legitimate concern to a bona fide French government. His principal sources were newspapers, radio broadcasts, and debates in the Canadian Parliament – hardly secret material. Any purely Canadian problems with Ristelhueber appear to have been potential rather than actual.

Gaullist concerns were another matter. The Gaullists were Canada's allies, but like their counterparts in South Africa, Ristelhueber and his consular subordinates did spy on them. Both Ristelhueber and consul Henri Bougeral in Winnipeg were enthusiastic Vichyites, and they monitored Gaullist activity in Canada. French citizens on the Prairies had enlisted and joined the Free French in London, Bougeral said, while "parishes and French societies" were raising goods and money for the Gaullists. To win support for Vichy, Bougeral proposed the circulation of Pétainiste French books and newspapers and the broadcasting of "certain programmes" in Canada. Ristelhueber himself mentioned Gaullist activity in a January 1941 dispatch; in July of that year, the Foreign Office asked Ristelhueber for "names of Frenchmen representing French firms in America who are suspected of Gaullist activities." In

Winnipeg, Consul Bougeral was particularly keen to monitor Gaullists, though he was convinced that most Prairie Gaullists were British or Canadian, not French. He reported a mid-August campaign to raise funds for Free French soldiers and their families.

Into 1942, Vichy's consulates in Canada continued to monitor and obstruct Gaullists. In response to letters from Ristelhueber, Gallat provided names and addresses of seventy-eight French draft-dodgers then living in British Columbia. Bougeral found only one in his jurisdiction, a rather high-profile individual – Edmond A. Poulain, president of the Gaullists in St. Boniface. Bougeral thought that Poulain should be stripped of his French citizenship.

Some of Ristelhueber's mail was in cipher, and as the interceptors did not know how to decipher it, they forwarded copies of the ciphered messages to cryptographers in the United Kingdom. At first the British planned to inform Ottawa only when they thought there would be something of interest. Lester Pearson, however, counsellor and official secretary at Canada's high commission in London, disagreed with this procedure. The British should report on all intercepted messages, he said, for Canadians were better qualified than they to determine what was relevant to Canada.

Although the British subsequently provided clear summaries of the French officials' ciphered messages, along with lists of those that they claimed to have been unable to decipher, Pearson remained less than satisfied. By 1941 Pearson thought that the British were giving the Canadian intercepts too low a priority. As they could not be bothered to make a serious effort to understand as many messages as they really could, thought Pearson, Canada ought to hire its own cryptographers. This it did in the form of the Wartime Examination Unit (WEU).

The WEU cooperated with British intelligence. Insofar as France was concerned, the Canadian government continued to send the bulk of its Vichy-related materials to the United Kingdom for deciphering, even after the WEU was up and running in the summer of 1941. Watching Vichy would be a cooperative effort. On its own, the WEU would concentrate on transoceanic messages, particularly those between Germany or Japan on the one hand, and South American contacts on the other. (A few months after Pearl Harbor, the British high commissioner in Ottawa, Malcolm Macdonald, asked that the WEU concentrate on Japan and the Pacific. Norman Robertson agreed to this provided that the United Kingdom would keep Ottawa informed about naval activities in the Atlantic. Thanks to Herbert Norman, a Canadian diplomat with considerable experience in Japan, the work of the WEU was first-rate.)

In May 1941, the Canadian government finally denied further use of the diplomatic pouch or cipher facilities to France's consular officials. This matter had been under consideration since July 1940 when Thomas A. Stone, the official at the Department of External Affairs who was responsible for postal censorship, had recommended that Ottawa reconsider the rights of any representatives of the Vichy government to communicate in cipher. Almost certainly, Stone thought, Germans would see their dispatches, and Canadians would not know what information was being transmitted. O.D. Skelton, Robertson's predecessor at the Department of External Affairs, saw merit in what Stone said but thought Ristelhueber and his consular subordinates trustworthy, unlikely to send sensitive information to Vichy. Skelton died in late January 1941, and on 26 May, Robertson and his staff withdrew cipher privileges from the consular officials – but not from Ristelhueber. They told the French minister that this was a reprisal for Vichy's denial of such amenities to Dupuy when he went to France. (Actually, withdrawal of cipher privileges was the result of a British suggestion designed both to express displeasure and to allow the French officials to remain in Canada so that Dupuy could continue to make his trips.) Ristelhueber explained, privately of course, that the German Armistice Commission had given the orders to deprive Dupuy of normal diplomatic amenities, and that the Pétain government had had no choice but to oblige. Nevertheless, Norman Robertson was well aware of the Canadian government's inability to control the flow of information across the border to Vichy's agents inside the United States.

In 1942, surveillance of Ristelhueber intensified. In September 1941, after the Department of External Affairs intercepted one of his telegrams to Vichy about the promotion within Canada of works by authors favourable to Pétain's regime, Ottawa reconsidered, then withdrew Ristelhueber's cipher privileges. Then, early in 1942, with the Free French in control of Saint-Pierre and Miquelon, ciphered messages continued to arrive from the French legation in Ottawa. This became a matter of deep concern to Canadian authorities. Stone sent copies of the Saint-Pierre telegrams, which the Gaullists had provided, to the WEU, but the WEU was so deeply involved in transatlantic and transpacific messages that it did not have the time to work on them. The navy sent copies to London by courier, and Stone indicated that if the British could decipher them, "it will probably be considerable help to the Unit." In other words, Ristelhueber's messages to Saint-Pierre were a concern but not the highest priority, at least once the Free French controlled Saint-Pierre and Miquelon.

Because information sent to Vichy might find its way to Berlin, there were limits on what Ristelhueber and the consular officials were supposed to report. On 22 October 1940 O.D. Skelton approached Ristelhueber with a request that French officials not report to their government on Allied or neutral shipping in Canadian waters. On the basis of the information available – both French correspondence intercepted by Canadian authorities and

French correspondence that managed to reach Vichy undetected – there is nothing to suggest that Ristelhueber and the consular officials violated that trust. On 31 August 1941 the *New York Herald-Tribune* reported that Vichy's embassy in Washington was forwarding such sensitive information to Europe, but if anyone in Canada was doing so, the documentation has been destroyed or remains hidden. On the contrary, in a note of 25 October 1940, Ristelhueber wrote that the French did not seek news that Canada's government did not think should be forwarded. He demanded that his consuls write nothing to Vichy about such matters.

By May 1942, shortly before the closure of the consulates, the WEU was monitoring Ristelhueber's telephone calls. On 19 May, when Coursier, the consul-general in Montreal, was about to become persona non grata because of his propaganda activities, Ristelhueber called Coursier "cher ami" and heard Coursier describe a quarrel with Abbé Lemoine of Stanislas College. Madame Ristelhueber and Madame Coursier planned to spend a few days with each other the following week.

What brought matters to a head between Canada and Vichy France was not espionage of any description but propaganda inside Quebec. As early as 31 July 1940, Canadian postal censors had intercepted a letter from Coursier to Ristelhueber. The letter revealed that *Le Devoir* had negotiated with Coursier for "an alternative news service," which Coursier then provided. The RCMP noted that Coursier had regular contacts with activists who opposed conscription and had made a "sizable" financial contribution to their cause. The Mounted Police also noted that information on Quebec public opinion which consular officials forwarded to France assisted Vichy's short-wave broadcasters as they selected and reported "the news" to Quebec audiences. These developments were consistent with the activities of Gaston Henry-Haye, Vichy's ambassador in Washington, who tried to arouse anti-British sentiment among New England's Acadians.

The Department of External Affairs then questioned the presence of France's consular posts, as distinct from the legation in Ottawa. On 3 October 1941, Stone had recommended closure of the consulates. Coursier at Montreal was antagonizing the Free French, and to leave a "semi-enemy" like Tambon at Halifax was positively dangerous. Surely the continued existence of the legation would be adequate compensation to Vichy for any visits that Dupuy might make. As a first step, the Canadian government banned Tambon from the docks, but Pearson – by this time located in Ottawa as assistant undersecretary of state for external affairs – suggested similar restrictions on Vichy's consular officials in other port cities.

On 8 May 1942 the minister of fisheries accused Consul-General Coursier of "engaging in Vichy propaganda" and demanded the closure of all French consular posts. On 22 May, the Cabinet War Committee agreed.

Evidently this factor more than offset any constructive efforts on the part of the consulate-general, such as forwarding news among family members separated by the war. Thus, propaganda rather than espionage determined the short-term course of the Vichy–Ottawa relationship. Yet, when it closed the consulates, Ottawa allowed the legation to survive in order that Dupuy might continue to go to Vichy.

There was another factor as well; the Free French were already active. In his memoirs, Pearson says that Canada would gladly have given formal recognition to the Free French and closed all Vichy's outlets, "for [which] we had scant respect," except that Ottawa did not want to upset Washington's delicate relationship with Vichy as the American landings in North Africa approached.

When the Vichyites had to surrender their legation, however, it was for reasons other than espionage and propaganda. The relationship even survived Pétain's congratulations to the German army for its victory at Dieppe. In early November 1942, when American forces landed in North Africa and Marshal Pétain ordered French troops to fire on them, the United States severed diplomatic relations. Canada followed suit, but granted Ristelhueber political asylum.

Conclusions

With benefit of hindsight and access to the French diplomatic archives, it is fair to say that the Vichyite diplomats and consular officials in Canada and South Africa were able to do more for their cause than Dupuy or Bain-Marais could do for the Allies in Vichy France. Indeed, Canada and the Gaullists paid a price and took risks so that Pierre Dupuy could visit Vichy and gather intelligence. That intelligence, on balance, was not very useful. In both Canada and South Africa, by contrast, the Vichyites were in a position to promote their cause and to keep themselves informed. The time and energy that Canadians devoted to the surveillance of Vichy's representatives were formidable. Nevertheless, Canada's role in intelligence matters in connection with Vichy France is indicative of a hallmark of twentieth-century Canadian diplomacy – that of firm support for the United Kingdom and the United States. Even when it seemed contrary to Canadian interests or the interests of Canada's Gaullist allies, Canadians continued to host Vichy's agents, to a considerable extent because authorities in London or Washington wanted them to do so.

If it was a mistake to maintain diplomatic relations with Vichy, the Canadian government deserves praise for its vigilance with Vichy's men, and that vigilance began a new phase of Canadian intelligence history. It was in large measure because of the presence of Vichy officials that Canada entered the fields of cryptography and electronic surveillance, and Canadians did develop and maintain considerable expertise in these areas. The WEU provided intelligence, first in connection with South America and Asia, then in connection with the Battle of the Atlantic in partnership with the United Kingdom and the United States. Skills developed in dealing with Vichy later proved useful during the Cold War. As part of the UKUSA intelligence network, Canadians eavesdropped on Soviet telephone calls from places like Alert on Ellesmere Island. However, between 1940 and 1942, nobody foresaw such an eventuality as a by-product of Dupuy's travels.

Fig. 1. It was in this section of Montreal's Tupper Street that Spanish diplomats Ramón Carranza and Juan Dubosc rented a house in 1898. Because of what American agents discovered when they broke in, the Canadian government ordered Carranza and Dubosc to return to Spain.

Photograph by the author

Fig. 2. Kingston Penitentiary became home to three Irish-Americans who tried to dynamite the Welland Canal in 1900. Security at the penitentiary was tightened when Colonel Sherwood heard reports that the terrorists' friends might dynamite a wall to allow them to escape.

National Archives of Canada PA-46242

Fig. 3. Colonel Arthur Percy Sherwood dominated the Dominion Police from 1885 until they became part of the RCMP in 1920. Pinkerton agents kept him informed about potential terrorists in the United States who might attack Canadian targets.

National Archives of Canada PA-44904

Fig. 4. William Jennings Bryan, U.S. Secretary of State from 1913 until 1915, demonstrated far more concern about possible violations of United States neutrality than about terrorist attacks on Canadian targets.
Courtesy of the Library of Congress

Fig. 5A. Canals along the Canada–United States border were favourite targets of terrorists in wartime. The canals at Sault Ste. Marie allowed ore-bearing ships from Duluth, Minnesota, to travel from Lake Superior to Lake Huron, and thence to Erie, Pennsylvania, near the steel mills of Pittsburgh. Draftsman Emil Wilhelm Lang made extensive blueprints of the canal locks, railway junctions, and railway bridge in the Sault Ste. Marie area, and then posted them to Germany from New York. This aerial view of the Sault Ste. Marie locks, facing downstream, vividly displays the bottleneck along the St. Mary's River. The Canadian shore is on the left, the American on the right. The railway bridge links the two shores.

Figure 5B. On the upper left is a close-up of the international railway bridge as it was being built, late in the nineteenth century. One German-sponsored terrorist did set off bombs on the cpr bridge at the Maine–New Brunswick border, but, despite Lang's blueprints, tight security prevented similar action at this bridge.

Both photographs courtesy of the Museum, Sault Ste. Marie, Ontario

Fig. 6. William E. Chapman, U.S. consul in North Bay, Ontario, during the interwar period. Chapman recruited a Canadian clergyman of Finnish origin, the Rev. Edwin Kyllonen, to spy on Northern Ontario's Red Finns.

Fig. 7. The Rev. Edwin Kyllonen kept the U.S. consulate in North Bay well informed about the activities and expressed opinions of Northern Ontario's Red Finns during the early years of the Depression. William E. Chapman, the U.S. consul, recruited Kyllonen through a mutual friend and arranged that Kyllonen should not sign his name to any correspondence in case it fell into the wrong hands.

Courtesy of the Finnish United Church, Copper Cliff, Ontario

Fig. 8. Riga, Latvia, from the River Daugava in 1941. In the 1920s, American moles working in the Riga post office on Aspazia Boulevard intercepted and read correspondence between Moscow and Canadian Communists, trying to keep themselves informed about the Communist threat north of the Canada–United States border.

Courtesy of Valija Dumpis

Fig. 10. Beatrice de Kobbe
Chinchilla, the Spanish consul's
beautiful young daughter. For
many years people believed
that Kobbe's espionage
activities had been uncovered
when "a young Canadian
secret agent" became friendly
with Beatrice and caught the
two coding information for
transmission. However, the
truth is more mundane;
interception of Kobbe's mail
paid off.

Fig. 11. René Ristelhueber, head of the French legation in Ottawa from 1940 until 1942, defended and promoted the policies of Marshal Pétain's government based at Vichy. Ristelhueber and his consular subordinates spied on the Free French and their supporters, but forwarded little useful information to Pétain's German allies. Fear that they might do precisely that caused Canadians to keep Ristelhueber and his staff under close surveillance.
Courtesy of the French Embassy, Ottawa

Fig. 12. In the aftermath of Fidel Castro's revolution, the CIA maintained surveillance of Cuban activities in Canada. One centre of such activity was the Consulate-General of Cuba, on Pine Avenue West in Montreal.
Photograph by the author

7
Pearl Harbor and Its Aftermath

During the last few months before Pearl Harbor, Canadian and American governments enjoyed first-hand accounts from their own diplomats of political developments in Tokyo. Scholarly accounts followed quickly. Now, however, with the release of Japanese cables intercepted by authority of the Canadian government, it is possible to discover how much Japanese authorities knew and what Canadian leaders knew that they knew.

In 1941 Canada entered the field of electronic surveillance, first of René Ristelhueber, then of Japanese diplomats and politicians. For various reasons, little of the data acquired that year proved particularly useful. Telephone eavesdropping on Ristelhueber and his consul-general in Montreal, Henri Coursier, was discussed in chapter 6; in late November and early December 1941, Canada's Wartime Examination Unit (WEU) intercepted Japanese messages that clearly indicated that something significant was about to happen. Unfortunately, by the time the unit had deciphered the intercepts and translated them into English (always English, never French), Pearl Harbor had come and gone. Shortly thereafter, the WEU intercepted a message from Tokyo instructing Japanese nationals in enemy countries to behave themselves and remain inoffensive. This did not, however, protect innocent Japanese, Japanese-Canadians and Japanese-Americans from arbitrary internment in Canada or the United States. Political pressure from paranoid or prejudiced voters proved more significant than documentary evidence.

One reason for delays prior to Pearl Harbor may have been a change of personnel. As noted in chapter 6, Lester Pearson and other Canadians aware of ciphered messages to and from Vichy France were critical of British cryptographers. In their opinion, the British cryptographers were not trying very hard to decipher what was available. This seeming indifference prompted the Canadian government to establish its own cryptographic service, the WEU. For reasons of economy and speed, the Canadian government hired an experienced American cryptographer eager for employment, Herbert Osborn Yardley. After more than a decade of service to the United States government, Yardley had lost his job in 1929. Secretary of State Henry Stimson thought the reading of other people's mail most ungentlemanly. (After all, Stimson became Secretary of State in 1929, one year after most nations adhered to the Kellogg–Briand Pact, which outlawed war as a means of settling disputes. A highly civilized man, Stimson fought adamantly and successfully to protect the art treasures of Kyoto. When others thought that Kyoto should be the target for the first nuclear bomb, Stimson — at that point Secretary of War — insisted that it must be some other place, such as Hiroshima.) Following his dismissal, Yardley published his memoirs, a book entitled *The Black Chamber*. Doing so earned some royalties, but it also earned enmity from his former employers who thought that he had revealed too many secrets. Once British and American authorities discovered that Yardley was Canada's chief cryptographer, they were reluctant to trust the WEU. Pressure from the Allies led Ottawa to replace Yardley with Oliver Strachey, a British cryptographer. Yardley's heated departure and Strachey's arrival amid controversy happened in late November 1941, at the worst possible time for delays.

The interception of Japanese correspondence began in the summer of 1941. At first processing was rather slow. On 20 August, Japan's consul in Vancouver advised Seijiro Yoshizawa, Japanese minister in Ottawa, to inquire about an alleged order to a Vancouver company not to receive reading material from Japan. The translation, processing, and filing at the Wartime Examination Unit were not complete until 2 October. A dispatch of 13 September from Japan's consul in New York detailing America's military build-up also was not translated and filed until 2 October. Yoshizawa's message of 27 July that Canada was opting out of an Anglo-Japanese Trade Treaty of 1911 was filed on 8 October. A report on American reactions to the German navy's attack of 11 September on the U.S. navy submarine *Greer* sat around from 18 September until 8 October, statements of President Franklin Roosevelt and of Senator Thomas Connally, Chairman of the Senate Foreign Relations Committee, on the probability of war between the United States and Japan, from 19 August until 15 October. Of course, this probably did not matter. Roosevelt and Connally were aware of what they had said, and Canadian authorities did not need to rely on Japanese officials to know what was happening in the United States.

By October, the process had accelerated. A message of 11 October from Kishisaburo Nomura, Japanese ambassador in Washington, to the Japanese legation in Ottawa on ship movements from Yokohama to ports in the United States and Canada was processed within four days. Yoshizawa's note of 9 October to the Japanese ambassador in London about a Canada National Defence order to requisition scrap iron and steel was processed within a week. Once the WEU hit its stride, it could usually move quickly.

When it opened for business on 9 June 1941, the WEU operated from a two-room suite in a remote building on the outskirts of Ottawa. The remote location was an advantage. Yardley and his wife and the nine subordinates who assisted him were less likely to bump into people and make conversation there than in the centre of the city. The unit had radio equipment for collecting messages right on location. The army had a station at Rockcliffe that could intercept messages between Hamburg and South America, while the navy had facilities for receiving the Japanese signals on the Pacific coast.

Officials in Ottawa had a very good idea of what their counterparts in Tokyo knew and were doing. Ottawa was aware that the Japanese were monitoring the possibility of Canadian and American aid to the Soviet Union, an ally of Canada's since the German attack on that country in June 1941. It knew that Tokyo was aware that President Roosevelt's cabinet had met to discuss the Konoye government's resignation, and that the stock market had declined. It knew that as early as 18 October Yoshizawa had advised the Japanese ambassador in London not to leave a cargo "any longer in a British Columbia port" in case Canada requisitioned it. Within days Ottawa knew that Tokyo knew that Canada was receiving Liu Shi Shun as Chinese ambassador. Even the state of the Canadian economy — specifically the imposition of price controls to combat inflation — did not escape Japanese scrutiny. The WEU could advise Canada's British ally on a number of vital issues. It intercepted an analysis forwarded by Nomura in Washington of the personalities in the new cabinet of Prime Minister Hideki Tojo. It also learned that Japan had spies and agents led by one Tatekawa Ki hidden in the Soviet Union.

The Canadian government knew that Yoshizawa was not dangerous. A career diplomat since 1917, he found his government's policy of arrogant militarism to be hazardous. On 4 November Yoshizawa warned the Foreign Minister that Japan's deliberate flaunting of military power in Asia and her support for Germany's attack on the Soviet Union might well provoke war with the United States, countries of the British Commonwealth (including Canada), and the Soviet Union. Such a war would be horrendously costly, warned Japan's minister to Canada. Japan's consul in Chicago sent a similar (and similarly intercepted) message to Tokyo. Yoshizawa's reputation as a peacemonger might well have contributed to the respect, even affection, that Prime Minister Mackenzie King had for him.

Professors J.L. Granatstein and Gregory A. Johnson have found evidence from British and American sources that by 1939 official Japan, particularly the Japanese consulate in Vancouver, was spying on British Columbia. The Canadian government had at least some knowledge of this. However, the WEU's intercepts indicate that most of Yoshizawa's information came from sources of a nonsecret nature: newspapers, publications of the government of Canada, and debates on the floor of the House of Commons. On 17 November, Yoshizawa notified his superiors in Tokyo and Japanese diplomats in Washington, London, and Hong Kong of a message that an unnamed person had cabled to him from Hong Kong: Canada had sent a number of soldiers, many of them from Quebec and Manitoba, to that British colony (to defend Hong Kong in the event of a Japanese attack). When the WEU processed this cable on 30 November, Ottawa had a good idea of what

Yoshizawa knew and did not know. That an unidentified person had telegraphed Yoshizawa news of the soldiers' arrival was not too serious, for the *Globe and Mail* and the *Ottawa Citizen* reported it on the 17th. Thanks to these newspapers, Yoshizawa could say that their commander was J.K. Lawson and that most of the troops came from Manitoba and Quebec. Yoshizawa's source did not know, and the *Globe and Mail* and the *Ottawa Citizen* did not publicize, the number that had gone (almost 2,000), nor the route their ship had taken. Yoshizawa suggested that the consul in Hong Kong try to determine the reason why they were there. Yoshizawa thought that Canada was really pursuing an activist foreign policy. In his words, "Canada deems it necessary to arm itself in preparation for eventualities in the Pacific."

The week before Pearl Harbor, the WEU intercepted ten messages about return travel arrangements to Japan for Japanese diplomats and their families in the United States, Mexico, and Panama. Unfortunately, none of these was processed until after 7 December. Messages went to the Japanese embassy in Washington and consular posts across the United States, but the WEU did not process most of them until December 17–18. Had they been deciphered earlier, someone in Ottawa might have been in a position to know that something serious was about to happen. Equally, the growing concern over the Japanese actions in Southeast Asia might have alerted the WEU to the importance of speed, even if earlier tensions and controversies had had little impact. Unfortunately it did not, and the controversy over Yardley right at this point could not have helped the situation.

Time does not excuse the decision to intern and evacuate innocent Japanese and Japanese-Canadians. Not only was information against them lacking; the WEU had evidence that they intended to do no wrong. On 11 December Japan's embassy in Buenos Aires forwarded instructions from Japan's vice-minister of home affairs to Japan's embassy in Rio de Janeiro. The Home Office instructed Japanese in enemy countries to avoid "reckless or malicious conduct towards the people of that country. They should always act with strict discretion." The antithesis of Germany's Foreign Office during World War I, which had wanted Germans in Canada and the United States to perform as terrorists, the Home Office warned:

> If, as a resident in an enemy country, a report is spread that some persons are receiving unjust treatment, exercise self-restraint and do not try to devise means for revenge. Display the necessary and true spirit of our nation. Have [special] consideration for those persons in any enemy country whose views and manners [are of a high order]. Always act in a manner that will guarantee and safeguard life and property.

This message was to have as wide a circulation as possible, in as many countries as possible.

The WEU processed this message by 19 December, but as far as the Japanese communities of Canada and the United States were concerned, innocence was not enough. Governments preferred to err on the side of caution rather than on the side of justice. It did not matter that Tokyo had instructed its expatriates not to make waves in the countries where they lived. Public opinion demanded action, and even had it been inclined, the Canadian government could hardly have defused public opinion by revealing the 11 December intercept. Publication might or might not have reassured Canadians: it would certainly have alerted the Japanese government to the reality that the enemy was reading its messages. In all probability, Tokyo would then have altered its procedures, at least for a time, and stopped the flow of information. No, even if the Canadian government had wanted to be fair to its Japanese community (a dubious presumption), Ottawa was limited as to what it could reveal. Japanese nationals and Japanese Canadians, like their counterparts in the United States, thus became innocent victims.

On balance, the WEU had a respectable, if not brilliant, beginning. The recruitment of Yardley was an understandable, if unfortunate, mistake. The unit should have operated with greater speed in the weeks before Pearl Harbor. However, it did gather information which, in the case of the evacuees, the political masters chose to ignore. That was not the fault of Yardley or anyone else in the WEU. More remarkable is the WEU's facility with Japanese ciphers at a time when British cryptographers were claiming such difficulty with Vichy France's messages. It would appear either that Yardley and Strachey were really good at their job, or that Pearson's suspicions of British indifference were well founded, or most probably both.

8
The Fight against Other Enemies, 1939–45

As World War II approached, Canadian authorities had reasons for concern about earlier opponents – Irish, Communist, and Fascist. Japan also joined the enemies list. In the end, however, the most significant cause for concern came from Franco's Spain.

Ireland-related challenges continued long after World War I. The Anglo-Irish treaty that partitioned Ireland and left six counties of Ulster inside the United Kingdom remained a sore point. Some Irish warriors – Liam Lynch, Joseph Plunkett and Joseph McGarrity – thought the treaty conceded too much and moved to the United States. They wanted to see Ireland a republic, not a dominion whose head of state was the British monarch, and they wanted a united Ireland. The Clann-na-Gael transferred its support to the newly formed Irish Republican Army (IRA), which prepared to fight for these objectives. Once released from Kingston Penitentiary, where he was serving time for his role in the Welland Canal bombings of 1900, Luke Dillon played an active role with the IRA.

In the early months of 1939, the IRA was exploding bombs in London. Its purpose was to convince the British that their continued occupation of Northern Ireland carried a price that they might not want to pay. One IRA protagonist, Sean Russell, had gone to the United States to explain why the IRA bombing campaign was taking place in Great Britain, and there he collaborated with Joseph McGarrity. Russell was in the Detroit area when King George VI and Queen Elizabeth visited Windsor, Ontario, and as a precaution, American authorities took him into custody. This made him a martyr of sorts, and Russell was never again to see his Irish homeland. After protests from members of Congress, Russell was released and ordered to leave the United States. From there he travelled to Nazi Germany in search of support. In 1940, while the Nazis were transporting him back to Ireland aboard a submarine, he died in transit, apparently from perforated ulcers. Other attempts at Nazi–IRA collaboration led to little, either because of general inefficiency or because the Nazis whom the IRA contacted lacked confidence in them. The IRA and its American supporters might have been a more significant threat to Canadian targets had Hitler and his cronies taken them more seriously.

As Canada entered World War II (10 September 1939), six men worked in the intelligence section of the RCMP. From the evidence of the monthly security bulletins (reports of possible security threats and action taken), some appear less than sophisticated – people who would spell the possessive of the third person plural pronoun as "their's," or the past tense of the verb "lead" as "lead." On one occasion, an RCMP bulletin informed the Canadian government that Czechs, as distinct from Slovaks, were "mainly Lutheran Protestants."

While the RCMP focused on alleged foreign agents and allegedly unpatriotic Canadians inside Canada, the RCMP security bulletins did include items from foreign (including American) publications, and letters smuggled out of occupied Europe or written in a neutral country. Until Hitler's June 1941 attack on the USSR, the RCMP paid far more attention to Communists than to alleged agents of Nazi Germany, Fascist Italy, or Imperial Japan. Communists might be Soviet agents, and the Ribbentrop–Molotov Pact and its aftermath seemed persuasive evidence that Stalin and Hitler were collaborators in aggression. The RCMP also monitored labour unions, Sudbury's Finnish-language newspaper *Vapaus*, Jehovah's Witnesses and Doukhobors, as well as schools and universities, but in the end, results were meagre. Most real Soviet agents went undetected until the defection of Soviet cipher clerk Igor Gouzenko in September 1945. Even Klaus Fuchs, later a key transmitter of U.S. nuclear secrets to the Soviets, spent time in a Canadian jail, but he won his freedom and went to work alongside J. Robert Oppenheimer, Edward Teller, and other fathers of the atomic bomb at Los Alamos, New Mexico.

The RCMP knew that Germany's consular posts, whose staff left Canada at the outbreak of hostilities, had promoted Nazi propaganda inside Canada. Also, before Italy became a belligerent in mid-1940, the RCMP had convincing evidence that that country's consul in Montreal, Signor Paolo de Simone, was encouraging Italian Canadians to support Benito Mussolini and his Fascists. In the early spring of 1940, de Simone presided at a secret meeting of Fascist sympathizers in Montreal, but the RCMP had been suspicious of Italian consular officials long before this particular indiscretion. As early as October 1939, the RCMP had noted that "Italian consuls [were] ... the centre for all Fascist activities among the Italian people throughout the Dominion." Indeed, it was "no mere coincidence [that] practically all these [Italian] Consuls" had made brief visits to Europe in the late summer or early autumn of 1939. The RCMP had specifically identified the Italian consul-general in Ottawa, Marquis A. Rosso-Longhi, as a potential troublemaker. Yet, the RCMP also reported that Japanese Canadians were overwhelmingly loyal to Canada, and that Japan's consul at Vancouver, Mr. Nakauchi, was urging them to live "as Canadians." After Pearl Harbor, of course, Canadian authorities disregarded these encouraging reports and interned large numbers of Japanese subjects and Japanese Canadians as potential enemies.

The Spanish Adversary

Irish, Communist, and Axis sympathizers were familiar enemies. There were also historic reasons for concern about Spain. For centuries Spain and Great Britain had been adversaries or potential adversaries. Even in the generation-long struggle against revolutionary France and Napoleon, Spain had proved an unreliable ally, twice switching sides. Spanish rulers sought to recapture Gibraltar, lost to Great Britain during the War of the Spanish Succession and then confirmed as British by the 1713 Treaty of Utrecht. In 1898 Spain had lost Puerto Rico, the Philippines and Guam to the United States and had had to leave Cuba under American control. Some of the generation of 1898 were still alive during World War II and remembered their nation's earlier humiliation.

Spain's government of the World War II era had come to power during a civil war won with military assistance from Hitler's Germany and Mussolini's Italy. Generalissimo Franco owed Hitler and Mussolini many favours. As World War II led to one German victory after another, Franco became increasingly supportive of the Axis cause. Following a precedent established by Mussolini's Italy, on 12 June 1940 he changed Spain's previously announced status of "neutral" to that of "nonbelligerent." Meeting with Hitler at Hendaye in October 1940, Franco agreed to enter the war on the Axis side, although he did not specify a date.

Official Spanish empathy with the Axis powers showed in many ways, as Allied observers noted. Throughout the war, Spain exported wolfram, a mineral vital to Hitler's war economy, to Germany. Franco's government allowed a German consulate to remain open at Tangier, where it could monitor Allied ships as they entered the Mediterranean. Spanish propaganda supported Germany's war effort, and after 7 December 1941, the Japanese one. On 17 October 1940, when Hitler's power was at its height, Franco replaced Foreign Minister Juan Beigbeder with a man more friendly to the Axis, Ramon Serrano Suñer. Crews and ships of the German navy enjoyed shore leave and refuelling privileges at Spanish ports. Franco sent Spanish forces, known as the Blue Division, to fight alongside German ones on the Russian front.

One explanation for the Franco government's behaviour is opportunism and self-interest. Franco saw advantages to a good relationship with the dominant power of Europe; in 1940 and for some time thereafter it appeared that that power would be Germany. After the United States entered the war and the German forces bogged down in the snows of Russia, Franco dismissed Serrano Suñer, and replaced him with a man friendlier to the Allies,

General Count Gómez Jordana. In 1943 Franco revised Spain's status from nonbelligerent to neutral, and withdrew most of the Blue Division. After the Normandy landings of 1944, Franco removed the autographed portraits of Hitler and Mussolini from his desk and closed the German consulate in Tangier.

Ideologically Franco shared many of the values of Hitler and Mussolini. He admired discipline and respect for authority. Casting himself in the tradition of King Ferdinand and Queen Isabella who had unified Spain in 1492, Franco lauded them for their expulsion of Spain's Jews, and said that they had spared Spain the Jewish problem that confronted Nazi Germany. Finally, Franco and his associates detested Communism, and Soviet aid to Franco's opponents during Spain's Civil War had reinforced the dislike. More than once Franco told U.S. Ambassador Carleton Hayes that he distinguished between Germany's war in western Europe against Great Britain and the United States, and the war in eastern Europe against the Soviet Union. He also expressed the fear that after an Allied victory, Great Britain and the United States would recall their forces and leave their Soviet ally to police the European mainland. The fact that Hitler was fighting the Soviet Union seemed, for Franco, good reason to support him.

Allied Reactions to Franco's Spain

Yet the Allies also had means to pressure the Spaniards. After the Civil War, Spain was nearly destitute, and the British – with their Canadian, American, and Argentinian connections – were in a better position than the Axis powers to provide the wheat and oil Spain desperately needed. Moreover, as Franco reminded Hitler at Hendaye, more than a year before Pearl Harbor, the possibility existed that the United States might enter the conflict and tilt the balance against Germany.

The British ambassador in Spain, Sir Samuel Hoare, found Gómez Jordana as friendly as he had found Serrano hostile. He even referred to him as "a wise friend." Other diplomats agreed. According to U.S. ambassador Carleton Hayes, Gómez Jordana sought to reverse the thrust of Serrano's policy, but he faced an uphill battle against ideological Falangists, supporters of Franco who disapproved of democracy and believed in government by a military-ecclesiastical-aristocratic elite. The papal nuncio also thought Gómez Jordana "thoroughly reliable and ... determined to pursue a policy of genuine neutrality with personal leanings toward [the United States] ... and the British."

Problems remained, because, as Hayes said, Gómez Jordana had limited influence in the Spanish government. At the end of 1943, one U.S. State Department official, Herbert Feis, tabulated a list of Allied grievances against Franco:

The Spanish government ... found new legal reasons for retaining Italian warships within Spanish ports. The Blue Division was being straggled out of the east rather than ordered out. German agents in Morocco and Tangier continued to inform about the movement of Allied convoys through the Straits [of Gibraltar]. Both General Eisenhower and the Combined Chiefs of Staff were sure that the heavy air attacks against Allied ships in these waters were guided by these secret reports.

Then Gómez Jordana, whose health was poor, died on 3 August 1944.

The Allies could not look forward to improved relations with Gómez Jordana's successor. One Spanish monarchist referred to José Felix de Lequérica as "more German than the Germans." A more recent writer has labelled him a "germanophile." Before his appointment as foreign minister, Lequérica had served as Spanish ambassador to France. Indeed, in that capacity he had served as an intermediary in June 1940 when Marshal Pétain's government wished to hear Hitler's armistice terms. Gómez Jordana's death and Lequérica's succession were to prove critical factors in Spanish-Canadian relations.

Franco and the Pacific

For Franco and his associates, events in the Pacific were not as significant as European developments. For a time, Spanish officials demonstrated a clear partiality toward Japan. They congratulated the Japanese on the success of their Pearl Harbor raid, and the Spanish press defended Japanese cruelties in the Philippines. Some time after assuming responsibility for protection of Japanese interests in the United States and elsewhere in the Western hemisphere, the Spanish government precipitated a first-class row with Washington in October 1943 by sending a congratulatory telegram to José P. Laurel, leader of a Japanese-backed government in the Philippines, on attainment of his country's "independence." (After discussions with Gómez Jordana, who accepted full responsibility for what the Spanish Foreign Office had done in his name, the U.S. embassy concluded that a subordinate had sent the letter on his own initiative without consulting the proper authorities.)

However, Spanish-Japanese relations were not always harmonious. On 29 July 1943, Hayes reported that for Franco, "Japan is the great enemy ... He would like to co-operate with us against the Japanese, although the relative weakness of Spain would prevent any effective aid." After the Laurel affair Hayes noted repeated assurances from both Franco and Gómez Jordana "that the Spanish Government sympathized with the United States in its war against Japan." Franco undoubtedly sought to protect Spanish nationals in the Japanese-occupied Philippines (Gómez Jordana hinted at this to Hayes), and when Spain did cut its ties with Imperial Japan in March 1945, it did so on the grounds of Japanese mistreatment of Spanish subjects there. This happened *after* Japan reportedly offered Franco repossession of the Philippines if Spain would remain loyal.

Spain's Japanese policy, like its Axis-Allied policies, appears unprincipled. As an ally of Germany and Italy, Japan was deemed worthy of support while the Axis stood a chance of victory, but once the Axis seemed headed for defeat, links between Spain and Japan deteriorated and eventually collapsed.

The Kobbe Chinchilla Affair

As it did on other war-related matters, Mackenzie King's government remained in close touch with both London and Washington concerning relations with Spain. It allowed Spanish representatives to operate on Canadian soil as long as they stayed within Canadian law, and that law allowed Spanish consular officials to promote Spanish interests. Once Canada and Japan became adversaries in December 1941 and severed diplomatic relations, Spain assumed the responsibility of protector power for Japanese interests in Canada.

When Spain assumed this responsibility, neither Spain nor Canada had legations in each other's capital. As the war began, Canada had legations in only five countries – the United States, France, Japan, the Netherlands, and Belgium. Until 1940, when Canada opened a consulate in Greenland – Danish territory – Canada also had no consulates, but many foreign countries had consulates across Canada; Spain had two, in Montreal and Vancouver. The British embassy in Madrid and British consular posts throughout Spain watched over Canadian interests in that country, while Juan Cárdenas, the Spanish ambassador in Washington, was the direct superior of Spain's consular officers in Canada. Like most Spanish envoys to Allied countries, Cárdenas was a career officer. Pedro E. Schwartz, Spanish consul-general in Montreal, was another career officer, and Schwartz's subordinate, Francis Bernard, was a Canadian who worked part time as vice-consul for Spain in Vancouver. Canada's counter-intelligence people discovered no hint of impropriety in any of these men, nor in the Count of Morales, who replaced Schwartz in the autumn of 1944. However, in January 1943 Bernard acquired a new superior, Fernando de Kobbe Chinchilla.

Because many Japanese lived in British Columbia, the duties of Spain's consular post in Vancouver increased considerably once Spain assumed responsibility for Japanese interests. The Spanish government suggested, with some reason, that the increased workload justified a full-time consul, and it nominated Kobbe Chinchilla to that post. Because the Department of External Affairs had heard rumours that Spanish officials in Latin America were "acting as agents for the Axis," Ottawa asked British and American sources whether Kobbe would be a safe person to have on Canadian soil. Washington warned Ottawa that he might be someone to watch; Ottawa's agents did watch him, and barely a year after his arrival, Kobbe Chinchilla faced expulsion on grounds of espionage.

Little mystery surrounds Canadian authorities' acceptance of a suspicious character at such a dangerous time. As early as 14 November 1942, Thomas A. Stone, a first secretary at the Department of External Affairs, explained to Colonel O.M. Biggar, the director of censorship, that there was little doubt that Kobbe was "prepared to act as an enemy agent." However, said Stone, the warning about Kobbe had reached Ottawa after Ottawa had already approved his appointment. Any reversal by Ottawa would require an explanation, and the explanation would "probably compromise the source" of the intelligence. Under the circumstances, the Department of External Affairs thought the wisest course of action was to let Kobbe come but to watch him closely.

The censorship bureau of the Canadian post office learned about Kobbe's unacceptable conduct as it intercepted Spanish consular mail. From May 1942 to January 1945, censors surreptitiously steamed open both incoming and outgoing mail. Someone read the mail, translated it, and then forwarded it with comments to the chief postal censor in Ottawa or one of his subordinates. In this way Ottawa monitored the actions of the consulate-general in Montreal and the vice-consulate in Vancouver with regard to such routine consular matters as promotion of bilateral Canadian-Spanish trade and of Spanish culture within Canada, plus two matters of interest to Japan: the internment of Japanese residents of Canada and the movement of ships along Canada's Pacific coast.

Spanish action on behalf of Japanese internees raised no objections from Ottawa, and almost anything Spain did on their behalf can be justified on humanitarian grounds. The story of Japanese and Japanese Canadians in British Columbia – interned and stripped of their property because of race rather than any wrongdoing on their part – is well known. Schwartz and Bernard received literally scores of letters from Japanese Canadians and Japanese residents of Canada whose breadwinner had gone to an internment camp and whose family faced destitution. Many of these letters, from dependants too ill or too busy with other dependants to work, are heart-rending. Once the Canadian government had seized their families' property and removed the breadwinners, only their limited savings and the Spanish officials stood between their families and destitution. As guardian of Japanese interests, the Spanish officials could legally represent only Japanese subjects, not Japanese Canadians, although this distinction did not become an issue. Schwartz and Bernard did what they could, dealing with Ottawa on behalf of the internees and arranging for those of Japanese background who had not been interned to provide charity for the dependants of those who had. They also tried to facilitate the repatriation of Japanese subjects to Japan and acted as a buffer between the interned people and the government of Canada. Even had Franco not been partial to Imperial Japan, humanitarian considerations would have bestirred all but the most heartless of recipients of those sad letters to do what they could to help. Certainly, the interests of the internees and their families provided the bulk of the work for Schwartz and Bernard.

From the moment of his appointment, Kobbe Chinchilla was a marked man. On 2 October 1942 Canada's chief postal censor, F.E. Jolliffe, informed the Department of External Affairs that the United States embassy in Madrid had warned the State Department about him, and that the State Department, in turn, had given the message to the Canadian legation in Washington. Under the circumstances, asked Jolliffe, should "we confidentially examine mail addressed to or posted by this party after he has reached Canada?" Thomas A. Stone replied in the affirmative.

Correspondence from the Department of External Affairs confirms that Ottawa disliked Spain seeking to upgrade its consular post in Vancouver during 1942. Yet, as Norman Robertson, who had succeeded Skelton as undersecretary of state for external affairs in 1941, wrote Lester Pearson, the minister-counsellor or second-in-command at the Canadian legation in Washington:

> In view of Spanish responsibilities as Protecting Power of Japanese Interests, it would have been very difficult to oppose their assigning a Consul de Carrière to Vancouver, where the bulk of their work as Protecting Power must be done.

On 30 October 1942, two weeks before Stone's letter to Colonel Biggar, King reported to the Secretary of State for Dominion Affairs – the British cabinet minister responsible for relations with sister Commonwealth dominions – on new information which indicated that Kobbe personified a risk. According to the new sources, Canada should receive the man only if it monitored his every activity and thought it could gain some advantage from this surveillance. The Department of External Affairs could and did insist that Kobbe must send all his correspondence by ordinary mail so that officials at the Canadian post office could steam it open, read it, and, if necessary, seize it. Unlike more trustworthy diplomats, Kobbe would not have permission to use the diplomatic pouch. Nowadays it would be illegal to deprive a diplomat of his pouch, a courier service that most governments operate in order to transport written messages in strict confidentiality between a diplomat's

Foreign Office and overseas post. Not even a customs officer has the right to examine the contents of the pouch. At the time, however, there were no such rules, although denial of pouch privileges was certainly unusual. The Canadian government wanted to scrutinize Kobbe's mail as it had the mail of Vichy's envoys. Some in Ottawa feared that mail dealing with Japanese prisoners of war might be delayed, and that the Japanese government would learn about the delay and might take reprisals against the Canadian prisoners of war it held. From Washington, Pearson reported that American officials doubted whether Canada could maintain constant surveillance over such an individual. Nevertheless, Ottawa permitted Kobbe to arrive in Vancouver and assume his duties there on 11 January 1943.

Who was Kobbe? A career diplomat for more than twenty years with a good command of English, he had worked at Spanish posts in Great Britain, France, and Cuba before going to Vancouver. During the Spanish Civil War he had defected from the Republican side and joined Franco's fledgling Foreign Office. After the collapse of the Spanish Republic in 1939, he had followed Franco to Madrid.

Because of Franco's attitudes to the Axis and Spain's role as protector of Japanese interests in Canada, many Vancouverites had strong negative opinions about Kobbe – quite apart from his personal background. It did not help his cause that only weeks after his arrival, Newsweek carried a report that Spanish diplomats worldwide were funnelling information to Berlin and Rome via Madrid. (Subsequent research has confirmed Newsweek's accusation. Late in 1942, one month after Allied forces liberated French Morocco, the Spanish chief of staff in Tangier gave a report on the American forces in Morocco to a representative from the German Foreign Office in the Spanish capital. Moreover, on 25 May 1943 Spain's ambassador in Washington wrote to the German ambassador in Madrid about a conversation he had had with President Roosevelt.)

The situation behind the suspicions can be clarified. On the basis of Canadian documents declassified at the request of the author, it is possible to tell the story of Kobbe's undoing and to correct earlier misconceptions. J.L. Granatstein and David Stafford attributed Kobbe's downfall to the Wartime Examination Unit. One of Kobbe's superiors in Madrid, Angel Alcázar de Velasco, asserted decades later that Kobbe was exposed after "a young Canadian secret agent" became friendly with his daughter. The truth is more mundane.

For months, Canadian authorities carefully scrutinized Kobbe's mail but found nothing untoward. Then, on 25 August 1943, the RCMP intercepted and forwarded to the Department of External Affairs the contents of a package that the Spanish Foreign Office had sent to Kobbe. The package had travelled via a circuitous route. From its point of origin in Madrid, it had gone to the Spanish embassy in Washington in the diplomatic pouch. Evidently without any awareness of the sensitivity of the contents, the Washington embassy had mailed it to the Spanish consul-general in Montreal. He in turn had sent it by registered mail to Vancouver. Along the way, Canadian postal censors discovered in the package two cipher keys "by means of which he will be able to transmit information to Madrid for retransmission to Japan within the texts of his normal reports to the Spanish Foreign Office either of an ordinary consular nature or in his capacity as representing Japanese interests." The package also contained "formulae for secret ink and developers," and $1,000 in U.S. currency. A sample telegram read: "Convoy left Port of Seattle for the Aleutians."

> There were also lists of Japanese proper names, each of which [was] given a value, which the secret agent might find it convenient to use in reporting ship and troop movements, defence installations, etc.

A covering letter to Kobbe bore the signature of one Gustavo Vallapalos.

The Department of External Affairs faced a dilemma. Would it expel Kobbe and reveal that it had been reading his mail? Or would it simply continue to keep him under tight surveillance? Mackenzie King thought it possible that neither the Spanish embassy in Washington nor the consulate-general in Montreal knew the contents of the parcel they had forwarded. In the short run, Canadian authorities decided just to keep Kobbe under surveillance. On 7 October 1943, the RCMP briefed Norman Robertson that to date Kobbe's activities appeared to have been totally routine or uncontroversial.

It was a British initiative that ultimately precipitated Kobbe's expulsion. The Department of External Affairs briefed the British Foreign Office about events in Vancouver, and the British government was delighted to have evidence of what it had long suspected: "that the Spanish Government w[as] giving assistance to the Japanese in intelligence matters." The British saw an opportunity and instructed their ambassador in Madrid, Sir Samuel Hoare, to make the most of the situation. A public exposé of the Canadian discoveries, Hoare warned the Spanish Foreign Office, would detract from the credibility of Spanish diplomats around the world. Spain had an interest in a quiet settlement.

Given that the Kobbe findings were likely part of a much wider network, one that involved officials at the Spanish Foreign Office and perhaps the Foreign Minister himself, London made several demands. Spain was to recall Kobbe at once. The Spanish Foreign Office must conduct an investigation to determine how Kobbe "was recruited into the Japanese Intelligence Service and permitted to receive instructions from the Japanese Government through the Spanish Foreign Office." The British wanted the Spanish investigation to include Gustavo Vallapalos, whose covering letter was part of the controversial package which Kobbe had received, and Alcázar de Velasco. Ottawa's one concern was that Madrid should not learn how it had obtained the incriminating evidence.

A few weeks later, on 16 January 1944, Hoare presented Gómez Jordana with the essentials of the Kobbe case (including some of the evidence), demanded Kobbe's "immediate recall," and suggested an investigation of the entire affair. Hoare reported that Gómez Jordana was "greatly shocked" and guaranteed that he personally would conduct "a most rigid enquiry." Within the hour, the Spanish Foreign Office ordered Kobbe to report to the Spanish embassy in Washington – but gave no reasons.

While allowing Spain to save face and remove Kobbe without publicity, the Department of External Affairs safeguarded Canadian interests. It instructed the commanding officer of the RCMP in Vancouver, C.R. Gray, to visit Kobbe on the morning of 23 January and inform him that "because of his having received instructions, codes and funds from a Japanese espionage organization in Madrid" he was persona non grata, and that a Mounted Policeman would "unobtrusively" board the train that evening and ride with him to Montreal. The RCMP were to search Kobbe's apartment, even his pockets, and to "impound" any incriminating evidence. They were also to tell Kobbe that he could not take "any papers whatsoever" out of Canada. Any official documents must be placed inside a sealed bag, which the RMCP and the Spanish consul-general in Montreal would open and inspect before the consul-general took them over. Before departure on the evening train for Montreal, Kobbe and his daughter – the only member of his family who had accompanied him to Canada – were not to leave their apartment without first telling the RCMP.

The Americans proved entirely cooperative. Notified by the Canadian embassy in Washington, Adolf Berle – the assistant undersecretary of state who looked after Canadian affairs – confirmed that the FBI would arrange for a security officer to meet Kobbe in Montreal and accompany him to the border. Inside the United States he would likewise remain under constant surveillance. At first Berle was uncertain whether his government would allow Kobbe to sail as scheduled from New Orleans.

Meanwhile Stone travelled from Ottawa to Montreal to tell Schwartz "of the facts in the de Kobbe case." According to Stone, "Schwartz was quite sincerely shocked and said that he was very sorry that such an incident should occur." Schwartz promised that during Kobbe's stopover between trains in Montreal, Kobbe would stay inside Schwartz's apartment.

Back in Vancouver, the RCMP searched Kobbe's apartment. They did not find either ciphers or instructions, but the police reported that Kobbe became agitated on three occasions – when they inspected a certain suitcase, when they seized a certain fountain pen, and when they found the $1,000 in U.S. bills. The fact that the money had not yet been spent may indicate either that Japan's agents on the Pacific coast had such dedication that they needed no financial compensation or, more likely, that little espionage of any consequence had taken place.

Despite the best efforts of the *Vancouver Sun* to learn what lay behind Kobbe's sudden departure, both the Department of External Affairs and the RCMP managed to keep the affair a secret. The *Sun* reported that Kobbe had received his marching orders from Madrid only Saturday, 22 January – two days before his actual departure – and that even he was in the dark about the reason for his expulsion. His appointment had always been controversial, noted the *Sun*, partly because of his responsibility for "Japanese evacuees and interned enemy Japanese," partly because of the dangerous way he drove his car. When the *Sun*'s Ottawa correspondent asked Stone for an explanation, Stone simply told him that

> the transfer of a Consul, if this was a transfer, was not a particularly important event and that no significance should be attached to it. He asked how and when we were notified of such transfers. I said that presumably the Senior Spanish Consular Officer in Canada [Schwartz] would inform us in due course if de Kobbe was, in fact, being transferred to another post.

Although Kobbe remained the centre of interest for Canadian officials, they could not be indifferent to the fate of his probable sponsors – including Gustavo Vallapalos and Alcázar de Velasco. Gómez Jordana quickly branded Alcázar as "one of [Serrano] Suñer's bandits." Gómez Jordana was right on target. In 1978, barely two years after Franco's death, Alcázar de Velasco made a public confession. According to *The Times* of London, Alcázar de Velasco admitted that he was the organizer of an espionage network consisting of four journalists and two other diplomats, all of them Spaniards. "Franco knew every detail of my activities," he said.

By his own admission, Alacázar had spied for the Axis at an earlier date when he was the Spanish press attaché in London. After his return to Madrid, he had organized an espionage ring in North America – primarily in the United States – which was supposed to collect information for Japan. The entire effort had failed, he told *The Times*, "when a young Canadian secret agent became friendly with the daughter of the Spanish consul in Vancouver and caught them coding information for transmission." Even in 1978, it does not appear to have crossed Alcázar's mind that Canadians would have been subtle enough to read someone else's mail. The Canadian government could rest assured. Their Spanish adversary had not discovered how they had learned the truth about Kobbe!

Nevertheless, one should not exaggerate the importance of Alcázar's admission. Professor John W.M. Chapman, who has studied German, Italian, and Japanese sources, has demonstrated there were limits to what each would say. Given the limited degree of trust among these formal Axis partners, it is most unlikely that any of them would have entered into a profound intelligence-sharing relationship with a more peripheral country such as Spain.

Gómez Jordana appointed a former Spanish consul-general in Montreal, who had resigned during the Civil War and was reportedly not at all friendly to either Japan or Germany, to investigate. "Señor Rolland can be trusted to take charge of the investigation," wrote Sir Samuel Hoare. By this time, Rolland had become head of the personnel department of the Spanish ministry of foreign affairs. Norman Robertson expressed his conviction "that the Spanish Government's investigation would establish Kobbe's guilt," but, unfortunately, Gómez Jordana died before the release of Rolland's report.

Hardly surprisingly, Rolland's investigation proved highly controversial. Rolland exonerated some of the people whom the British considered suspicious, but thought that "Alcázar de Velasco was probably leader of the ring." About Kobbe himself, Rolland was very cautious. Arthur Yencken, British chargé d'affaires in Madrid, told Rolland that Kobbe had "received microfilms which ... could be read with a magnifying glass":

It was unthinkable that an experienced diplomatist receiving such microfilms would not study them carefully and, if he were innocent, at once inform his superiors. The instructions in them were even more damning than the message in secret [invisible] ink ... Kobbe, moreover, having seen the formula for the secret ink in the instructions, would certainly have used it.

Kobbe, however, made a denial that even the British embassy found "plausible." He denied ever receiving a covering letter or microfilms and noted that when the police had searched his Vancouver apartment they had not found any. As for the American dollars, he had simply assumed that a friend must have sent them for purchases in the United States and that a request would follow in the next bag in two or three months. Meanwhile he had not wanted to inquire about them for fear of giving the sender away.

Unlike the British, Rolland thought that proof that Kobbe had received the microfilms would have meant little, for he might have received them without "his fore-knowledge." More plausibly, Rolland could not "understand why the Canadian authorities had allowed so long a time [from 25 August 1943 to 23 January 1944] to elapse before they had had Kobbe searched." Moreover, Kobbe's previous track record with the Foreign Office had been without blemish, and there was no evidence that he had actually forwarded anything to the Japanese.

The official Spanish investigation cleared Kobbe of any wrongdoing except the illegal retention of the $1,000, for which he was to receive a mild reprimand. He should have reported the money to Madrid, said a Spanish memo, but there was no conclusive evidence of his having received any "secret message or microfilm" or of any other impropriety. As might be expected, the British embassy found Rolland's findings unacceptable. Like the Department of External Affairs, it considered the case against Kobbe conclusive, and it doubted the innocence of some of the people Rolland had cleared.

Epilogue

Absence of archival material in Madrid on the Kobbe Chinchilla affair may be only a coincidence, but it may indicate a cover-up in higher places. Spanish historian Angel Viñas has suggested judicious editing by those in charge of archives for the Franco period, and in November 1989, when the present author asked at the Spanish Foreign Office for the file on the Vancouver consulate, it had disappeared. Shortly before the Spanish rupture with Japan, the Foreign Office circulated a list of Spanish diplomatic and consular posts worldwide that had assisted in the protection of Japanese interests. The Vancouver consulate was one of two such posts omitted from the list, although Lequérica, the Foreign Minister who approved the list, had personally reassigned Kobbe. (Kobbe's curriculum vitae at the Spanish Foreign Office states that he officially ceased to be his country's consul in Vancouver as of 5 October 1944.) It was the Japanese who reminded Lequérica that the Vancouver post had been helpful and that it, as well as Rabat in Morocco, ought to be included.

After the war the Department of External Affairs had an opportunity to express its continuing anger. In the autumn of 1945 Franco's Spain suggested upgrading Spain's representation to the status of legation or embassy. Canada was opening legations and embassies in capitals of countries to which it had been allied, and the Allies were opening missions in Ottawa. Other neutrals received permission for high commissions, legations or embassies. Argentina opened a legation in 1941, Sweden in 1943, and Switzerland in 1945. Ottawa informed Madrid, however, that it could not follow suit and that Canadian rejection of the Spanish overture was linked to the Kobbe affair. Not until 1953 did Canada and Spain exchange embassies.

In brief, the World War II years saw increased Canadian cooperation with intelligence agencies in the United States as well as the United Kingdom. Such cooperation led to the preventive detention of Sean Russell and the Kobbe Chinchilla fiasco. It does not appear to have helped in the fight against Communism.

9
The CIA in Canada during the 1960s*

Even friendly countries keep an eye on each other. Peter Wright, the author whose book Margaret Thatcher tried to ban, tells that after 1958, the government-owned British telephone company deliberately disrupted service at the French embassy in London. Charles de Gaulle, hero of World War II, had become president of France, and he did not want British membership in the European Economic Community. When British authorities wanted to know what de Gaulle's diplomats were saying to each other, the British telephone company cut off their phone service. French embassy officials then reported that their telephones were not working, and agents from the British security service MI5 (Military Intelligence 5) disguised themselves as repairmen, gained access to the building, and bugged the French embassy. Similarly, J.L. Granatstein and David Stafford have described efforts of French officials in the 1960s and 1970s to support Quebec independence and destabilize Canada. Granatstein and Stafford have also described Canadian surveillance of those same French diplomats and agents. While France of that era was hardly "friendly" toward Canada, it certainly was not an enemy in the sense that Nazi Germany, Imperial Japan, or even the Soviet Union and Vichy France had been.

Many readers will remember Dr. Ewen Cameron and the experiments of the U.S. Central Intelligence Agency (CIA) at Montreal's Allan Memorial Institute from 1957 to 1963. Drugs administered by Dr. Cameron erased his patients' memories and created heartbreak and litigation that continue to this day. Presumably the CIA experimented with Canadians because its mandate directed it to work with foreigners, not Americans. (The agency had been founded in 1947 to coordinate United States foreign intelligence; the Federal Bureau of Investigation and other police forces dealt with U.S. citizens.) If the CIA was still involved in such activities during the presidency of Lyndon Baines Johnson (1963–69), this author was unable to find any documentary evidence at the LBJ archives in Austin, Texas. By that time, the CIA had a new director; Allen Dulles, who had been director when Dr. Cameron's experiments began, had resigned in 1961. However, other revelations were available.

---

*The author is grateful to the United States Information Agency, which financed his trip to the Lyndon Baines Johnson Archives in Austin, Texas.

Recently declassified documents have confirmed that during the 1960s, the CIA kept Canada and Canadians under surveillance, and that these activities began long before 1 May 1965, when terrorists dynamited the U.S. consulate-general in Montreal. Although the CIA certainly demonstrated more restraint in its Canadian actions than the Soviets had in the 1920s or the French would in the late 1960s and 1970s, it helped the U.S. government to exploit a Canadian diplomat without the full cooperation of the Canadian government. While there are parallels between Consul W.E. Chapman's recruitment of the Rev. Edwin Kyllonen in Northern Ontario in the interwar years and the recruitment of Blair Seaborn, this time the recruiting agent was not a minor consul in North Bay but the United States Secretary of State, Dean Rusk. His target was a Canadian diplomat paid by the Canadian government.

From the standpoint of American authorities, it was vital to keep Canada under surveillance. Canada physically occupied the territory between the United States and the Soviet Union. It hosted officials from Fidel Castro's Cuba, whose relationship with the United States had been adversarial since 1959 or 1960. Canada supplied oil, uranium, nickel, and other strategic resources to the United States, and it was the United States' largest trading partner. Economic setbacks in Canada would cause unemployment in the United States. Canadians shared many American values, could travel to certain places where Americans could not go, and were willing and able to tell what they had seen and heard.

What the CIA had to say about Lester Pearson, Canada's prime minister from 1963 to 1968, was not complimentary. Before Pearson met President Kennedy at Hyannisport in May 1963, the CIA said:

> In his search for political issues ... [Pearson] has in the past flirted with propositions which have been disturbing from the U.S. point of view. He originally opposed nuclear weapons for Canadian forces, questioned the whole course of U.S.-Canadian defense relations and Canada's role in NATO, and advocated a significant limitation on the extent of Canadian participation in NORAD.

Nevertheless, Diefenbaker had made such a negative impression on Washington that the White House felt it must support Pearson. Despite the CIA's apprehensions, Pearson was the best alternative to Diefenbaker available.

In retrospect, this was significant. At the very least, Pearson's acceptability represented a difference of opinion between the Central Intelligence Agency on the one hand and the State Department and the White House on the other. The CIA's chief of counter-intelligence was James Jesus Angleton, whose convictions were so far to the right that he failed to distinguish between Communists and socialists. To him they were all part of the same bad bunch. Angleton became convinced that Pearson was "an active Soviet agent," but the number of people whom he managed to convince was small. He had similar thoughts about many of Pearson's contemporaries: Harold Wilson, the British prime minister; Olof Palme, Swedish prime minister; Willy Brandt, who would soon be Chancellor of West Germany; Averell Harriman, a former American ambassador to the Soviet Union; Henry Kissinger, a future Secretary of State. In 1967, Pearson authorized RCMP participation in an intelligence partnership (then called CAZAB) with intelligence organizations in the United States, Great Britain, Australia, and New Zealand.

Canada's geographic location had been fatal to the relationship between Pearson's predecessor, John Diefenbaker, and President John F. Kennedy. Diefenbaker's government had agreed to accept Bomarc-B missiles armed with nuclear warheads at North Bay, Ontario, and at La Macaza, Quebec. It also accepted a nuclear strike role for the Royal Canadian Air Force (RCAF) in Europe. The United States subsequently agreed to locate the bases at North Bay and La Macaza rather than at sites in the United States, and the NATO allies adjusted their responsibilities to accommodate the RCAF. While the bases were under construction, Diefenbaker came under pressure from antinuclear activists and prepared to renege on his commitments. In January 1963, officials at the State Department and the White House issued a statement that refuted, point by point, every argument for hesitation or sober second thought advanced by Diefenbaker. When Diefenbaker's Conservatives lost a vote of confidence over the defence issue and the Governor General dissolved Parliament for a general election, President Kennedy's pollster, Lou Harris, went to work for the Canadian Liberals (according to John English, at the invitation of Walter Gordon and Keith Davey). Pearson, the Liberal leader, had agreed to fulfil the nuclear commitments. For years he had opposed them as unnecessary and unwise but, once the Canadian government had accepted them, he believed that Canadians had an obligation to their allies to do what they had promised. When Pearson won the election, he allowed the Americans to arm their Bomarcs with nuclear weapons, and he accepted the nuclear strike role.

With Kennedy's assassination in November of that same year, his vice-president and successor, Lyndon Baines Johnson, inherited his predecessor's chief foreign policy advisers – Secretary of State Dean Rusk, Secretary of Defense Robert McNamara, and National Security Adviser McGeorge Bundy. They most definitely preferred Pearson to Diefenbaker. Bundy even joked about the way he and Under-Secretary of State George Ball had "knocked over the Diefenbaker government by one incautious press release." In 1965, when Pearson and Diefenbaker fought another election, the Johnson team did not want Diefenbaker to win. If Pearson won, recommended Rusk, Johnson should telephone to congratulate him. If Diefenbaker surprised everyone and won, a perfunctory telegram should be good enough. The Liberals engaged an American pollster, Oliver Quayle, "the best pollster we could find," according to Pearson. Quayle's friends in the White House called him "Olly." Olly both advised Pearson – who did not always accept the advice – and kept the Johnson team aware of the way Canada's election campaign was progressing. (Unlike Erich Windels and René Ristelhueber, American authorities did not need to rely on the media.) When Pearson won a plurality rather than a majority, the State Department and President Johnson decided that a congratulatory telegram would be more appropriate than a telephone call after all.

While Angleton failed to weaken the position of Prime Minister Pearson, he brought the career of another Canadian, Leslie James Bennett, to a tragic conclusion. Because Bennett, a senior officer in the RCMP's counter-intelligence service, frequently met Angleton to share information and to discuss common problems, Bennett's loyalty was a matter of great concern to Angleton. Finding that he could not trust Bennett to follow the party line, Angleton successfully engineered his downfall. Bennett failed to share Angleton's hostility to socialism or his admiration for the notorious Republican senator of the 1950s, Joseph McCarthy of Wisconsin. Bennett's sympathies went to McCarthy's victims, people whom he had slandered on little or no evidence and whose careers he had ruined. Bennett was also less enthusiastic than Angleton about KGB defector Anatoliy Golitsyn, whom Bennett first met in Washington in 1962.

Bennett actually defied Angleton in the case of Olga Farmakovskaya, who had served as a translator for Peter Worthington, Moscow correspondent of the *Toronto Telegram*. On a visit to Beirut in 1966, Farmakovskaya defected and sought political asylum at the United States embassy. Convinced that she had not really defected and remained a KGB agent, Angleton successfully blocked Farmakovskaya's entry into the United States and warned Bennett not to let her into Canada. Rather than take Angleton's word, Bennett asked the British intelligence agencies, MI5 and MI6, for a second opinion. They found her to be clean, and she moved to Canada, where she still resides.

Angleton suspected Bennett of being a Soviet mole, an spy with access to Western security information. He wanted Bennett removed as deputy chief of RCMP counter-intelligence. The RCMP deferred to his wishes: after all, there were reasons for thinking that the CIA was more knowledgeable and more experienced in such matters than they were. On Angleton's suggestion, the RCMP planted microphones in Bennett's office, and also in his home. RCMP investigators began to suspect that Bennett was homosexual. They found that in 1940 (when "gay" still meant "cheerful"), Bennett had referred to an army buddy as a "gay bird." The microphones in Bennett's home fed these suspicions: Bennett and his wife had separate bedrooms. In reality, their marriage was on the rocks, but those who wanted to jump to conclusions jumped to conclusions. Because of a sore knee, Bennett often woke at night and turned on the lights. His detractors said that the lights at strange hours had to be signals to Soviet agents. Bennett's earlier acquaintance with the British spy, Kim Philby, also worked to his disadvantage. (Before Philby's defection to the Soviet Union, Angleton had also been a very close friend of Philby's.) There was enough such "evidence" that in 1972 the Trudeau government dismissed Bennett without warning and forced him to take early retirement, despite the fact that he passed a lie-detector test administered by the RCMP and the CIA. Subsequently he has been totally exonerated.

Angleton was not totally wrong. In 1985, another KGB defector, Vitaliy Sergeyevich Yurchenko, confirmed that the KGB had indeed had an agent inside the RCMP during the Angleton-Bennett years. Unfortunately, that agent was not Bennett.

Canada's links with Cuba were another source of concern. They came up at Pearson's first meeting with Kennedy at Hyannisport, Massachusetts, barely a month after Pearson defeated Diefenbaker in the 1963 election. Canadian trade with Cuba was on President Johnson's list in January 1964 as he and Pearson met for talks in the American capital. Two years later the Johnson administration was so concerned about a possible Canadian-Soviet air agreement that would have allowed continuation flights to and from Cuba that veteran negotiator Averell Harriman went to Ottawa for talks with the prime minister. (This was the same Harriman whom Angleton had thought to be, like the prime minister, a Soviet agent.) Rejecting Pearson's suggestion that this was "just another commercial agreement which had little political significance," Harriman told Pearson that since the Cuban missile crisis, "the Soviet Union was using Cuba as a base for subversive activity against Latin American countries ... including Venezuela, Colombia, and Peru." Canada's granting of transit privileges would set a dangerous precedent, and the United States expected better of a close ally. In the end, for reasons the White House did not understand, the Soviets decided that they did not want transit rights after all. (They did not want to grant transit rights to a Canadian airline that might overfly the USSR on a route between Japan and western Europe.) Commented Walt Rostow, who in March 1966 had succeeded McGeorge Bundy as national security adviser, "It appears that the Soviets, rather than the Canadians, helped us out of the onward rights to Cuba problem."

According to Granatstein and Stafford, Montreal and Ottawa became the centres of Cuban espionage operations in North America once the United States and Cuba severed diplomatic relations early in 1961. Another author, John Sawatsky, has noted that Cubans acted as Soviet surrogates in various parts of the world, including Canada, where Cuban "diplomats" had greater mobility than their Soviet counterparts. Because Canadian diplomats in

Moscow were on a short leash, a Soviet official in Canada needed permission from Canadian authorities to travel more than twenty-five miles from the diplomat's embassy or consular post. The request for permission alerted the RCMP, who could then follow. As Canadian diplomats had freedom to travel in Cuba, Cuban officials faced no restrictions in Canada. The CIA watched the Cubans and warned President Johnson that it might be dangerous for him to visit Expo 67, Montreal's 1967 world fair. They feared that Miami-based Cubans would dynamite the Cuban pavilion, sponsored by Fidel Castro's government, around the president's estimated time of arrival.

A White House memo of 17 May 1967, barely one week before the presidential visit, warned President Johnson that the CIA and FBI were seeking "new information" on security at Expo 67. Marvin Watson, President Johnson's appointments secretary, wrote on White House stationery; "As of this time, neither CIA nor FBI has further information. (There is still talk of the Cubans bombing the Cuban exhibit, possibly this weekend.) If the President could delay his decision [to visit Montreal] until Monday ... other information will be available for consideration."

An event five years later demonstrated that the Johnson team's concern about Cuban espionage was well founded. On 4 April 1972, somebody (probably Miami-based Cubans) bombed the offices of the Cuban Trade Commission in Montreal, located in a building which was shared with other tenants. Fearing that subsequent blasts might threaten other occupants of the building, the Montreal police sought entry to the trade commission's unit. Its Cuban occupants did not want to let them in and, invoking diplomatic immunity, threatened to shoot them if they entered. The police forced their way in. Fidel Castro protested, and the Canadian government apologized. It is a fair assumption that if the trade commission's sole purpose had been trade, the Cubans' reaction would have been different.

In addition to observing Cubans and other potential troublemakers at Expo, the CIA continued to watch Canadian politicians. As Canada's 1968 federal election approached, President Johnson asked CIA director Richard Helms to prepare a briefing paper with "basic information about the upcoming Canadian election." Rostow wrote a covering letter to the president: "Herewith CIA notes on Canadian politics including the name of the Conservative candidate [sic], Robert Stanfield, that none of us could remember."

The leading threat to Canadian stability during the Johnson presidency lay in the possible secession of Quebec. Jean-François Lisée's excellent book, In the Eye of the Eagle, says that an otherwise brilliant 1961 CIA forecast for Canada in the 1960s failed totally in its predictions about Quebec. While the document predicted "the political agendas of Diefenbaker ... Pearson ... and Pierre Trudeau before they could ever possibly have been drafted," it also stated that

Canada could anticipate "a sharpened sense of national unity, including an improved relationship between the major English- and French-speaking communities." However, the situation quickly became sufficiently serious that early in the Johnson presidency Ray Cline of the CIA visited the White House to discuss Quebec. Premiers Jean Lesage (1960–66) and Daniel Johnson (1966–68) demanded increased power for their province at the expense of federal authority, and in July 1967, while visiting Montreal, President Charles de Gaulle of France proclaimed the separatist slogan, "Vive le Québec libre!" A new political party pledged to Quebec independence, the Parti québécois, was born the next year. For much of the decade a terrorist group, the Front de libération du Québec (FLQ), was dynamiting mailboxes and other symbols of federal authority, and there were casualties.

On 1 May 1965, witnesses saw a man leave a package outside the U.S. consulate-general in Montreal, then drive away in a waiting car. A few minutes later a bomb exploded, breaking windows and doors. The blast appears to have been the work of the FLQ, possibly opposing the "imperialist" U.S. war in Vietnam. Paul Martin, the minister for external affairs, expressed his regrets to the American ambassador in Ottawa, Walton Butterworth.

Ambassador Butterworth – as might be expected and as was his duty – kept the White House well informed of developments in Canada. Early in 1968, the ambassador warned the State Department that a united Canada was in America's interest:

> The possibility of Quebec independence has implications for Canada – and of course the United States – which are legion and monumental. It seems apparent that our own best interest is in having a united Canada on our northern border, not two or more states sharing a legacy of bitterness over separation, but the Embassy has requested the Department to undertake a contingency study to examine our stake in Canada and the problems which division would create for us.

Lisée says that American officials at the consulates-general in Montreal and Quebec City were highly competent people who spoke and understood French, some of them very well, and who could tell Washington what was happening. Dean Rusk was familiar with the situation, and late in 1967 President Johnson discussed events in Quebec and the mischievous role of the French president with Charles Bohlen, the United States ambassador to France. Perhaps because Canada still lacked intelligence agents in foreign countries, Lisée is convinced that American authorities were more knowledgeable than their Canadian counterparts about the links between the French government and Quebec nationalists, but that the State Department failed to warn Ottawa. The primary reason was Washington's obsession with Vietnam, but there were other factors. Some officials were amused that the moralizing, self-righteous Canadians had a problem of their own. Willis Armstrong, a one-time associate of Ambassador Butterworth at the embassy in Ottawa and subsequently a key official at the State Department who controlled appointments to the consulates-general in Montreal and Quebec City, sympathized with the separatists. Lisée quotes him: "I felt that to some extent Quebec had colonial status and I am against colonial status." By contrast, Leonard Marks of the United States Information Agency lamented that in 1968 the French government was spending $6.5 million in Quebec alone, while the total budget of the United States Information Agency across all Canada was a mere $161,000. "We must expand our information and cultural program if we are to keep our friends throughout the world and try to answer the charges made by those who disagree with us," said Marks.

Although the White House did not inform the Canadian government about Quebec matters, it tried to get information via a Canadian route on Vietnam. In 1964, the Johnson administration sought to persuade or warn the government of Communist North Vietnam to stop its military efforts in South Vietnam. Its chosen means for delivering the appropriate messages and for learning of North Vietnamese reactions was a Canadian diplomat. The messenger needed credibility in both Hanoi (the North Vietnamese capital) and Washington, and Henry Cabot Lodge, U.S. ambassador in South Vietnam, did not want anyone from the other possible countries: the United Arab Republic (Egypt's name at the time), Yugoslavia, Poland, or even the United Kingdom.

On 19 April 1964, Rusk and McGeorge Bundy travelled to Saigon, the South Vietnamese capital, for talks with Lodge. On his return to Washington, Bundy met at once with President Johnson, and the Executive Committee of the National Security Council – Rusk and Bundy, McNamara and CIA director John McCone – agreed that a Canadian should be the messenger. This proved quite possible. Since 1954, Canada – along with Poland and India – had belonged to the International Control Commission (ICC), a body established at Geneva that year to monitor cease-fires in Vietnam and its neighbours, Laos and Cambodia. Moreover, Rusk had already agreed to visit Ottawa on 30 April for a discussion of bilateral Canadian-American relations. While in the Canadian capital, the Secretary of State could ask Pearson to appoint an experienced and competent diplomat to the ICC. That diplomat would have "the specific mission of conveying to Hanoi both warnings about its present course and hints of possible rewards in return for a change."

In Ottawa, Rusk found Prime Minister Pearson and the minister of external affairs, Paul Martin, totally sympathetic. In Rusk's words, "I found our Canadian friends in close concert with the thoughts you and I discussed in

Saigon and they assure me they are most willing to cooperate with us." They would appoint Blair Seaborn, "an expert on Communist affairs," who had just returned from a tour of duty at the Canadian embassy in Moscow. According to Rusk, Pearson and Martin agreed that Seaborn would spend more time in Hanoi than had his predecessors and would cultivate a close personal relationship with Ho Chi Minh and other North Vietnamese officials. Seaborn would also attempt to persuade Polish members of the ICC to be more objective, less partisan in their defence of any and all North Vietnamese actions. While Pearson's memoirs are silent on the 30 April meeting, Martin's explain the Canadian government's willingness to oblige. It hoped that Canada's ICC membership might prove useful in averting a conflict, and it thought that Canada had a unique role to play as "a close friend of the United States, with an entrée to Hanoi." Unfortunately, according to CIA official Chester Cooper, who had responsibilities for both Asia and Canada, "The sights we had on the Seaborn effort were pretty low."

Paul Martin presented a problem. As minister of external affairs he was Seaborn's boss and thought, not surprisingly, that Seaborn should take orders from him and report to him. Seaborn insists that this is what he did, and that his visits were diplomacy, not espionage. When the U.S. embassy in Saigon contacted him directly, Seaborn "cleared ... any requests from that source with Ottawa before I would act upon them. Also, my reports of visits were always filed with Ottawa before I gave information to the local Americans." Before Seaborn's first visit to Hanoi, Martin thought the State Department's approach too belligerent, and American authorities thought official Ottawa too timid. These differences of opinion led to a breakdown in communications. Ambassador Lodge wanted Seaborn to warn Hanoi "that they will be punished." Rusk thought this so blunt as to be counterproductive "in light of present Canadian attitudes." Lodge then agreed that the State Department should exploit, but not level with, Seaborn. Seaborn "does not need to tell North Vietnam that the bomb is about to come. What I propose ... is that the bomb does come just prior to his arrival in Hanoi. There is no question whatsoever of consulting the Canadians."

In order to arrange what Seaborn was to say to Ho Chi Minh and other Communist officials, William H. Sullivan of the State Department and Chester Cooper of the CIA visited Ottawa on 27–29 May. Paul Martin's memoirs do not mention Cooper, but they do insist that Martin forced Sullivan to soften the message that Seaborn was to carry to Hanoi; Martin thought the original too threatening.

In June, before any aerial bombardment of North Vietnam had taken place, Seaborn made his first visit to Hanoi. His reports of that and subsequent visits remain classified, but the *Canadian Forum* did manage to publish extensive excerpts in its issue of September 1973. Seaborn met Premier

Pham Van Dong during the June visit and gave him a letter from the Canadian prime minister. Seaborn told the North Vietnamese premier that the United States held his government responsible for Communist insurgency in South Vietnam, and that American patience was limited. Seaborn believed that Pham Van Dong understood the consequences of further defiance. Ambassador Lodge received a copy of Seaborn's report immediately after Seaborn returned to Saigon, and cleared the contents with his superiors in Ottawa.

On 13 July Sullivan did meet Seaborn and a Canadian brigadier who had just returned to Saigon from Hanoi. The brigadier told Sullivan and General Maxwell Taylor, who had replaced Lodge as United States ambassador in Saigon, that the North Vietnamese were building air-raid shelters and camouflaging possible targets in Hanoi. Taylor thought the brigadier's information so sensitive that he took special precautions to prevent it from falling into the wrong hands. Seaborn, by contrast, thinks that the brigadier was simply stating the obvious. "It was quite evident to any observer in Hanoi that air-raid shelters were being built and possible targets camouflaged. We had reported this to Ottawa and others (British and French) had no doubt done the same to their capitals. Perhaps Taylor personally had not heard of this development."

By the time Seaborn actually returned to Hanoi on 10 August 1964, the war had entered a new phase. On 30 July, naval commandos from South Vietnam under the direction of General William Westmoreland of the U.S. army had raided the North Vietnamese islands of Hon Ngu and Hon Me. Since 19 May the Pentagon had been orchestrating such unpublicized raids as part of Operation Plan 34A. On 2 August, North Vietnamese PT boats "began their high speed runs" at the U.S. navy destroyer *Maddox* which was gathering intelligence off the North Vietnamese coast. The Pentagon believed that the North Vietnamese "had mistaken *Maddox* for a South Vietnamese escort vessel." President Johnson then ordered another destroyer, the *C. Turner Joy*, close to the *Maddox*, while South Vietnamese PT boats attacked a radar installation at Vinh Son and targets at the Ron River estuary. On 4 August North Vietnamese torpedo boats attacked the *Maddox* and the *C. Turner Joy* for reasons that are not altogether clear. One may nevertheless reasonably assume that the North Vietnamese associated the presence of the two destroyers with Operation Plan 34A. Yet, without disclosing Operation Plan 34A to Congress, President Johnson used the attacks on the *Maddox* and the *C. Turner Joy* as evidence of North Vietnamese aggression, and on 7 August won from Congress a resolution authorizing the use of virtually unlimited force against North Vietnam.

Much as American authorities wanted Seaborn's cooperation, Dean Rusk was less than candid with him. (According to Paul Martin, Rusk was annoyed at Martin's insistence that Rusk and Seaborn communicate through

Martin, not directly, since Seaborn was a Canadian, not an American diplomat.) On 8 August Rusk rushed a message to the United States embassy in Ottawa. The embassy was to forward the message to Seaborn before he left Saigon for Hanoi. Seaborn was to tell North Vietnamese officials that the two destroyers were not "in any way associated with the attacks" on Hon Ngu and Hon Me. Rusk asked Seaborn to say that while the United States could accept the 2 August attack on the *Maddox* as a case of mistaken identity, "the Americans were and are at a complete loss to understand" the 4 August attack on the two destroyers. Rusk said nothing about Operation Plan 34A, of which Seaborn remained totally unaware.

Seaborn's second trip appears to have been quite unproductive. According to the *Pentagon Papers*, Seaborn told Pham Van Dong that "North Vietnam must halt the Communist-led insurgencies in South Vietnam and Laos or 'suffer the consequences.'" Seaborn thought Pham "unintimidated" by this ultimatum.

In all, Seaborn made five trips to Hanoi. Their impact was, at best, marginal. On 2 March 1965 a re-elected President Johnson launched Operation Rolling Thunder, bombing raids on the North Vietnamese panhandle south of the 19th parallel. A few days later Seaborn visited Hanoi; this time Pham Van Dong refused to receive him, so Seaborn had to deal with a lesser official. On his return he reported that North Vietnamese leaders remained defiant and unlikely to make concessions. In their opinion, according to Seaborn, President Johnson's government faced greater pressure than Ho's to negotiate. Seaborn also delivered to Hanoi a warning about the American government's plans for additional massive bombing in North Vietnam, a warning which he believes American embassy officials in Warsaw had already conveyed to their Chinese colleagues in the Polish capital. (Whether the Chinese had forwarded the message to North Vietnamese officials remains unclear.) Seaborn's usefulness was ending as the war became more destructive. CIA official Cooper later commented on the manner in which U.S. officials had used Seaborn: "It was done in a way that was probably not quite legit from their [Canadians'] point of view, of using their ambassadors for in a sense American intelligence agents."

Nor was Seaborn the only Canadian to provide information on North Vietnam. On occasion, Canadians in Vietnam with the ICC operated on their own initiative, quite independently of Ottawa. John C. Powell, at that time administrative officer of the Canadian delegation of the ICC, says: "I personally paid for subscriptions to buy Hanoi newspapers, which were then transferred to American intelligence." Because none of the Canadians in Vietnam could read Vietnamese, Powell asked why he should continue to provide money from ICC accounts for that purpose. Every week an ICC aircraft went to Hanoi, and the Canadian crew and passengers could purchase North

Vietnamese newspapers while there. One Canadian sergeant commented, "If Lester Pearson knew what we were doing, there would be hell to pay in Ottawa."

Yet another Canadian diplomat – Chester Ronning – would visit Hanoi with the blessing of the Johnson administration, but his trips were certainly not espionage efforts. Ronning was one of the foremost Asian authorities at the Department of External Affairs, and his task was to determine whether there was any common ground between Hanoi and Washington that might serve as the basis of a peace settlement. Ronning went to Hanoi in March and June 1966, and on his return William Bundy, brother of McGeorge Bundy and assistant secretary of state for far eastern affairs, debriefed him in Ottawa. Bundy saw no hope in what Ronning reported and said so, although the CIA's Cooper, who had known and admired Ronning for years, was more optimistic.

The State Department observed diplomatic niceties with Ronning in a way that it had not with Seaborn. Bundy later told an interviewer, "I was very careful to debrief Ronning in front of Paul Martin, always a man looking for an easy interpretation, and to have Canadian professionals there and to compare my notes with them." Back in Washington, Walt Rostow would complain to the president: "Martin, without revealing any substance, is trying to keep us hemmed in on the grounds that the channel is 'still open.' " The North Vietnamese knew that Ronning was sounding them out in attempts to find common ground and, despite its distrust of Paul Martin, the White House did not try to avoid him this time.

Nor were Canadians the only nonbelligerents to provide information to the United States government. In his memoirs, Secretary of State Dean Rusk noted other futile efforts to find common ground. When President Kennedy met Soviet leader Nikita Khruschev at Vienna in May 1961, they discussed the matter. Besides Canadians, said Rusk, mediators included "Poles, Rumanians, Hungarians, Soviets, and others, both representatives and private citizens ... Despite the absence of formal talks until 1968, we were never out of contact with the North Vietnamese." Walt Rostow has said that papal nuncios as well as neutral diplomats provided information from Hanoi.

On the commercial front, the CIA monitored Canada's wheat industry. The United States government wanted to sell wheat to the Soviet Union and other Communist countries in Eastern Europe, and its greatest competitors were Canada and Australia. To that end, those responsible for U.S. sales had to be aware of the wheat situation in Canada and Australia and of those countries' methods of operating, as well as of the potential market in the Communist countries. In 1964, the CIA presented information on all these markets.

Conclusions

Even the United States – a "friendly" country by any standard, Canada's most powerful ally and most important trading partner – found reasons for its intelligence organization, the CIA, to collect information in Canada. Conventional U.S. diplomats, even with the help of a professional pollster, could not necessarily find the required data in the media and in the area around Parliament Hill. The United States also felt it had reasons to circumvent the proper Canadian authority, Paul Martin, in its dealings with Blair Seaborn and the brigadier on the ICC. If even a close ally resorts to such measures, it is easy to envision all sorts of possibilities for officials from less friendly countries. Finally, once again a Canadian government knew less than it should have (on this occasion about the French government's encouragement of Quebec nationalists) because Ottawa depended on an ally and did not collect its own foreign intelligence. Admittedly, however, there is no guarantee that such knowledge would in any way have affected the outcome.

10
The Future

The passage of time has led to declassification of secret documents in such democracies as Canada, the United States, the United Kingdom, and France, and thus made possible chapters 2, 3, 4, 6, 7, and 9. The defeat of Nazi Germany and the capture of its archives released the material for chapter 5. Without the death of Generalissimo Francisco Franco and the desire of his successors not only to be democratic but to be perceived as democratic, chapter 8 would not have been possible in its present format.

Revelations from these archives demonstrate that intelligence did prove helpful to Canadian interests, while lack of adequate intelligence has sometimes proved harmful. Agent X, working for the British, prevented destruction on Vancouver Island during the Boer War; lack of adequate intelligence left the Welland Canal vulnerable. Hopkinson served British, not Canadian, interests, and Sir Courtney Bennett's paranoia wasted many people's time. Although Colonel Sherwood and the Dominion Police allowed Ottawa some sense of perspective during World War I, faulty intelligence created inconvenience for some at a time when terrorists were successfully attacking Canadian targets near the international border. The Communist threat of the interwar years was less potent than it then appeared to be, so Canadian intelligence in that era probably mattered little. Because Nazi Germany's consular officials spied on fellow Germans rather than on Canadians, and restrained themselves in other ways, official Canadian indifference cost Canadians little. Similarly, Nazi Germany's failure to exploit the Irish Republican Army and its connection with Vichy France was good news for Canada. Had Hitler's priorities been different, the results might have been devastating. The CIA and the U.S. State Department were selective in what they told Blair Seaborn, and withheld information from Ottawa about links between France and Quebec City. Whether full information would have changed the course of events is arguable, but one would think that Canadian governments ought to be knowledgeable about events involving Canadians.

It was Vichy France that energized Canada's intelligence community and introduced Canadians to cryptography, mail interception, and electronic eavesdropping; some of these skills proved useful in the surveillance of Imperial Japan and the more marginal Fernando de Kobbe Chinchilla. Whether the information collected in either of these instances was of much value may be open to debate, but the mere possession of such knowledge seemed vital at the time. However, despite the less-than-satisfactory track record of Britain and the United States with regard to Vichy France and Kobbe Chinchilla, Canada retained an unhealthy dependence on the British and American intelligence communities – as researcher Alti Rodal would reveal a couple of generations later. In the aftermath of World War II, American and British intelligence officers debriefed some Nazis who appeared knowledgeable about the Soviet Union. Once the Nazis had reported what they claimed to know, the CIA told Canadian authorities that they were trustworthy people who would make worthy citizens. Obviously, Ottawa should not have trusted others, whose interests might have been different, to do Canada's screening.

Future intelligence disclosures should prove fascinating. With the collapse of the Soviet Union and its European empire, new chapters may soon be available. Boris Yeltsin and other post-Communist leaders of Russia may not feel the same need as their predecessors to protect the image of Communist politicians, and revelations are likely to pour out of Moscow. What additional strikes in Canada did Moscow subsidize? Did Soviet Communists create and promote, or merely exploit, labour strife in Canada? How deep was the relationship between Soviet authorities and the International Union of Mine, Mill and Smelter Workers? Were there other spies to replace those exposed and arrested in the aftermath of the Gouzenko disclosures, or did Gouzenko place roadblocks at the end of many trails? To what extent did Soviet authorities recruit Canadians who had relatives in the Soviet Union? To what extent did they use those relatives as bargaining chips to intimidate Canadians? Which Canadians who were short of money or who were closet Communists sold secrets to the Soviet Union? To what extent did Soviet knowledge of Canada, indeed of North America, improve once Fidel Castro's diplomats, who faced fewer restrictions than their Soviet counterparts, were willing to provide information? What secrets were Soviet officials so desperate to hide when their embassy in Ottawa and their consulate-general in Montreal caught fire? It is not likely that Moscow's secrets will remain secret much longer.

Revelations will undoubtedly be forthcoming from Moscow's Warsaw Pact allies, particularly Poland, Czechoslovakia, Hungary, and East Germany. New rulers have taken office in Warsaw, Prague, Bratislava, and Budapest. The Federal Republic of Germany plans to release East German documents subject to the Thirty Year rule; that is, thirty years after the time they were written. There may be greater continuity in other Warsaw Pact countries than in East Germany, which no longer exists and is now governed by its adversaries in Bonn, but one should not have to wait much longer to learn which refugees really were refugees. Once Fidel Castro is history, Cuban archives may reveal a harvest of information about Canada and Canada–U.S. relations – unless Castro, like Franco, has sanitized his archives.

The former Yugoslavia may be a somewhat more difficult nut to crack. In the aftermath of attacks by dissidents on Yugoslav airliners and diplomats around the world, Marshall Tito and his successors had good reasons to monitor activities of expatriate Croatians, Slovenians, and even Serbs. What additional aircraft did they hope to hijack? What additional diplomats did they plan to kill? What funds were they raising abroad to finance the secession of Croatia or Slovenia, and what were they doing with the money? How much Canadian money went for weapons in Texas or Florida gunshops? Canadians will be interested in the means whereby Yugoslav officials pursued answers to these questions, and they will have questions of their own. How many immigrants from the former Yugoslavia saw Canada not as a new homeland but as a battleground for the liberation of their true homeland? Unfortunately, most of the answers are buried in Belgrade and Zagreb. Belgrade, capital of the principal successor state to Tito's Yugoslavia, will, for the foreseeable future, probably not want to reveal Tito's secrets – unless to embarrass Croats or Slovenes. Highly nationalistic Croatians, who played the decisive role in the initial stages of dismantling Yugoslavia, may not want to air their own dirty laundry. Because of the presence of Canadian forces in Croatia and Bosnia, Canadians are likely to learn from their own sources about postindependent Croatia and the Bosnian war long before they learn what Serbs and Croats were doing before Yugoslavia disintegrated.

Certain non-Communist governments also have stories to tell. Democratic Chile must have documents on the Pinochet regime's surveillance of Chilean refugees in Canada. India's government, mindful of the 1985 bombing of an Indian Airlines flight from Toronto to Europe and the attempted assassination of a cabinet minister on Vancouver Island, must have files on Canada's Sikhs. Because of recent reactions by Canadian Armenians to old animosities, Turkish authorities have almost certainly been vigilant. It does not stretch the imagination to think that Arabs and Jews have filed reports on each other's Canadian communities with governments in the Middle East. The RCMP and CSIS will eventually release their files on these subjects, but the foreign governments will take longer. Unlike the Soviet Union, East Germany, and Yugoslavia, these non-Communist countries have survived, and unlike the Warsaw Pact regimes, their governments have maintained considerable continuity with their past. The non–Warsaw Pact countries have more incentive to maintain their secrets for some time to come. Canadians are more likely to learn the contents of telephone conversations monitored from Ellesmere Island before they learn the whole story about Chilean, Indian, Turkish, or Middle Eastern activities in Canada.

Nevertheless, espionage is a long-standing fact of life in Canada and is likely to remain so. Canadians should learn from past mistakes, avoid both paranoia and complacency, and do their own research when their own interests are at stake.

Abbreviations

AA	Auswärtiges Amt, Bonn
AAFC	Archives de L'Ambassade française au Canada, Ottawa
AQO	Archives du Quai d'Orsay, Paris
CADN	Centre des Archives diplomatiques, Nantes
CO	Colonial Office, London (see PRO)
DCER	Canada, Department of External Affairs, *Documents on Canadian External Relations*
DEA	Department of External Affairs, Ottawa
FO	Foreign Office, London (see PRO)
FRUS	United States, Department of State, *Foreign Relations of the United States*
LBJ	Lyndon Baines Johnson Archives, Austin, Texas
MAE	Ministerio de Asuntos Exteriores, Madrid
NA (Ottawa)	National Archives of Canada, Ottawa
NA (Washington)	National Archives of the United States of America, Washington, D.C.
NSF	National Security File (in LBJ)
PABC	Provincial Archives of British Columbia, Victoria, B.C.
PRO	Public Record Office, London (housing the records of both CO and FO)
RSS	Records of the Secret Service, Correspondence 1863–1950 (Re Spy Suspects during the Spanish-American War), National Records Center, Suitland, Md.
UBC	University of British Columbia Library – Special Collections Division, Vancouver, B.C.
WHCF	White House Central Files (in LBJ)

Notes

The number on the left is the page where the quoted phrases (set here in boldface) appear. Wherever appropriate, i.e., where the quoted phrase covers the subject matter of the whole paragraph, all notes for that paragraph are grouped under one phrase.

Introduction

vii **F.H. Hinsley:** Hinsley, II, 551, 636–37.
John Sawatsky: Sawatsky, 1–8.
Hoy and Ostrovsky demonstrate: Hoy and Ostrovsky, 162, 74–75.
Charles Taylor and James Eayrs: Taylor, 22; Eayrs, *In Defence of Canada – Indochina*, 247–51.

viii **a study of UKUSA:** Richelson and Ball; see also Sawatsky, 9.
appeared in late sumer 1993: *RCMP Security Bulletins: The Depression Years, Part I, 1933–1934* and *The War Series, Part II, 1942–1945.*

Chapter 1. The Secret Operations of Spanish Consular Officials during the Spanish-American War

2 **of concern to … CSIS.** *Globe and Mail*, 22 Feb. 1986.
Contrary to what … : Jeffreys-Jones, *American Espionage;* Lowenthal; Wilkie; *Boston Sunday Herald,* 2 Oct. 1898.
Norman Penlington: Penlington, 101–8. O'Toole, whose otherwise excellent book discusses American intelligence around the world, fails even to mention Montreal in its index.
Phyllis Sherrin: Sherrin, 23–33.
Nathan Miller: Miller, 171.
The present writer: Mahant and Mount, 78–80; Mount, 59–76.
foreign intelligence: O'Toole, 194.
had a spy at Cadiz itself: Ibid., 228.
American agents travelled: Corson, 595.

Domingo Villaverde: O'Toole, 19, 32–33.

3 **the U.S. consul in Victoria … quickly became aware of Cabrejo's presence:** Abraham E. Smith, Victoria, to A.A. Adee, Assistant Secretary of State, Washington, 18 June 1898, Despatch 64, Department of State, Records of the U.S. Consulate in Victoria, B.C., microfilm T-130-12, NA (Washington).
From Gibraltar: Trask, 374.
in Hong Kong: Ibid., 68, 97, 375.
U.S. consulates … fed information to the U.S. Secret Service: William R. Day, Secretary of State, Washington, to the Secretary of the Treasury, 25 June 1898, RSS; Thomas W. Cridler, Third Assistant Secretary of State, Washington, to the Secretary of the Treasury, 24 and 28 May 1898, RSS; John Bassett Moore, Assistant Secretary of State, Washington, to the Secretary of the Treasury, 1 July 1898, RSS. Moore forwarded a telegram from John L. Bittinger, U.S. consul-general in Montreal. See also Cridler to the Secretary of the Treasury, 18 June 1898, RSS. Cridler advised about the activities of Spain's agent in Victoria, who was sending ciphered telegrams to Montreal.

4 **the Secret Service … received assistance from the post office:** E.g., Agnes Harrison, Santa Cruz, California, to Prime Minister Praxedes Sagasta, Madrid, 20 Apr. 1898, RSS.
"Spanish spies disguised as priests": John W. Kimball, Kimball's Detective Agency, New York, to Wilkie, Washington, 1 July 1898, RSS.
Mrs. Cora Hemer: Hemer, Pittsburgh, to President William McKinley, 6 July 1898, RSS.

R.E. Logan: Logan, Kansas City, to Adjutant-General, U.S. Army, Washington, 17 June 1898, RSS.

a letter from a Spaniard in Houston: Lena Huhn me Agguirra, Houston, to General Ramón Blanco, Havana, 29 May 1898, RSS.

Wilkie received a warning: G.B. Hamlet, Chief Inspector, Post Office Dept., Washington, to Wilkie, 27 May 1898, RSS.

the Secret Service intercepted Spanish consular mail: José Buigar de Delmar, Kingston, Jamaica, to Pedro Solís, Quebec City, 2 Aug. 1898, RSS; the Spanish Consul in Nassau to the Spanish Consul-General in Montreal, 21 May 1898, RSS.

Polo … did not trust: Toronto *Globe*, 22 Apr. 1898.

Polo "received … messages": Toronto *Mail and Empire*, 22 Apr. 1898.

5   **working … at Tampa, Florida:** Polo, Toronto, to the Minister of State, Madrid, 27 Apr. 1898, Document no. 118, Legajo no. H1481, MAE.

to Santiago de Cuba: Polo to the Minister of State, Madrid, 28 Apr. 1898, in *Spanish Diplomatic Correspondence and Documents, 1896–1900 Presented to the Cortes by the Minister of State* [translation of title] (Washington: Government Printing Office, 1905), 180.

interference from the host government seemed unlikely: This was a reasonable assumption, though there was a Canadian Secret Service in 1898, quite distinct from the Dominion Police, and it did assist the Americans in Halifax.

6   **on Dominion Square:** *Montreal Star*, 17 May 1898.

a possible U.S. invasion of Cuba: Polo to the Minister of State, 13 May, Legajo no. H2420, subfile Aprovisionamientos en el Canadá, document 13, MAE.

Polo assigned specific intelligence … duties: Bonilla, Montreal, to the Minister of State, 3 June 1898, Legajo no. H1973, MAE.

Polo evidently … : The author has checked the 1898 records of both the premier and the lieutenant-governor of British Columbia (PABC). For evidence of Bonilla's contacts with Cabrejo, see Bonilla to the Minister of State, 15 May, Legajo no. H1973, despatch no. 22, MAE; also, the Minister of State to Bonilla, summary of despatch no. 24 (11 July 1898), July summary, Legajo no. H1973, MAE.

Joaquín Torroja … Halifax: E.g., Minister of State to Bonilla, 15 April 1898, Legajo no. H1973, despatch no. 10, MAE.

for intelligence and telegrams: Minister of State to Bonilla, summary of despatch no. 13 (21 May 1898), May summary, Legajo no. H2420, MAE.

before destroying the Spanish fleet: Between 23 May and 31 May, Subosc and Bonilla sent sixteen cables to the Ministry of State, Legajo no. H2420, MAE.

target for invasion: Dubosc, Montreal, to the Minister of State, 4 June 1898, Legajo no. H2420, subfile Aprovisionamientos en el Canadá, document 12, MAE.

Downing … was found dead: Jeffreys-Jones, *American Espionage*, 31.

Secret Service intercepted a letter: Marqués Puente de Loma, Madrid, to Dubosc, Toronto, late Apr. 1898, RSS.

overheard a conversation: W.A. Wallace, Denver, to George D. Meiklejohn, Washington, 28 May 1898, RSS.

7   **The letter purportedly contained:** This summary is taken from a version of the letter, Carranza to José Gómez Ymay, 26 May 1898, published in Wilkie, 433–36.

embellishing its contents: *La Presse* and the *Montreal Star*, 6 June 1898. See also the Toronto *Globe* and the

Toronto *Mail and Empire* of the same date.

remains in some doubt: Jeffreys-Jones, *American Espionage*, 41.

St. Pierre: Jeffreys-Jones, "The American spy ring," 125–27. There are several letters between Prime Minister Sir Wilfrid Laurier and St. Pierre in vol. 79 of the Laurier Papers, MG 26, G, NA (Ottawa). See also a letter from Sir Julian Pauncefote, Washington, to the Governor General, Lord Aberdeen, 9 June 1898, Laurier Papers, MG 26, G, vol. 750, no. 215006. See also the Colonial Office memo of 12 June 1898, CO 42/862, 493.

Dubosc threatened: *Montreal Star*, 10 June 1898.

Dubosc had also established contacts: Dubosc to the Minister of State, 21 June, cable no. 35, Legajo no. H2420, MAE.

8 **Dubosc was still active:** 3 July, Legajo no. H1973, MAE; 6 July, cable no. 51, Legajo no. H2420, MAE.

"using Canadian territory ... government": Colonial Office memo of 28 July 1898, CO 42/859, 237–38. See also letter from the Foreign Office to the Colonial Office, 27 Oct. 1898, CO 42/864, 209.

Rejecting the charge: The expulsions attracted attention in both the Spanish Cortes and the Madrid press. A Cuban deputy, Rafael Maria de Labra, raised the matter on the floor of the Cortes 19 June 1898; Valentin Gomparre to the Minister of State, 21 June 1898, document E29, Legajo no. H2420, subfile Discusión Parlamentaria. There were front-page stories in the Madrid newspaper *El Liberal*, 12 and 13 June and 12 Aug. 1898; see also *El Tiempo* (Madrid), 8 June 1898.

Thanks to a "patriotic" employee: Bonilla to Mellor, Vancouver, 13 and 15 July 1898; Bonilla to Cabrejo, 15 July 1898; A.W. Greely, Chief Signal Officer, Washington, to the Assistant Secretary of War, 16 July 1898; all in RSS.

So Bonilla continued ... to cable Madrid: Bonilla to the Minister of State, cables no. 55–66, Legajo no. H2420, MAE.

"a clear violation of [Canadian] neutrality": Minister of State to Bonilla, summary of despatch no. 18, 13 June 1898, June summary, Legajo no. H1973, MAE.

9 **"in strict compliance with neutrality":** Count of Rascón, London, to the Minister of State, 27 June 1898, Legajo no. H2420, MAE. See also Pauncefote, Washington, to Lord Aberdeen, 26 April, Laurier Papers, M6 26, G, vol. 750, no. 214945.

vigilancias: E.g., Minister of State to Bonilla, money for Angel J. Cabrejo, Victoria, no. 22, 15 May 1898; £2,000, no. 27, 29 May 1898; May summaries, Legajo no. H1973, MAE; £150 to be paid monthly for a special commission to Manuel Martínez Aquiar for responsibilities in Canada and the United States, 2 July 1898; £1,800, no. 42, 15 July 1898; July summaries, ibid.

The Spanish Foreign Office stated: Minister of State to Bonilla, no. 22, 30 June 1898, June summary, ibid.

news of ship movements: Bonilla to the Minister of State, no. 54, 8 Aug. 1898, Aug. summary, ibid.

In that speech: Canada, House of Commons, *Debates*, 13 June 1898, p. 7890. Bonilla to the Minister of State, no. 18, 13 June 1898, no. 27, 15 June, June summary, Legajo no. H1973, MAE; Minister of State to Bonilla, no. 23, 11 July 1898, July summary, ibid.

Bonilla supervised: Bonilla to the Minister of State, no. 40, 14 July 1898, July summary, Legajo no. H1973, MAE; Minister of State to Bonilla, no. 10, 11 June, June summary, ibid. Bonilla to the Minister of State, June summary; Bonilla to the Minister of State, no. 43, 8 Aug. 1898, August summary, ibid.

peace talks: Bonilla to the Minister of State, 14 and 21 Sept. 1898 (cables no. 69 and no. 70), Legajo no. H2420, MAE.

10 **Spanish withdrawal from Cuba without a war ... would probably be fatal:** Trask, 59; O'Toole, 65–66, 109, 121, 379.
enthusiasm alone was no match: O'Toole, 179, 141, 167, 168.
geography, natural resources and people were on the side of the United States: Ibid., 97–98, 216, 170, 211, 214–18. Havana was one important exception to the problem of mobility.

11 **Without effective naval power:** This is certainly O'Toole's opinion: ibid., 357.
Igor Gouzenko: Smith, 94–109.
Nazi and Fascist infiltrators: Avery, "Canada's Response," 182.
British and American intelligence agencies were able: The findings of the researcher Alti Rodal on this point created considerable media consternation in Canada late in 1987. See, for example, Littman, 24–27; de Graff, 317–26, especially 318.

Chapter 2. Agent X and the Boer War, 1900

12 **Fenians:** For an up-to-date summary of Fenian and counter-Fenian activity in 1866, see Keshen, 355–81.
secret agents inside the United States: Andrew, 26; Popplewell, 51; Porter, 99–113.

13 **but used Pinkerton:** For more on Pinkerton, see Nathan Miller, 93, 98–106, and Morn.
Controversial ... in Canada and in Britain: Carman Miller, 422–38. James A. Hobson's polemic, *Imperialism,* first published in 1902, was in large measure a reaction to this war; see Philip Siegelman's introduction to the 1965 edition.
in Britain's forces: Granatstein et al., 62.
Other Americans ... disagreed: For a sample of conflicting American opinions, read the letters-to-the-editor columns of the *New York*

Times throughout the war.

14 **on which side they fought:** This opinion was originally expressed by Captain William Wyndham, British consul in Chicago, to Lord Pauncefote, the British ambassador in Washington, 6 Jan. 1900; FO 115/1174/39–40, Public Record Office, Kew Gardens, UK (hereafter, Foreign Office documents in the Public Record Office are identified simply as FO). Some of the recruits of the so-called Irish-American Ambulance Corps who left the United States to fight for the Boers early in 1900 were veterans of 1898; Pinkerton report, issued to Sir Percy Sanderson, British consul-general in New York, 16 February 1900, FO 115/1175/241–43. A Methodist clergyman in Portland, Oregon, the Reverend Alfred Thompson, approached the *British* consulate in that city and offered to use his powers of persuasion to have veterans of 1898 enlist on the British side; James Laidlaw, British consul, Portland, Oregon, to Pauncefote, 28 Dec. 1899, FO 115/1134/244–46.
The Fenian Spirit: Beckett, 365, 371, 376–78, 384–85, 392, 415–16, 437; Foster, 61–82; Blake, 7.
Bourke: Letter to the editor, the *New York Times,* 24 Dec. 1899.

15 **"of immense value":** J.E. Blunt, British consul in Boston, clipped this editorial and forwarded it to Pauncefote; FO 115/1134/214–15.
"the Irish Joan of Arc": A clipping from the *New York Sun,* forwarded by Sanderson to Pauncefote, so labelled Miss Gonne; Sanderson to Pauncefote, 30 Jan. 1900, FO 115/1175/14. The *Boston Herald* also described her that way; Blunt to Pauncefote, 19 Feb. 1900, FO 115/1175/256–58. See also Bell, 8–9, 42–44, 184; McCaffrey, 169.
arms shipments to the Boers: Sanderson to Pauncefote, 23 December 1899, FO 115/1134/205–7. There are several Pinkerton reports

that Sanderson forwarded to Pauncefote in FO 115/1176–1178.

recruitment to the Boer armies: E.g., Sanderson to Pauncefote, 7 Feb. 1901, FO 115/1215/170–71.

an alleged plot: E.g., Sanderson to Pauncefote, 20 Apr. 1901, FO 115/1217/114–19.

watch the Irish-American community: Robert Pinkerton to Wilfred Powell, British consul in Philadelphia, 29 Dec. 1899, FO 115/1174/66.

New York Herald: Sherwood renewed his subscription to the *Herald* 18 Sept. 1900; Records of the Federal Police Forces, RG 18, E, vol. 3106 (microfilm C-13, 857), NA (Ottawa).

Daly: Sherwood to Daly, 5 Jan. 1900, and Sherwood to Pinkerton, 13 Jan. 1900, both RG 18, E, vol. 3129 (microfilm 13874), NA (Ottawa).

16 **Laidlaw took the matter seriously:** Memo from James Laidlaw, 8–9 Jan. 1900, FO 115/1174/45; Laidlaw to Pauncefote, 10 Jan. 1900, FO 115/1174/46–48.

cooperated with Clayton Pickersgill: Laidlaw to Pauncefote, 29 Jan. 1900, FO 115/1175/51.

an amateur detective identified only as Agent X: Pickersgill to Pauncefote, 2 Feb. 1900, FO 115/1175/52; F.S. Hussey to H.A. Maclean, Deputy Attorney-General of British Columbia, 9 May 1900, GR 429, Box 5, File 5, PABC.

X's gender: Hussey to Maclean, 9 May 1900, GR 429, Box 5, File 5, PABC; Cormac & Donohoe & Baum to Pickersgill, 7 Mar. 1900, FO 115/1176/355; Hussey to Maclean, ibid.

17 *after* **months of effort:** Hussey to Maclean, 23 May 1900, GR 429, Box 5, File 5, PABC.

to protect X: Cormac & Donohoe & Baum to Pickersgill, 28 Apr. 1900, FO 115/1177/118, and 7 Mar. 1900, FO 115/1176/355; Hussey to Maclean, 23 May 1900, GR 429,

Box 5, File 5, PABC.

"blowing up 'the works at Esquimalt' ": Oral report of Agent X reduced to writing, 18 Jan. 1900, FO 115/1176/336–37; Report of X, 28 Jan. 1900, FO 115/1176/339.

JFM: JFM to Pickersgill, 5 Feb. 1900, FO 115/1176/340; Cormac & Donohoe & Baum to Pickersgill, 8 Feb. 1900, FO 115/1176/342, and 17 Feb. 1900, FO 115/1176/348.

Clann-na-Gael: See Coogan, 15–58; Bell, 3–15.

18 **"generously provided with funds":** Report of X, 16 Jan. 1900, FO 115/1176/360.

JFM promised: Cormac & Donohoe & Baum to Pickersgill, 8 Feb. 1900, FO 115/1176/342–45.

to the ... naval officer at Esquimalt: Pickersgill to Pauncefote, 9 Feb. 1900, FO 115/1176/209–11.

investigation by American authorities: State Department Files, Notes from the British Legation in the United States to the Department of State (1791–1906), microfilm series M-50, roll 132; Department of Justice, RG 60, Box 1189, File 18549/99 and Instructions to United States Attorneys and Marshalls, vol. 123, roll 136, NA (Washington).

Hussey was later to report: Hussey to Maclean, 9 May 1900, RG 429, Box 5, File 5, PABC.

stand guard ... in Victoria: Hussey to the Attorney-General of British Columbia, 9 Feb. 1900, GR 64, PABC.

X continued to entertain her ... sources: Cormac & Donohoe & Baum to Pickersgill, 7 Mar. 1900, FO 115/1176/355.

19 **[David Starr] Jordan:** Reports of X, 16 Jan. 1900, FO 115/1176/360; 15 Feb. 1900, FO 115/1176/346–47.

"The man of whom I made a report": Report of X, 22 Feb. 1900, FO 115/1176/349.

Pickersgill relayed all this news: T.E.K. Cormac to Pickersgill, 1 Mar. 1900, plus Pickersgill's written mar-

ginal comments, FO 115/1176/350.
Funds were pouring: Report of X, 4
Mar. 1900, FO 115/1176/351.
The next day ... on 13 March:
Reports of X, 5 Mar. 1900, FO
115/1176/353; 13 Mar. 1900, FO
115/1176/354.

20 **[to] a grateful F.S. Hussey:** Hussey
to Pickersgill, 10 Mar. 1900, FO
115/1176/357.
Donovan: Moore to Pauncefote, 20
June 1900, FO 115/1178/245–46.

21 **the two men arrested ... were innocent:** Report of X, 28 Mar. 1900, FO
115/1177/19.
The visit: "Précis of a conversation
held with Agent 'X' by telephone"
by "one of the members" of Cormac
& Donohoe & Baum, forwarded by
Moore to Pauncefote, 3 July 1900,
FO 115/1178/411–14.

22 **could have caused extensive damage:** Pickersgill to Pauncefote, 26
Apr. 1900, FO 115/1177/113. See
also the Toronto *Globe*, 23, 24, and
25 Apr. 1900.
to find the evidence: Sherwood to
Robert Pinkerton, 30 Apr. 1900;
Sherwood to Robert Pinkerton, [day
illegible] May 1899; RG 18, E, vol.
3105 (microfilm C-13857), NA
(Ottawa).
**to determine the real identity of
Karl Dullman:** S.P. Atkins [? – name
illegible] to R.J. Bryan, 17 Nov. 1900,
ibid., vol. 3106 (microfilm C-13857),
NA (Ottawa). Sherwood and Bryan
did not succeed in identifing Dillon,
but books on the IRA (see **Dillon**
below) state that Dillon had been in
Kingston Penitentiary for the
Welland Canal bombing.
a confidential warning: Sherwood
to the Warden, Kingston
Penitentiary, 4 July 1900, RG 18, E,
vol. 3105, 399, NA (Ottawa).
Dillon: Coogan, 49, 52, 137–38; Bell,
156; Bishop and Mallie, 21–34; Blake,
passim.
Donovan: Report of X, 27 Apr. 1900,
FO 115/1177/119.
Pickersgill had some difficulties:

Pickersgill to JFM, alias "100," 16
Mar. 1900, FO 115/1176/358; JFM,
alias "100," to Pickersgill, 22 Mar.
1900, FO 115/1176/359; Pickersgill
to Pauncefote, 28 April 1900, FO
115/1177/122–23; Moore to
Pauncefote, 20 June 1900, FO
115/1178/245–46.

23 **Pickersgill ... became ill and died:**
Moore to Gerald Lowther, chargé
d'affaires, Newport, Rhode Island,
8 Aug. 1901, FO 115/1219/109.
concluded that Donovan had lied:
Cormac & Donohoe & Baum to
Moore, 20 June 1900, FO
115/1178/247–48.
to be "making charts": Report of X,
19 June 1900, FO 115/1178/249.
**defended his force's expanded esti-
mates:** Sherwood to the government
auditor, 11 July 1900, vol. 3105
(microfilm C-13857), NA (Ottawa).
**Donovan had "no suspicion ... of
Agent X":** Cormac & Donohoe &
Baum to Moore, 14 July 1900, FO
115/1179/26.

Chapter 3. Terrorist Threats and Conspiracies during World War I

25 **A prominent ... historian:** Kealey,
"Surveillance State," 179–210. The
quotation comes from 179.
an anarchist plot: Sherwood to Silas
H. Carpenter, Chief of Detectives,
Montreal, 19 March 1903, RG 18, E,
vol. 3111 (microfilm C-13861), NA
(Ottawa).
"most of their people": Sherwood
to Bopp, 26 March 1903, ibid.

26 **Sherwood also authorized Bopp:**
Sherwood to Bopp, 30 March 1903,
ibid.; Sherwood to Carpenter, 30
March 1903, ibid.
British intelligence: Andrew, *Secret
Service*, 30, 50, 77. Another excellent
source on the origins of British intel-
ligence in the twentieth century is
the first chapter of Hinsley.
**British concern began to focus on
Sikhs:** For a history of British
Columbia's Sikh population

between 1905 and 1914, see Peter Ward; also Johnston, 3–27.

28 *Komagata Maru:* Johnston, 3–27; also Popplewell, 49–76.

Well before hostilities began: Hadley and Sarty, 64–65, 69–70, 81, 93.

29 **The German Navy:** Ibid., 46–49, 68.

One recent author: Elliott, 50–51.

Right at the beginning: Witcover, 58–61. See also Nathan Miller, 184–94.

German immigrants: International Migration and Naturalization (Series C 88-114), Immigrants by Country, 1820–1857, in U.S. Department of Commerce, 56–57.

30 **Lang had posted his drawings:** George Shotts, U.S. Consul, Sault Ste. Marie, Ontario, to the Secretary of State, 27 April 1915, item 342.62/183, Department of State, Record Group 59, Series 342.62, NA (Washington).

Albert Kaltschmidt: Horace Nugent to Spring Rice, 23 June 1915, FO 115/1904/308–9. For information about the explosions and attempted explosions, see successive issues of the Windsor *Evening Record* from 21 June until 13 Aug. 1915. The British correspondence concerning Kaltschmidt is in file FO 115/1904/284–309.

Bernstorff himself placed $10,000: Doerries, 181–82.

31 **German documents released after World War II reveal:** Kitchen, especially 257, 258.

Welland Canal: Ibid., 246.

Von der Goltz ... went to jail: Witcover, 58–61.

"interruption of traffic": Witcover, 68.

32 **von Papen summoned Werner von Horn:** Kitchen, 254. A photograph of the cheque von Papen wrote to von Horn (no. 87) appears in the records of the American Embassy in the United Kingdom – 1914, Military Affairs, xliv, 820 German, C8.15, 74, NA (Washington). See also the *New York Times,* 3 Feb. 1915, and the *Canadian Annual Review,* 1915, 447–49, 453.

hard evidence: Witcover, 67–69.

von Horn served time: Kitchen, 256.

Paul Koenig: Witcover, 126–33.

Reinhard R. Doerries: Doerries, 178–80.

33 **Von Papen then sailed:** Witcover, 134–35.

Wolf von Igel: Witcover, 147.

von Papen also tried to recruit Sikhs: Ibid., 79–80.

34 **Reid:** Johnston, 19–25.

Balwant Singh ... and Harnam Singh: Johnston, 26–27. That H.F. Bopp, consul-general of Imperial Germany in Montreal, and Franz Bopp, consul-general of Imperial Germany in San Francisco, were one person is confirmed in a letter to the author from Axel Saurer, Third Secretary, German Embassy, Ottawa, 3 Jan. 1992. For further information about the German embassy's connection with Sikhs, see Doerries, 154 and 186.

With the outbreak of war: While the files of the Dominion Police for this period burned when Canada's Parliament Buildings went up in flames in 1916, certain authors have discovered and analysed Dominion Police correspondence with other branches of the federal government in the files of those branches. See Hadley and Sarty, 107–13.

35 **One Irish-American organization:** Alan J. Ward, 27–28, 59–60. Regarding cooperation between Irish and German communities in the United States, see the microfilm *Die Irlaender in den Vereinigten Staaten,* Record Group 242, T-149, Roll 380, published by the NA (Washington). It consists of German embassy correspondence captured at the end of World War II. For a summary in English of the German embassy's relations with Irish-Americans, see Doerries, 72–76, 155–65, 179–93.

British and Canadian authorities:
See FO 115/2073 and FO 115/2074.
Leay: Spring Rice to Leay, 17 May
1916, FO 115/2073/97.
Armstrong: Spring Rice to Lord
Hardinge, London, 24 June 1916, FO
115/2073/202. Home Office records
are housed at the Public Record
Office, Kew Gardens; the author
searched in Sept. 1989.

36 *Gaelic-American:* Alan J. Ward, 17.
"There are hundreds ...": Quoted
by Spring Rice to Lord Hardinge, 30
June 1916, FO 115/2073/204; Lord
Hardinge to Spring Rice, 27 June
1916, FO 115/2073/203.
Casement: The correspondence is
available in FO 115/2074.
Canadian officials did exaggerate:
Sarty and Armstrong. For a list of
the German embassy's conspiracies
– successful and unsuccessful –
against Canadian targets, see
Doerries, 178–82.

37 **Bryan's primary concern:** Bryan to
Spring Rice, 1 June 1915, FO
115/1869/303; Spring Rice to
Lansing, 9 July 1915, FO
115/1869/337–38.
Bryan ... rejected a request: Bryan to
Spring Rice, 27 Feb. 1915, FO
115/1869/144–45.

38 **Ball:** FO 115/2018/284–323.
**"You will notice ... that Mr. Reat
has been transferred":** Spring Rice
to Governor General, 22 Nov. 1915,
FO 115/1904/52; Governor General
to Spring Rice, 16 Dec. 1915, FO
115/1904/154; Horrigan to the
Commissioner, RNWMP, Regina,
5 Nov. 1915, FO 115/1904/155–58.

39 **There is nothing:** Various letters in
RG 59, decimal file 1910–29, File 123,
Reat, Samuel C., Box 1612, NA
(Washington), including Reat to the
Secretary of State, 26 July 1915; A.S.
Nimmo, Calgary, to the Secretary of
State, 17 Nov. 1915; Reat, Rangoon,
to the Secretary of State, 8 Feb. 1916;
Hagan Cavell, Guatemala City, to
the Secretary of State, 21 May 1917;
John G. Foster, U.S. consul-general,

Ottawa, to the Secretary of State,
7 Aug. 1918.
Reat's correspondence: Reat,
Rangoon, to the Secretary of State,
[day omitted] Feb. 1916, and to H.C.
Hengstler, Department of State,
20 Feb. 1916, ibid.
**Reat had reprimanded his subordi-
nate:** Montgomery to Reat, 25 Jan.
1915 and Reat to Montgomery, 27
Jan. 1915, RG 84, Correspondence,
American consulate, Calgary, 1915,
part 3, class 7, file 703.
**American authorities ... appeared
satisfied:** Count J.H. von Bernstorff
to the Secretary of State, 5 Nov.
1915; Wilbur J. Carr (for the
Secretary of State) to Samuel C. Reat,
25 Nov. 1915; Frank L. Polk (Acting
Secretary of State) to Bernstorff, 27
Nov. 1915; all in RG 59, decimal file
1910–1929, 342.62/331, NA
(Washington). Also, P.A. Jackson,
U.S. vice-consul, Calgary, to the
Secretary of State, 3 Dec. 1915,
RG 59, decimal file 1910–1929,
342.62/365, NA (Washington).

40 **imaginations ran wild:** Bennett
Memorandum, "German Raid on
Canada," 2 Mar. 1915, FO
115/1169/156.
These men denied: Anonymous let-
ter, New York, to Sherwood, 20 Feb.
1915, FO 115/1869/139.
"I am inclined": Joseph Pope
(Under-Secretary of State for
External Affairs) to Spring Rice, 11
Feb. 1915, FO 115/1869/122; Bennett
to Spring Rice, 19 Feb. 1915, FO
115/1869/130A.
Henry Muck: Bennett to the Foreign
Office, the British embassy
(Washington), and the Governor
General (Ottawa), 22 May 1915, FO
115/1869/280.

41 **"a German named Henry Muck":**
Lansing to Spring Rice, 19 June 1915,
FO 115/1869/319.
"tons of explosives": Bennett to
Spring Rice, 4 June 1915, FO
115/1869/308–10.
Bradbury told ... Mortimer:

A. Carnegie Ross, British consul-general, San Francisco (Mortimer's superior), to Spring Rice, 12 Jan. 1915, FO 115/1869/79–80; S.R. Bradbury to C. White Mortimer, 3 Feb. 1915, FO 115/1869/121; Memo of the State Department, signed by Robert Lansing, 1 Apr. 1915, FO 115/1869/219–20; Spring Rice to the Governor General, 5 Apr. 1915, FO 115/1869/223.

the Countess Dekomiss: Leay to Spring Rice, 29 Jan. 1917, FO 115/2165/177.

42 **Pope reported:** Joseph Pope to the Secretary of the Governor General, 2 Feb. 1917, FO 115/2165/209–10.
Krenz: Pope to Spring Rice, 15 Feb. 1917, FO 115/2165/224. The quotation comes from the actual report, FO 115/2165/225.

State Department officials ... were aware: Memorandum of the War Trade Intelligence Department, 2 Oct. 1917, RG 59, decimal file 1910–1929, 862.20241/5, NA (Washington). See also items 862.20241/17 and 20241/18.

Devoy: Lansing to the U.S. embassy, London, 2 July 1918, RG 59, 862.20241/22a and Laughlin, U.S. embassy, London, to the Secretary of State, 10 July 1918, RG 59, 862.20241/23, NA (Washington). For confirmation of Devoy's importance, see Coogan, 19, 131–33.

Guvrick: G.R. Taggart, U.S. Consul, Cornwall, to the Secretary of State, 4 Feb. 1916, RG 59, 862.20242, NA (Washington).

Schopper: Harold D. Clum, U.S. consul, Calgary, to the Secretary of State, 7 Aug. 1917, RG 59, 862.20242/2, NA (Washington), plus related documentation within that file. Also Clum to the Secretary of State, 26 Dec. 1917, RG 59, 862.20242/3, plus related documentation.

A.M. Mealy and Dr. C.H. Johnson: Even E. Young, U.S. consul-general, Halifax, to the Secretary of State,

17 Apr. 1918, RG 59, 862.20242/5, and Young to the Secretary of State, 3 July 1918, RG 59, 862.20242/7, NA (Washington).

43 **Harry B. Weber and Erwin W. Weber:** Raymond Phelan, acting U.S. vice-consul, Port of Spain, to the Secretary of State, 16 May 1918, RG 59, 862.20242/6, and Statement of the War Department, 18 June 1918, RG 59, 862.20242/8, NA (Washington).

when the U.S. consulate ... reported: Chester W. Martin, U.S. consul, Toronto, to the Secretary of State, 28 Aug. 1918, and the Secretary of State to Martin, 11 Sept. 1918, RG 59, 862.20242/11, NA (Washington).

Chapter 4. American Surveillance of Canadian Communists, 1921–33

44 **Soviet interest in Canada:** There is extensive literature on Gouzenko. One of the latest interpretations is that of Granatstein and Stafford, 47–75. Regarding Canadian Communists, see, for example, Balawyder, 171–207.

The RCMP has long been vigilant: Fetherstonhaugh, a fervent admirer of the Mounted Police, admits as much, 185–86. Sawatsky, 66-67; Kealey, "Surveillance State"; see also Kealey, "State Repression of Labour." A forthcoming book edited by Kealey and Whitaker, *RCMP Security Bulletins: The Early Years, 1919–1929* (Toronto: Canadian Committee on Labour History), deals with the domestic surveillance of Canadian Communists. See also Hannant.

Woodsworth: Canada, House of Commons, *Debates*, 4 April 1922, 670–72.

45 **Third International:** Lenin, 240–41; Possony, 405, 448–98 (especially 468).

Across the world: Suvorov, 6–30; see also Andrew and Gordievsky, 65–232.

met in Guelph: Angus, 86; see also Buck, *Years in the Struggle.* Sawatsky, 43, 66–67.

Ian Angus: Angus, 78, 118–27, viii.
The Workers Party of Canada: Ibid., 97–102, 199. The quotation on page 46 comes from 98.

46 **The Canadian, British, and American governments:** Two very different interpretations of the intervention are those of Buck, *Canada and the Russian Revolution,* and Swettenham. On Canada, see Balawyder, 22–34. See also Eayrs, *Northern Approaches,* 116–17. On Great Britain, see Keith Neilson, "'Pursued by a Bear': British Estimates of Soviet Military Strength and Anglo-Soviet Relations, 1922–1929," *Canadian Journal of History* 28, no. 2 (August 1993). Two American classics on the red scare in the United States are Hicks, 13–16, and Leuchtenburg, 66–83.

In the aftermath of World War I: Horrall, 169–90. Kealey, "Surveillance State," is often critical of Horrall's interpretations: see 180 and 201. Elliott, 65.

Although ... self-reliant: Volkman and Baggett, 23. For a warning not to exaggerate the U.S. intelligence cuts, see Angevine.

47 **In all three countries:** Hannant, 711–35. See also Nathan Miller, 202–13; Eayrs, *Northern Approaches,* 119.

On 16 March: Balawyder, 37, 43.
The Soviets' baggage: Ibid., 42.
O.D. Skelton: Ibid., 82–87.

48 **"The delegation came":** Halstead, Montreal, to the Secretary of State, 11 March 1924, RG 59, 842.00B/7, NA (Washington).
Foster soft-pedalled: Foster to the Secretary of State, RG 59, 842.00B/10, ibid.
Despite the literature issue: Balawyder, 87–92; Dominions Secretary, London, to the Governor General, 19 May 1927, *DCER* 4, 994; Foster to the Secretary of State, 26

May 1927, RG 59, 842.00B/22, NA (Washington). See also Andrew, 376, 458–59, 469–70. For more information on the controversy inside Canada, see Balawyder, 92–104.

49 **Riga:** Commissioner of the United States, Riga, to the Secretary of State, 4 Mar. 1922, RG 59, 842.00B/1, NA (Washington); Commissioner of the United States, Riga, to the Secretary of State, 18 Apr. 1922, RG 59, 842.00B/2; MacLachlan, United States legation, Riga, to the Secretary of State, 25 Mar. 1925, RG 59, 842.00B/15.

Radnik: Frost to the Secretary of State, 2 Aug. 1929, RG 59, 842.00B/30, NA (Washington); Statement of R. Brodeur, Commissioner of Customs, sent by Frost to the Secretary of State, 6 Aug. 1929, RG 59, 842.00B/31; State Department to the U.S. consul-general in Montreal, n.d.; ibid.

50 **Brittain sent ... a copy of *Manifesto No. 1:*** Angus, 96; Brittain to the Secretary of State, 22 Dec. 1921, RG 59, 842.00B/-, NA (Washington); Slater to the Secretary of State, 26 Nov. 1924, RG 59, 842.00B/12. For confirmation about Popovitch's role in the Communist party, see Angus, 71, 80, 173, inter alia. Stewart to the Secretary of State, 8 April 1930, RG 59, 842.00B/33. For more about Ryan, see Angus, 83, 222, 227–29.

Consular officials depended heavily upon ... newspapers: Perusal of decimal file 1910–1929 of RG 59, 842.00B will confirm that statement.

even greater use: E.g., H. Dorey Newsom, U.S. legation, Ottawa, to the Secretary of State, 4 Apr. 1928, RG 59, 842.00B/26, NA (Washington).

Kyllonen: For further information on Kyllonen, see Jalava, 165–66. Chapman to the Secretary of State, 14 Nov. 1931, RG 59, 842.00B/61, 16 Apr. 1931, RG 59, 842.00B/38 (Chapman forwarded a copy of the *Ottawa Journal* with this letter), and

20 Aug. 1931, RG 59, 842.00B/46, NA (Washington).

Hill was an active … Communist: Jalava, 83–84, 116–17.

The State Department … asked him to monitor: W.R. Castle, Jr., for the Secretary of State, to Chapman, 24 Sept. 1931, RG 59, 842.00B/46, NA (Washington).

Chapman continued to report: Chapman to the Secretary of State, 7 Nov. 1931, RG 59, 842.00B/57 and 9 Nov. 1931, RG 59, 842.00B/58, ibid.

"a prominent Finnish Communist": Angus, 300; J.B. Jackson, U.S. consul, Fort William, to Chapman, 5 Nov. 1931, 842.00B/57, NA (Washington); Chapman to the Secretary of State, 10 March 1932, RG 59, 842.00B/71. For further information on Ahlquist, see Angus, 296–97 and 301, inter alia.

51 **Canadian police departments:** Frost to the Secretary of State, 11 Nov. 1931, RG 59, 842.00B/59, NA (Washington); Chapman to the Secretary of State, 14 Nov. 1931, RG 59, 842.00B/62.

These talks: Balawyder, 113 (Balawyder is quoting a contemporary source), 181.

to go to El Salvador: See Levenstein.

following a tradition: Winks, passim; Mount, 31–48.

Chapter 5. Nazi German Consular Posts as Sources of Information, 1933–39

53 **More than thirty years ago:** Eayrs, "'A Low Dishonest Decade,'" 74.

The information that these men … forwarded to Berlin: For an example of Nazi influence on Canadian Adrian Arcand *before* 1933, see Robin, 87–88.

54 **"The [German] Foreign Office":** Geyer, 311–12. This is also the opinion of Wagner, 31.

Wagner agrees: Wagner, 23–24.

Ludwig Kempff: Kempff to Heinrich Dieckhoff, Ministerial

Direktor, Auswärtiges Amt (AA), Berlin, 24 Sept. 1935, file R77315, AA. When Kempff or his contemporaries wrote to AA, they wrote to Berlin, then the capital. However, when the present author did his German research (June 1991), AA operated from Bonn, still the seat of government of the Federal Republic of Germany. Wagner, 32–33; Robin, 256, 255.

55 **Hans Ulrich Granow:** Wagner, 44.

Heinrich Seelheim: For an indication of Seelheim's extensive travels across the Prairies and British Columbia, see the report attached to his letter to AA, Berlin, 3 Sept. 1935, file R77333, AA. *Vancouver Sun*, 11, 18, 19 March 1935; Vancouver *News-Herald*, 13 March 1935; *Vancouver Province*, 18 March 1935.

When Seelheim won promotion: Wagner, 41, 42; Robin, 256–57.

Both Kempff and Seelheim: File R77326, AA. Kempff to AA, 20 Dec. 1933 and 28 Oct. 1935, file R77326, AA; Kempff to AA, 13 April 1934, 4 April 1935, and 23 April 1935, file R77350, AA.

56 **For years Kempff had been monitoring:** Kempff to AA, 18 June 1935, file R77315, AA.

Kempff's interest in Canadian foreign relations: Kempff's correspondence with AA: file R77317, AA; 17 June 1935, file R77323, AA; 5 and 7 March 1935, file R77320, AA; 21 and 26 Sept. 1935, file R77320, AA; 21 May and 29 June, 1935, file R77320, AA; 1 Nov. 1935, file R77330, AA; 14 Dec. 1935, file R77326, AA.

57 **Echlin's thirteen articles:** Toronto *Globe*, 26, 27, 28, 29 and 31 July, 1, 2, 3, 19, 22, 29 and 31 Aug., and 7 Sept. 1933.

a letter from Eisendrath: Toronto *Globe*, 31 Aug. 1933.

Official German correspondence: RG 242, series T-120, microfilm roll 3217, NA (Washington).

58 **a 1937 report … on the League of Nations Society:** Granow to AA,

Berlin, 27 April 1937, file R102392, AA.

a revised version of Kempff's 1935 letter: Granow to AA, 14 Aug. 1937, file R102392, AA.

"In the face of the latest developments": Windels to AA, 28 Feb. 1938, file R102392, AA.

59 **Kempff notified Berlin:** Kempff to AA, Berlin, 27 March, 4 and 8 Apr. 1933, file R77315, AA. Graner's letter of protest is included with Kempff's 8 April report.

Some prominent people participated: Kempff to AA, 8 April 1933, file R77315, AA.

"There are 80,000 Jews": *Montreal Gazette,* 21 April 1933.

Laurendeau expressed doubt: *La Patrie* (Montreal), 21 April 1933.

60 **Through the pages:** Letter of Dandurand to the editor of *Le Devoir,* 25 April 1933.

had founded ... *Le Patriote:* Kempff to AA, 26 Oct. 1933, file R77326, AA. There is further information in Robin, 89.

a report on Fascism in Ontario: Kempff to AA, 26 Aug. 1933, file R77316, AA.

For his part, Windels: Windels to the German consulate, Montreal, 5 April 1938, UBC; Windels to AA, 17 May 1938, UBC; Eckner to Windels, 14 Sept. 1938, UBC.

prompted Granow to appeal to German Canadians: Granow to L.G. Mickles of the F.P. Weaver Coal Company, Montreal, 13 Aug. 1937, UBC.

61 **The consuls' second type of activity:** Seelheim to AA, 24 Nov. 1933 and Kempff to AA, 4 Dec. 1933, file R77348, AA; Kempff to AA, 16 Jan. 1934, file R77375, AA.

This practice continued: Seelheim to AA, 6 March 1935, file R77346, AA.

In the same report: Kempff to AA, 20 Dec. 1935, file R77315, AA.

Adam Sharrer: RCMP report filed in the UBC collection, n.d.

62 **In great detail, Kempff narrated:**

Kempff to AA, 3 July 1933, file R77326, AA.

63 **also failed to materialize:** Muller, German consulate-general, Montreal, to AA, 9 July 1933, file R77326, AA.

Kempff continued: Kempff to AA, 26 Aug. 1933, file R77326, AA.

64 **Arcand's purpose:** Betcherman, 128. Betcherman's source was an American one: the Dies Committee on Un-American Activities.

In western Canada: Seelheim to AA, 4 Nov. 1933, file R77326, AA; Wagner, 64–65.

the Deutscher Bund: Wagner, 68, 80–81. Wagner summarizes the history of the Bund, 64–84.

65 **Kempff approached a Montreal law firm:** Kempff to Hackett, Mulvena, Moster, Hackett and Hannen, 4 Jan. 1934, file R77347, AA.

Much of what the consuls did: Kempff to Dieckhoff, AA, 24 Sept. 1935, file R77315, AA; Kempff to AA, 21 Sept. 1935, file R77320, AA; Seelheim to AA, 29 Oct. 1934, file R77370, AA; file R77375, AA.

66 **The intelligence:** Borchers to Abwehr, 29 June 1940, file R102046, AA; Kahn, 69. For further information on Nazi Germany's consulates in the United States, see Kahn, 42–72. Julio to Abwehr, 20 June 1940 and Winter [Julio's superior] to Abwehr, 3 July 1940, file R102046, AA; Koecher, Berne, to Abwehr, 29 Aug. 1940, file 102047, AA; Hempel to Abwehr, 6, 15, and 23 Sept. 1940, file 102047, AA.

sources other than diplomatic ones: Kahn, 222, 491–92. Granatstein and Stafford, 27–28; Kealey and Whitaker, Introduction to *RCMP Security Bulletins: The War Series, Part II, 1942–1945;* Kahn, 1–26, 285.

a weather station: Newman, 152. *Operation Watchdog:* Kealey and Whitaker, *RCMP Security Bulletins: The War Series, Part II, 1942–1945,* 9–12.

67 **Canada had no foreign intelligence**

organization: Wagner, 123–24.
"a low, dishonest decade": Eayrs, 74.
German sources: Keyserlingk, 221.

Chapter 6. The Futility of the Dupuy Missions: Vichy-France and Canada, 1940–42

68 **"a precaution ...":** Canada, House of Commons, *Debates*, 12 Nov. 1940, 62.
69 **information has been available:** Baudouin, 282, 283, 291; Xavier de Bourbon, 11, 32–49, 59, 62, 66–68, 70–71; Thomas, 75–82; Hinsley, 149–58.
Canadians too: Dawson, 260–67; Lingard and Trotter, 118–29, 154–59; Couture, "The Vichy–Free French Propaganda War" and "The Politics of Diplomacy."
When Philippe Pétain replaced Paul Reynaud: Vanier to the Secretary of State for External Affairs, 22 June 1940, *Documents on Canadian External Relations*, VII, 322. Cited hereafter as *DCER*.
70 **set sail for England:** Vanier to the Secretary of State for External Affairs, 22 June 1940, *DCER*, VII, 323; Speaight, 190–243.
The terms of the Franco-German armistice: The terms appeared in the *New York Times*, 26 June 1940; they also appear in Baudouin, 301–5.
to prevent that: Churchill, 224–41; Paxton, 57.
Nevertheless: Churchill, 508.
Early in 1942: Memorandums of Conversations (with the British Ambassador) by the Secretary of State, 25 April 1942 and 4 May 1942, *Foreign Relations of the United States, 1942*, vol. II, 179–89, 183. Cited hereafter as *FRUS*.
the relationship between South Africa and Vichy: Simonin to the French legation, Lisbon, 16 July 1940; letters of Simonin to Baudouin, 21 Aug. and 26 Sept. 1940. Simonin wrote yet another letter to the Foreign Office in Vichy with this

message, 12 Dec. 1940. All these letters are available in the file Archives de Postes, Pretoria, vol. XVI, Centre des Archives diplomatiques, Nantes. Cited hereafter as Pretoria, CADN.
monitored the South African political scene ... and Free French activity: E.g., Simonin to Baudouin, 3 Sept. 1940 and Simonin to Laval, 8 Nov. 1940, Archives des Postes, Pretoria, sac 10, carton 38, CADN; Simonin to Baudouin, citing a report from Armand, 22 July 1940 and Simonin to Baudouin, 4 Sept. 1940 and 15 Oct. 1940, ibid. See also Armand to Simonin, 25 July 1941, Pretoria, sac 16, carton 61, CADN. Indeed, sac 16, cartons 61–64 and part of carton 65 deal with such matters. Simonin to Baudouin, 12 Oct. 1940 and Simonin to Flandin, 15 Dec. 1940, Pretoria, sac 10, carton 38, CADN; Simonin to Darlan, 16 May 1941, Pretoria, sac 16, carton 38, CADN; See also Simonin to Darlan, 5 June 1941, ibid.
71 **In Canada, these included:** Norman Robertson, Department of External Affairs, Ottawa, to Ristelhueber, Ottawa, 30 May 1942, and Ristelhueber to Robertson, 2 June 1942, both in the file Fermeture des Consulats, 1 juin 1942, stored at the French Embassy, Ottawa. Cited hereafter as AAFC.
cause for concern: *New York Times*, 27, 28 June 1940; 16 July and 12 Sept. 1940; 10, 20, 28 Aug. 1940; 11 Nov. 1940.
These were justifiable concerns: Kahn, 96; Koecher, Berne, to Abwehr, 29 Aug. 1940, Abwehr file, AA; Strache, German Embassy in Rome, to the Foreign Office, Berlin, 2 July 1942, microfilm T-0120, Roll 2486 (captured German documents available at the NA [Washington]).
72 **Paxton:** Paxton, 68, 95–96, 112–15, 123–26, 129, 134–35, 305. The quotation is from 305. Tournoux agrees. He quotes Hitler as telling Mussolini that Vichy had a reactionary regime

dominated by the Roman Catholic Church, which he considered hostile to Germany: Tournoux, 220.
Chapman: Chapman, 268–69.
He completely mislead ... Mackenzie King: *Mackenzie King Diaries,* 17 May 1941, typescript edition, fiche 159, sheet 402.
Ristelhueber was an intellectual: The books are Ristelhueber, *Les Traditions Françaises au Liban* and *Mission Française, "Dieu le Veut"* (about the crusades), *Aventure de Fridtjob Nansen,* and *Histoire de France Illustrée.*
two Vichy laws: Ristelhueber to Gallat, 25 Nov. 1940, Archives des Postes, Vancouver, Vol. X, File 10, CADN; Gallat to Ristelhueber, 30 Nov. 1940, ibid; Ristelhueber to Gallat, 18 Dec. 1940, ibid.; Gallat to Ristelhueber, 24 Dec. 1940, ibid. For further information about the 3 October 1940 law and other anti-Semitic actions of Vichy in 1940, see Marrus and Paxton, 3, 4, 12.

73 **Ristelhueber's career as a ... diplomat ended:** Foreign Office, Algiers, to Ristelhueber, 16 Nov. 1942 (received in Ottawa 26 Nov. 1942), file Fermeture des Consulats puis de la légation de France, AAFC; Ristelhueber to Foreign Office, Algiers, 27 Nov. 1942, ibid.; Ristelhueber to Governor General, Algiers, 26 Dec. 1942, ibid.
Through contemporaries and historians: Even Mackenzie King called Darlan a "traitor": *Mackenzie King Diaries,* 16 May 1941, fiche 159, sheet 400. On 5 June 1941 an editorial in the *Ottawa Citizen* denounced Darlan's collaborationist policies; the *Montreal Gazette* denounced him 19 June. Frank, "Vichy et Le Monde," 107; Aron, 367.
wrote to Darlan's ... successor: Ristelhueber to Gen. Henri Giraud, Algiers, 7 Jan. 1943, in file Représentation Diplomatique de la France au Canada, AAFC.
Ristelhueber's subordinates:

France, Ministère des Affaires Étrangères, *Annuaire Diplomatique et Consulaire, 1964,* 582; Paxton, 57, 89; Rochereau de la Sablière to Ristelhueber, 4 June 1942, in file Fermeture des Consulats, 1 juin 1942, AAFC.

74 **[To avoid] such controversy ... the Canadian government:** Couture, "The Politics," 34–43; Pickersgill, 147–48, 208–9, 216. For details on Ottawa–Vichy relations, see *DCER,* VIII, 534–91, and IX, 11–25. See in particular the letters of the High Commissioner for Canada in the United Kingdom (Massey) to the Secretary of State for External Affairs (Mackenzie King), 29 July 1940 and 1 Aug. 1940, *DCER,* VIII, 556–58; Order-in-Council (21 May 1940), *DCER,* VII, 106; Massey, London, to the Acting Secretary of State (Ernest Lapointe), Ottawa, 22 Aug. 1941, *DCER,* VIII, 582 (the quotation is from this letter). For French perspectives on Dupuy's trips, see Dreyfus, 329–32, 387; Lacouture, 287; Lottman, 336–39, 366, 393, 455, 557; Vulliez, 48–58, 253. The most recent account is that of Robert Frank, "Vichy et les Britanniques," in Azéma and Bedarida, 153–55.
several factors to remember when evaluating Dupuy's reports: Tournoux, 247; Year-end report of Pierre Dupuy, 31 Dec. 1941, reprinted in Tournoux, 375; Tournoux, 222, 197, 393.
Some he included in other reports: Tournoux quotes from Dupuy's year-end report of 1941, months after his final visit: 279, 323, 375.
Dupuy first went to Vichy: Dupuy, 396. For information on the Gaullist takeover of Black Africa, see Lacouture, 270–81.
Dupuy offered a plausible agenda: Ristelhueber to Diplomatie Vichy, 7 Nov. 1940, no. 44; Memo, Monsieur Dupuy, 23 Nov. 1940, no. 51; and Note sur le Cabinet du Maréchal, 25 Nov. 1940, no. 52; Note, Vichy, 30

Nov. 1940, no. 57, all Guerre 1939–1945, Vichy-Amérique: Canada, Box 1, AQO. See also letter of Skelton to Ristelhueber, 6 Nov. 1940, file Représentation Diplomatique du Canada en France, AAFC.

75 **there were several clues:** Both the clipping and Ristelhueber's summary (Ristelhueber to Diplomatie Vichy, 6 Aug. 1940), appeared in an unnamed file, AAFC; Ristelhueber to the Foreign Minister (Flandin), 27 Dec. 1940, ibid.; Ristelhueber to Diplomatie Vichy, 8 Sept. 1941 and 22 Jan. 1942, ibid.

Ristelhueber seemed to miss ... the clues: Ristelhueber to Diplomatie Vichy, 19 May 1942, file Représentation Diplomatique de la France au Canada (39–43), AAFC; Ristelhueber to Pierre Laval, 12 June 1942 and 30 Aug. 1942, and a clipping from Canada, House of Commons, *Debates*, 1 Aug. 1942, 5691, all ibid.

When gathering information: Dupuy, 396–97.

76 **Dupuy's first report:** Dupuy to the Secretary of State for External Affairs, 25 Dec. 1940; *DCER*, VIII, 642; the Chargé in France (Matthews), to the Secretary of State (Cordell Hull), 16 Nov. 1940, *FRUS, 1940*, II, 411–14; Frank, "Vichy et les Britanniques," 144–63; Frank, "Vichy et le monde," 99–121, especially 118.

Pétain and ... Darlan: Taken from Dupuy's report, 25 Dec. 1940, *DCER*, VIII, 642–43.

One may well question: Aglion, 120.

the third question: Dupuy's report, 25 Dec. 1940, *DCER*, VIII, 642–43; Lacouture, 287.

"nice but ingratiating": Matthews, Vichy, to the Secretary of State, 31 Dec. 1940, *FRUS, 1940*, II, 434–35.

American officials in France agreed: E.g., Murphy, Vichy, to the Secretary of State, 16 Aug. 1940, *FRUS, 1940*, II, 381.

might be useful ... reported Dupuy: Dupuy, London, to the Prime Minister, 15 Jan. 1941, *DCER*, VIII, 651–52.

77 **Dupuy made two additional trips:** Aron, 367; Frank, "Vichy et le Monde," 107.

Dupuy was unjustifiably optimistic: Dupuy, London, to the Secretary of State for External Affairs, 14 March 1941, *DCER*, VIII, 657–58; Dupuy, London, to the Prime Minister, 3 April 1941, *DCER*, VIII, 659.

William Langer ... agrees: Langer, 254, 350, 353, 375.

78 **Darlan was the real villain:** Massey to the Secretary of State for External Affairs, 27 Sept. 1941, *DCER*, VIII, 662–65.

when Dupuy made his 1940 visit: Tournoux, 196–97, 246–47.

Dupuy's third visit: Memorandum from Robertson to the Prime Minister, 13 Aug. 1941, *DCER*, VIII, 580–81; Pickersgill, 216, 241–42; Massey to the Acting Secretary of State for External Affairs (Lapointe), 22 Aug. 1941, *DCER*, VIII, 582.

79 **S.T. Wood:** Commissioner RCMP, Ottawa, to Robertson, 4 Aug. 1941, *DCER*, VIII, 836–37.

Eberts' task: The quotation is from Anglin, 61–62. For information about Eberts' appointment, see the correspondence in *DCER*, VII, 115–21; Ristelhueber to Foreign Office, Vichy, 16 Aug. 1941, a British translation of a cipher, RG 25, G1, vol. 1927, file 724, 39c, NA (Ottawa); Eberts to the Secretary of State for External Affairs, 2 Oct. 1941, *DCER*, VIII, 840–42, and 5 Nov. 1941, *DCER*, VIII, 849–50.

80 **was controversial:** To appreciate some of the controversy surrounding the presence of the Vichy officials, see Dawson, 261–67, and Lingard and Trotter, 118–23. While these accounts rely on incomplete information and contain several inaccuracies, they do report the

differences of opinion among Canadians over the ongoing relationship with Vichy France.

Canadian postal censors: Unsigned memo of Skelton, 15 July 1940, RG 25, G1, vol. 1924, file 724-V, part 1, NA (Ottawa). Also Ristelhueber to Skelton, 22 Aug. 1940, ibid. See also Stone to Skelton, 1 Sept. 1940, RG 25, G1, vol. 1924, file 724-V, part II, NA (Ottawa); Stone to Ristelhueber, 3 Sept. 1940, ibid.; Ristelhueber to Skelton, 5 Sept. 1940, ibid; A. Gagnon, Assistant Chief Postal Censor, Ottawa, to Stone, 24 Sept. 1940, ibid.; Ristelhueber to the Foreign Minister (Baudouin), 19 Sept. 1940, no. 25, Guerre 1939–1945, Vichy-Amérique: Canada, Box 1, AQO; intercepted letter of the French Ambassador in the United States to Charles de Fontnouvelle, consul-general of France, New York, 8 July 1940, RG 25, G1, vol. 1924, file 724-V, part II, NA (Ottawa); Gagnon, Ottawa, to Stone, 24 Sept. 1940, RG 25, G1, vol. 1924, file 725-V, part II, NA (Ottawa).

Henri Bougeral: Ristelhueber, Ottawa, to Diplomatie Vichy, 28 May 1942; Ristelhueber to Robertson, 2 June 1942; Ristelhueber to Laurent Beaudry, Dept. of External Affairs, 29 June 1942; Ristelhueber to French Ambassador (Henry-Haye), Washington, 29 June 1942; Robertson to Ristelhueber, 3 July 1942; Ristelhueber to Diplomatie Vichy, 11 July 1942; Ristelhueber to Pierrepont Moffat, U.S. Legation, Ottawa, 22 July 1942; Robertson to Ristelhueber, 21 Aug. 1942; Ristelhueber to Robertson, 27 Aug. 1942; all in the file Fermeture des Consulats, 1 juin 1942, AAFC.

If war-weary Canadians hoped: Ristelhueber to Diplomatie Vichy, 4 Oct. 1940, unnamed file, AAFC; *Mackenzie King Diaries*, 25 Sept. 1940, fiche 153, sheet 894, and 26 Sept. 1940, fiche 153, sheet 895; Ristelhueber to Diplomatie Vichy,

29 Oct. 1940, unnamed file, AAFC; Ristelhueber to Diplomatie Vichy, 29 July 1941, file Représentation Diplomatique de la France au Canada (39–43), AAFC; Ristelhueber to Laval, 12 June 1942, ibid.

81 **Ristelhueber's correspondence:** Ristelhueber to Diplomatie Vichy, 11 Oct. 1940, ibid.

Gaullist concerns: Ristelhueber to the French consul-general, New York, 28 Aug. 1940; Ristelhueber to Diplomatie Vichy, 5 Sept. 1940; Ristelhueber to the French consul-general, New York, 21 Oct. 1940, all in Représentation Diplomatique de la France au Canada (39–43), AAFC; Bougeral to Ristelhueber, 12 Oct. 1940, RG 25, G1, vol. 1925, file 724-V, part III, NA (Ottawa); Ristelhueber to Diplomatie Vichy, 17 Jan. 1941; RG 25, G1, vol. 1925, file 724-V, part IV, NA (Ottawa); Diplomatie Vichy to Ristelhueber, 20 July 1941, RG 25, G1, vol. 1925, file 724-V, 39c, NA (Ottawa) (translated by British cipher clerks); Bougeral to Ristelhueber, 13 Aug. 1941, ibid.

82 **French draft-dodgers:** Gallat to Ristelhueber, 12 Feb. 1942, RG 25, G1, vol. 1927, file 724-V, 39c, NA (Ottawa); Bougeral to Ristelhueber, 20 Feb. 1942, ibid.

Some of Ristelhueber's mail was in cipher: The Secretary of State for External Affairs, Ottawa, to the Secretary of State for Dominion Affairs, London, 5 July 1940, RG 25, G1, vol. 1924, file 724-V, part 1, NA (Ottawa); Lester B. Pearson, London, to Skelton, 30 Sept. 1940, ibid., part II.

Canada ought to hire its own: Pearson to Robertson, 1 Feb. 1942, RG 25, G1, vol. 1925, file 724-V, part IV, NA (Ottawa).

Wartime Examination Unit (WEU): For further information on the Wartime Examination Unit, see Wark, 639–65; Hilliker, 269; Volkman and Baggett, 62–70. For more information on Canada's first

cryptographer, Herbert Osborn
Yardley, see Nathan Miller, 194–96,
210–13, 230.
**The WEU cooperated with British
Intelligence:** See the unsigned letter
written on behalf of the Secretary of
State for External Affairs to Massey,
8 July 1941, RG 25, G1, vol. 1926, file
724-V, part VII; see also Stone to
Herbert Osborn [Yardley], 26 July
1941, and Stone to Lt. Col. W.W.
Murray, Department of National
Defence, Ottawa, 31 July 1941, ibid.
See also the correspondence in RG
24, vols. 20306 and 20307, NA
(Ottawa).

83　**had been under consideration since
July 1940:** Memo of Stone, 25 July
1940, RG 25, G1, vol. 1924, file
724-V, part 1, NA (Ottawa); Skelton
to Stone, 26 July 1940, ibid.
**was the result of a British sugges-
tion:** Pickersgill, 208–9. See also correspondence in *DCER*, VIII, 571–81.
Ristelhueber explained: Pickersgill,
210–11.
**inability to control the flow ... to
Vichy's agents:** Robertson to the
Prime Minister, 1 Sept. 1941, *DCER*,
VIII, 582–84.
Surveillance ... intensified: The
Under-secretary of State for External
Affairs (Robertson) to the Prime
Minister, 1 Sept. 1941, *DCER*, VIII,
582–83; Stone to Robertson, 20 Feb.
1942, RG 25, G1, vol. 1927, file
724-V, part XII, NA (Ottawa); Naval
message to Robertson, 17 Feb. 1942,
ibid.; Stone to Robertson, 20 Feb.
1942, ibid.
**limits on what ... officials were
supposed to report:** Skelton to
Ristelhueber, 22 Oct. 1940, *DCER*,
VIII, 564–65. See also the
Memorandum from the First
Secretary (T.A. Stone) to Skelton, 25
July 1940, *DCER*, VIII, 555–56;
Aglion, 122; Ristelhueber to
Bougeral, 25 October 1940, RG 25,
G1, vol. 1925, file 724-V, part III, NA
(Ottawa). On 2 Nov. 1940, Bougeral
signed the pledge not to do any-

thing that would hurt British or
Canadian interests nor to create suspicion by Canadian authorities, ibid.

84　**Ristelhueber's telephone calls:**
Transcripts of calls of 19 and 23 May
appear in RG 25, G1, vol. 1927, file
724-V, 39c, NA (Ottawa); intercepted
telephone transcript, Ristelhueber to
Coursier, 19 May 1942, ibid.
What brought matters to a head:
Couture, "The Vichy–Free French
Propaganda War," 207, 213–14;
Aglion, 121–22.
**questioned the presence of France's
consular posts:** First Secretary
(Stone) to the Under-secretary of
State for External Affairs, 3 Oct.
1941, *DCER*, VIII, 584–85; Assistant
Under-secretary of State for External
Affairs (Pearson) to the Under-
Secretary of State for External
Affairs (Robertson), 17 Nov. 1941,
DCER, VIII, 586.
**the closure of all French consular
posts:** Extracts from the Cabinet War
Committee, 8 May 1942, *DCER*, IX,
17, and 22 May 1942, *DCER*, IX, 19.

85　**forwarding news:** Coursier to
Baudouin, Sept. 1940, no. 140,
Guerre 1939–1945, Vichy-Amérique:
Canada, Box 1, AQO.
**Ottawa allowed the legation to
survive:** Pickersgill, 424.
and closed all Vichy's outlets:
Pearson, 200.
Pétain's congratulations: Paxton,
304.

86　**The WEU provided intelligence:**
Wark, passim; Hinsley, II, 551,
636–37.
As part of the UKUSA ... network:
Richelson and Ball, 82–95, 174, 337.

Chapter 7. Pearl Harbor and Its Aftermath

87　**first-hand accounts:** The American
ambassador in Japan, Joseph C.
Grew, wrote reports that appeared
in book form as early as 1944;
187–489. See also *FRUS, 1941*, IV,
389–729; and *DCER*, VIII, 1355–1561.

Scholarly accounts: E.g., Dawson, 273–78; Reischauer, 95–102.

88 Yardley's heated departure: Granatstein and Stafford, 29–36; Wark, 646–52; Nathan Miller, 194–96, 205, 210–13.

The interception: Kawasaki to Yoshizawa, Ottawa, 20 Aug. 1941, RG 24, vol. 20307, file 1, no. 4, NA (Ottawa). Subsequent references to intercepted Japanese messages come from this same file. Morishima to the Foreign Minister, Tokyo, 13 Sept. 1941, nos. 1–3; Yoshizawa to Foreign Office, Tokyo, 27 July 1941, no. 7; Muto, San Francisco, to the Foreign Minister, Tokyo, 18 Sept. 1941, nos. 5–6; Kishisaburo Nomura, Japanese embassy, Washington, to the Foreign Office, Tokyo, 19 Aug. 1941, no. 10.

By October: Nomura to Yoshizawa, 11 Oct. 1941, nos. 11 and 12; Yoshizawa to the Japanese ambassador, London, and the Japanese consul, Vancouver, 9 Oct. 1941, no. 13.

the WEU operated: Granatstein and Stafford, 31–32.

89 Officials in Ottawa: Yoshizawa to the Foreign Minister, Tokyo, n.d., no. 14; Nomura to the Foreign Minister, Tokyo, 15 Oct. 1941, no. 28, and 16 Oct. 1941, no. 31; Yoshizawa to the Japanese ambassador, London, 18 Oct. 1941, no. 33; Yoshizawa to the Foreign Minister, Tokyo, 27 Oct. 1941, processed 1 Nov. 1941, no. 38; Yoshizawa to the Foreign Minister, Tokyo, 20 Oct. 1941, nos. 42–43; Nomura to the Japanese minister, Ottawa, 20 Oct. 1941, nos. 47–48; Nomura to the Japanese minister, Ottawa, 17 Oct. 1941, no. 59.

The Canadian government knew: Pringsheim, 56–57; Yoshizawa to the Foreign Minister, Tokyo, 4 Nov. 1941, nos. 68–69; Japanese consul, Chicago, to the Foreign Minister, Tokyo, 24 Oct. 1941, nos. 70–71; Pringsheim, 57–58.

Granatstein and ... Johnson: J.L. Granatstein and Gregory A. Johnson, "The Evacuation of the Japanese Canadians, 1942: A Realistic Critique of the Received Version," in Hillmer, Kordan, and Luciuk, 106–8.

most of Yoshizawa's information: Yoshizawa to the Japanese consulate in Vancouver, the Japanese embassies in Washington and London, and the Foreign Office, Tokyo, 16 Nov. 1941, no. 78; Yoshizawa to the Foreign Minister, Tokyo, 18 Nov. 1941, nos. 83–84; Yoshizawa to the Foreign Minister, Tokyo, 18 Nov. 1941, no. 79; Yoshizawa to the Foreign Minister, Tokyo, 16 Nov. 1941, no. 80; Vincent, 1. For an account closer to the era, see Lingard and Trotter, 50–59. Yoshizawa to the Foreign Minister (Tokyo), the Japanese ambassadors in Washington and London, the Japanese consul (Hong Kong), 17 Nov. 1941, no. 76.

90 The week before Pearl Harbor: Miura, Mexico City, to Foreign Office, Tokyo, 6 Dec. 1941 (processed 11 Dec.), no. 98; Chiba, Lisbon, to the Japanese consulate, Los Angeles, 5 Dec. 1941 (processed 18 Dec.), no. 99; Shigenori Togo (the Foreign Minister), Tokyo, to the Japanese consulate, Chicago, 3 Dec. 1941 (processed 18 Dec.), no. 100; Togo to the Japanese consulate, Honolulu, 3 Dec. 1941 (processed Dec. 18), no. 101; Togo to the Japanese consulate, New Orleans, 3 Dec. 1941 (processed 18 Dec.), no. 101; Togo to the Japanese consulate, Portland, Oregon, 3 Dec. 1941 (processed 18 Dec.), no. 102; Togo to the Japanese legation, Panama City, 5 Dec. 1941 (processed 18 Dec.), no. 102; Togo to the Japanese consulate, Houston, 3 Dec. 1941 (processed 18 Dec.), no. 103; Togo to the Japanese consulate, New York, 5 Dec. 1941 (processed 18 Dec.), no. 103; Togo to the Japanese embassy, Washington, 3 Dec. 1941 (processed 18 Dec.), no. 104.

Earlier tensions and controversies: For a review of these tensions and controversies, see Dawson, 273–78. **Time does not excuse:** Lingard and Trotter, 60–65; Adachi, *The Enemy That Never Was* and *A History of the Japanese in British Columbia;* Broadfoot; Sunahara; Peter Ward; Wilson and Hosokawa, 188–285. A recent, controversial interpretation of the episode is that of Granatstein and Johnson, in Hillmer, Kordan, and Luciuk, 101–29. **"If, as a resident":** Foreign Office, Tokyo, to Japanese embassy, Buenos Aires, 11 Dec. 1941, no. 107.

Chapter 8. The Fight against Other Enemies, 1939–45

92 **Clann-na-Gael ... IRA:** Bishop and Mallie, 21–34; Blake, passim; Coogan, 68, 136–37, 139–40. **In the early months of 1939, the IRA:** Ibid., 156–173; Bell, 159, 189–190; Coogan, 268–272; Fisk, 333–43. **Other attempts at Nazi–IRA collaboration:** Coogan, 260–279; Bell, 168–235.

93 **the intelligence section of the RCMP:** Kealey and Whitaker, 11; Bulletin No. 13, 15 Jan. 1940, 116. All citations of RCMP security bulletins in this chapter are to Kealey and Whitaker, *RCMP Security Bulletins: The War Series, 1939–1941,* and end with the page number. Bulletin No. 1, 23 Oct. 1939, 23; Bulletin No. 40, 17 Feb. 1941, 327. **the RCMP security bulletins did include:** Bulletin No. 25, 8 April 1940, 198; Bulletin No. 40, 17 Feb. 1941, 326; Bulletin No. 46, 16 Aug. 1941, 392–93; Bulletin No. 38, 11 Nov. 1940, 303; Kealey and Whitaker, 10–11, 16; Bulletin No. 4A, 14 Nov. 1939, 53–54; Bulletin No. 28, 29 April 1940, 222–24; Bulletin No. 1, 23 Oct. 1939, 28–29; Bulletin No. 2, 30 Oct. 1939, 31–32, 35; Bulletin No. 10, 26 Dec. 1939, 95–96; Bulletin No.

35, 15 July 1940, 283–84; Bulletin No. 44, 19 June 1941, 369–70; Bulletin No. 2, 30 Oct. 1939, 32; Bulletin No. 10, 26 Dec. 1939, 98; Bulletin No. 17, 12 Feb. 1940, 141–42. **The RCMP knew:** Bulletin No. 2, 30 Oct. 1939, 38; Bulletin No. 28, 29 April 1940, 228; Bulletin No. 30, 13 May 1940, 240; Bulletin No. 1, 23 Oct. 1939, 21; Bulletin No. 38, 11 Nov. 1940, 304.

94 **Franco owed Hitler and Mussolini:** Thomas, passim; Whealey, 229–54. **Official Spanish empathy:** Feis, 186–88, 210–12, 215–32, 247–53; ibid., 230, 238, 256, 264; *New York Times,* 9 and 18 May and 2 June 1944; Feis, 144–46, 151, 192, 229; ibid., 63–64, 92; Gallo, 107.

95 **Ideologically Franco shared many of the values:** Feis, 26; the Ambassador in Spain to the Secretary of State, 1 June 1942, *FRUS*, 1942, III, 288; the Ambassador in Spain to the Secretary of State, 10 June 1942, ibid., 290; the Ambassador in Spain to the Secretary of State, 29 July 1943, *FRUS*, 1943, II, 615. **found Gómez Jordana ... friendly:** Lloyd, *Franco,* 185–86, 189, 183; the Ambassador in Spain to the Secretary of State, 24 Dec. 1942, *FRUS, 1942*, III, 319; the Ambassador in Spain to the Secretary of State, 29 March 1943, *FRUS*, 1943, II, 598; the Ambassador in Spain to the Secretary of State, 4 Jan. 1944, *FRUS,* 1944, IV, 288–89; the Ambassador in Spain to the Secretary of State through the Under-Secretary of State (Sumner Welles), 9 Nov. 1942, *FRUS*, 1942, III, 309–11.

96 **"The Spanish government":** Feis, 238. **José Félix de Lequérica:** Gallo, 21, 22; Barrio, 120. **a clear partiality toward Japan:** Feis, 229; *FRUS*, 1943, II, 722–38; Memorandum by the Chargé in Spain (Beaulac), 12 Nov. 1943, *FRUS, 1943,* II, 736–38.

Spanish-Japanese relations: The Ambassador in Spain to the Secretary of State, 29 July 1943, *FRUS,* 1943, II, 615; Memorandum by the Ambassador in Spain of a Conversation with the Spanish Minister for Foreign Affairs, 9 Dec. 1943, *FRUS,* 1943, II, 719–21; the Ambassador to Spain to the Secretary of State, 5 Nov. 1943, *FRUS,* 1943, II, 727–30; *New York Times,* 18, 19, 23, 24, 25, 30 March 1945, and 1, 12, 14 April 1945; also the Ambassador in Spain (Armour) to the Secretary of State, 24 March 1945, *FRUS,* 1945, V, 669; *New York Times,* 31 Jan. 1944.

97 **Cárdenas was a career officer:** Feis, 9, 67.

no hint of impropriety: Schwartz to Miguel Espelius, Conde de Morales, Caracas, 7 Sept. 1944, RG 25, G1, vol. 1933, file 724, BS, Part II, NA (Ottawa).

98 **asked ... whether Kobbe would be a safe person:** Robertson to Massey, 20 Sept. 1943, DEA, file 123s. Cited hereafter as 123s. In response to a request from the present author in late December 1988, the Department of External Affairs partially declassified file 123s. F.E. Jolliffe to Robertson, 2 Oct. 1942, Censorship Bureau, RG 25, G1, vol. 1933, file 724, BS, Part I, NA (Ottawa).

Little mystery: Stone to Colonel O.M. Biggar, Ottawa, 14 Nov. 1942, 123s.

censors ... steamed open ... mail: RG 25, G1, vol. 1933, file 724, BS, Parts I–IV, NA (Ottawa).

Japanese internees: Adachi, *The Enemy That Never Was* and *A History of the Japanese in British Columbia;* Broadfoot; Sunahara; Granatstein and Johnson, in Hillmer, Kordan, and Luciuk, 101–29; Peter Ward. See the correspondence in the Censorship Bureau Records, RG 25, G1, vol. 1933, file 724, BS, Parts I–IV, NA (Ottawa). The numbers of people involved are not altogether clear,

in part because the census returns often tabulated people of Japanese extraction along with other Asians. The Census of 1941 indicates that there were 23,149 people of Japanese background living in Canada in 1941. Granatstein and Johnson estimate that of these, 22,000 were living in British Columbia, and that of those, 7,200 were subjects of the emperor. Many of the rest held dual citizenship (British and Japanese), but Granatstein and Johnson say that the number in that category is "unknown" (103–6). Official Canadian statistics indicate 782 Japanese and Japanese Canadians were actually arrested (as distinct from those "merely" relocated from the coast), of whom 420 were still in custody at the end of the war. A statistical table appears in Hillmer, Kordan, and Luciuk, 63.

99 **Kobbe Chinchilla was a marked man:** F.E. Jolliffe, Ottawa, to the Under-secretary of State for External Affairs, Ottawa, 2 Oct. 1942, Censorship Bureau, RG 25, G1, vol. 1933, file 724, BS, Part I, NA (Ottawa); Stone to Jolliffe, 2 Oct. 1942, ibid.

"In view of ...": The Under-secretary of State for External Affairs (Robertson) to Pearson, 29 Oct. 1942, 123s.

King reported ... on new information: The Secretary of State for External Affairs, Ottawa, to the Secretary of State for Dominion Affairs, London, 30 Oct. 1942, 123s.

100 **From Washington, Pearson reported:** Pearson, Washington, to Robertson, 25 Nov. 1942, 123s.

Who was Kobbe? *Vancouver News-Herald,* 12 Jan. 1943.

strong negative opinions about Kobbe: *Vancouver Daily Province,* 13 Jan. 1943; *Vancouver News-Herald,* 16 Jan. 1943.

Spanish diplomats ... were funnelling information to Berlin and Rome: *Newsweek,* 1 Feb. 1943, 12.

Mentioned in the *Vancouver News-Herald*, 4 Feb. 1943. The Department of External Affairs clipped this news item and stored it in file 123s. Kahn, 69.

earlier misconceptions: Granatstein and Stafford, 36; *The Times*, 21 January 1978.

101 **Canadian postal censors discovered in the package:** Stone to Robertson, 9 Sept. 1943, 123s; Memorandum from the Prime Minister, n.d., ibid.; Robertson to Massey, 20 Sept. 1943, ibid.

faced a dilemma: King to the Minister (Leighton McCarthy) at the Canadian Legation in Washington, no date indicated but from circumstantial evidence approximately 9 Sept. 1943, 123s.

"that the Spanish Government": Charles Ritchie, High Commissioner of Canada in London, to the Secretary of State for External Affairs, 13 Nov. 1943, 123s.

London made several demands: Draft letter of the British Foreign Office to His Majesty's Ambassador in Madrid, no day specified, Nov. 1943, copy enclosed with the Ritchie letter of 13 Nov. 1943, 123s; F.K. Roberts, Foreign Office, London, to Sir Samuel Hoare, British Embassy, Madrid, 5 Dec. 1943, ibid.; a letter of the British Embassy in Madrid to the Spanish Foreign Office, 15 Jan. 1944, ibid.

102 **Ottawa's one concern:** Robertson to Massey, 23 Nov. 1944, 123s.

External Affairs safeguarded Canadian interests: King to the Canadian Ambassador, Washington, 23 Jan. 1944, 123s.

The Americans proved entirely cooperative: The Canadian Ambassador, Washington, to the Secretary of State for External Affairs, Ottawa, 24 Jan. 1944, 123s.

Meanwhile Stone travelled: Stone to the Prime Minister, 24 Jan. 1944, 123s.

Back in Vancouver: King to Massey,

26 Jan. 1944, and Most Secret Memorandum for the Prime Minister, 29 Jan. 1944, both in 123s; C.K. Gray, RCMP, Vancouver, to the Commissioner of the RCMP, Ottawa, 25 Jan. 1944, 123s.

103 **Despite the best efforts:** *Vancouver Sun*, 25 Jan. 1944; Stone to Robertson, 25 Jan. 1944, 123s.

his probable sponsors: Hoare to the Foreign Office, London, 12 Jan. 1944, quoted in correspondence of the High Commissioner for Canada in the United Kingdom, London, to the Secretary of State for External Affairs, Ottawa, 19 June 1944, 123s; *The Times* (London), 21 Jan. 1978.

104 **Chapman:** Chapman, 268–69.

Gómez Jordana appointed …

Rolland: Hoare to the Foreign Office, London, quoted in correspondence of the High Commissioner for Canada in the United Kingdom, London, to the Secretary of State for External Affairs, Ottawa, 25 Jan. 1944, 123s; Robertson to King, 11 March 1944, 123s.

"It was unthinkable": Hoare to the Foreign Office, London, 4 Mar. 1944, quoted in correspondence of the Acting High Commissioner for Canada in the United Kingdom to the Secretary of State for External Affairs, 6 Mar. 1944, 123s.

that a friend must have sent them: Hoare to the Foreign Office, London, 23 Mar. 1944, quoted in correspondence of the High Commissioner for Canada to Great Britain to the Secretary of State for External Affairs, 1 April 1944, 123s.

Rolland thought: P. Garran, British Foreign Office, London, to John Holmes at the High Commission for Canada in the United Kingdom, London, 13 April 1945, 123s.

105 **The official Spanish investigation:** Holmes, London, to Robertson, 8 Sept. 1945 (plus enclosure of the Spanish *note verbale* both in the original Spanish and in the English trans-

lation), 123s; Memorandum of the British Embassy, Madrid, 6 March 1944, sent to the Secretary of State for External Affairs, Ottawa, by Charles Ritchie at the High Commission for Canada in the United Kingdom, London, 7 April 1944, 123s.

Absence of archival material: Viñas, 239; Curriculum vitae of Kobbe y Chinchilla, 2 Dec. 1948, Legajo P-152, exp. 773, MAE; Foreign Office List no. 44 and Note Verbale of Japanese Legation, Madrid, to Spanish Foreign Office, 3 Feb. 1945, Legajo 5863, exp. 3, MAE.

After the war: Acting High Commissioner in Great Britain to the Secretary of State for External Affairs, 10 and 27 Oct. 1945, *DCER*, X, 67–68.

Chapter 9. The CIA in Canada during the 1960s

106 **Even friendly countries:** Wright, 110–11; Granatstein and Stafford, 200–5.

The agency had been founded in 1947: For a history of the CIA, see Jeffreys-Jones. See also Nathan Miller, 301–444.

107 **"In his search":** Central Intelligence Agency Office of Central Reference Biographic Register, Vice Presidential Security Files, Box 12, Folder: Visit of P.M. Pearson, Briefing Memorandum, 5/10–11/63, No. 41, LBJ.

James Jesus Angleton: Mangold, 280–83.

108 **at the invitation of Walter Gordon and Keith Davey:** English, 231.

he had opposed them ... but: Newman, 267, 355–68; Sorensen, 648–49; McLin.

"knocked over the Diefenbaker government": McGeorge Bundy to President Johnson, 1 May 1964, in White House Central Files (WHCF), Countries (CO), Box 18, Folder: CO 43, LBJ.

If Pearson won: Rusk to Johnson, 6 Nov. 1965, in National Security File (NSF), Head of State Correspondence File, Box 1, Folder: P.M. Pearson, vol. I, no. 65e, LBJ.

109 **Oliver Quayle:** Pearson, 203; Hayes Redmon to Bill Moyers, 14 and 28 Oct. 1965, WHCF, CO, Box 19, CO 43, Folder 6/1/65-7/19/66, LBJ.

a congratulatory telegram: Benjamin Read, Executive Secretary, Dept. of State, to McGeorge Bundy, White House, 9 Nov. 1965; NSF, Head of State Correspondence File, Box 1, Folder: P.M. Pearson, vol. I, no. 67, LBJ. Also, telegram of Johnson to Pearson, ibid., no. 69.

110 **Angleton was not totally wrong:** Mangold, 255–73.

Canada's links with Cuba: Vice Presidential Security Files, Box 12, Folder: Visit of P.M. Pearson, Briefing Memorandum, 5/10–11/63. Cuba was item 2 in the General Index for the Hyannisport meeting, and the index included a background paper entitled "Canadian Policy Toward Cuba." Unfortunately, when the author visited the LBJ archives in May 1993, the document had not yet been declassified. List of Talking Points, NSF Country File: Canada, Box 167–168, Folder: Pearson Visit Briefing Book, 1/21-22/64 [1 of 2], nos. 52 and 55, LBJ; Harriman report, NSF Country File: Canada, Box 166, Folder: Canadian Memos, vol. III, part 2, no. 130a, LBJ; Rostow to Johnson, 11 July 1966, NSF Country File: Canada, Box 166, Folder: Canadian Memos, vol. III, part 1, no. 124.

Montreal and Ottawa became the centres: Granatstein and Stafford, 189–90, 197; Sawatsky, 1–8.

111 **The CIA ... warned President Johnson:** Memo of Marvin Watson, 17 May 1967, in NSF, International Meetings and Travel File, Box 20, Folder: President's Trip to Canada –

EXPO 67 5/25/67, no. 15a, LBJ.
In addition to observing Cubans:
Rostow to Johnson, 29 April 1967, in
NSF Country File, Canada, Box
167–168, Folder: Canada Memos,
vol. V, 1/67-10/68 [1 of 2], LBJ;
Richard Helms, CIA, to Johnson, 17
May 1968, in NSF Country File:
Canada, Box 166, Folder: Canada
Cables, vol. V, part 1, no. 28a, LBJ;
Rostow to Johnson, 17 May 1968, in
NSF Country File: Canada, Box 166,
Folder: Canada Cables, vol. V, part
1, no. 28.
**an otherwise brilliant 1961 CIA
forecast for Canada:** Lisée, 29, and
National Intelligence Estimate (NIE)
99–61, quoted ibid.

112 **a bomb exploded:** Toronto *Globe and
Mail*, 3 May 1965, 10.
**Butterworth ... kept the White
House well informed:** Annual
Report (for 1967, written 2 Jan. 1968)
(Butterworth to Dept. of State), NSF
Country File: Canada, Boxes
167–168, no. 116a, p. 23, LBJ. Most of
Butterworth's year-end reports
appear in various files at the LBJ
archives. For 1964 and 1965, see
NSF, Files of McGeorge Bundy,
Folder: Correspondence with
Ambassadors, Box 16, nos. 5a and 6a
respectively. For 1967, see NSF
Country File: Canada, Boxes
167–168, no. 116a. The statement
about the benefits of a united
Canada appears in the 1967 report,
p. 23.
Lisée says: Lisée, 29–67.

113 **Willis Armstrong:** Quoted in
Lisée, 30.
Leonard Marks ... lamented:
Leonard H. Marks, USIA, to
Douglass Cater, White House, 8 Feb.
1968, in WHCF, Countries, CO 43,
Box 19, Folder: 6/20/67-6/30/68.
**the White House ... tried to get
information:** Memorandum of a
Conversation, U.S. Embassy, Saigon, 19
April 1964, *FRUS, 1964–1968,* I, 249.
On 19 April 1964: The Editors of the
New York Times, The Pentagon Papers,

257–58 (hereafter cited as *The
Pentagon Papers*); Memorandum
from the President's Special
Assistant for National Security
Affairs (McGeorge Bundy) to the
President, 21 April 1964, *FRUS,
1964-1968,* I, 253.

114 **"they assure me they are most willing":** Telegram from the Department
of State to the Embassy in Vietnam,
1 May 1964, *FRUS, 1964–1968,* I,
281–82. Blair Seaborn supplemented
the information on his activities with
a personal letter to the author,
21 June 1993. Martin, 424; Oral
Histories, Chester Cooper, Interview
I, p. 23, LBJ. For background on
Cooper, see ibid., pp. 1–3.
**"my reports ... were always filed
with Ottawa":** Seaborn to the
author, 21 June 1993.
These differences of opinion:
Telegram from the Department of
State, Washington, to the Embassy
in Vietnam, Saigon, 22 May 1964,
FRUS, 1964–1968, I, 348; Lodge to
Rusk (Telegram 2318), 26 May 1964,
FRUS, 1964–1968, I, 348–49.
what Seaborn was to say:
Memorandum from the Secretary of
State's Special Assistant for Vietnam
(Sullivan) to the Secretary of State,
23 May 1964, *FRUS, 1964–1968,* I,
351; Martin, 425.
**In June ... Seaborn made his first
visit:** When the appropriate volume
of *FRUS* was published in 1992, this
material remained classified: *FRUS,
1964–1968,* I, 525; Lodge to the
Department of State, 24 June 1964,
FRUS, 1964–1968, I, 525–26. A copy
of Seaborn's report appears in
Martin, 426–27. See also Martin, 428,
and *The Pentagon Papers,* 264.

115 **On 13 July:** Maxwell Taylor to the
Department of State, 14 July 1964,
FRUS, 1964–1968, I, 546.
"It was quite evident": Seaborn to
the author, 21 June 1993.
**By the time Seaborn actually
returned:** *The Pentagon Papers,*
266–68.

Dean Rusk was less than candid: Martin, 429; Rusk to the U.S. Embassy in Canada, 8 Aug. 1964, *FRUS 1964–1968*, I, 651–53.

116 **Seaborn's second trip:** *The Pentagon Papers*, 244, 277.

In all, Seaborn made five trips: Rusk, 461. See also *The Pentagon Papers*, 373, 376, and Telegram from the Department of State to the Embassy in Vietnam, 3 Dec. 1964, *FRUS, 1964–1968*, I, 978–79; *The Pentagon Papers*, 404–5; Seaborn to the author, 21 June 1993; Rusk, 461–62; Girard, 338–39; Martin, 430–34; Oral Histories: Chester Cooper, Interview III, pp. 1–2, LBJ.

a warning which he believes: Seaborn to the author, 21 June 1993.

John C. Powell ... says: Interview with the author, Sudbury, Ont., 21 Aug. 1993.

117 **Yet another Canadian diplomat:** Oral Histories: William Bundy, pp. 33–36, LBJ; *The Pentagon Papers*, 489. See also English, 371–74, Martin, 437–40; Oral Histories: Chester Cooper, Interview III, pp. 1–2, LBJ.

"I was very careful": Oral Histories: William Bundy, pp. 35–36, LBJ.

Back in Washington: Rostow to LBJ, 20 June 1966, in NSF Country File: Canada, Boxes 167–168, folder: Ronning Mission, no. 5a.

Nor were Canadians the only non-belligerents to provide information: Rusk, 460; Dr. Rostow, interview with the author at the LBJ archives, 11 May 1993.

Canada's wheat industry: The CIA wrote a paper, "Prospects for Purchase of US Grain by the USSR and the Eastern European Satellites," which was still classified when the author visited the LBJ archives in May 1993. Summaries, however, appear in a covering letter of Francis M. Bator, who joined the National Security Council (NSC) staff that year, to McGeorge Bundy, 6 May 1964: Papers of Francis M. Bator, Box 1, Folder Chronological File (NSC) 4/7/64-8/31/64, no. 142, LBJ. A confidential memorandum for the president (no. 128, n.d.) has similar information.

Chapter 10. The Future

120 **Once the Nazis had reported:** de Graff, 317–26, especially 318; Littman, 24–27.

Bibliography

Archives and Archival Collections

Canada
Department of External Affairs, Ottawa (DEA)
National Archives of Canada, Ottawa (NA [Ottawa])
Provincial Archives of British Columbia, Victoria, B.C. (PABC)
University of British Columbia Library – Special Collections Division, Vancouver, B.C. (UBC)

France
Archives de l'Ambassade française au Canada, Ottawa (AAFC)
Archives du Quai d'Orsay, Paris (AQO)
Centre des Archives diplomatiques, Nantes (CADN)

Germany
Auswärtiges Amt, Bonn (AA)

Spain
Ministerio de Asuntos Exteriores, Madrid (MAE)

United Kingdom
Public Record Office, London (PRO)

United States
Lyndon Baines Johnson Archives, Austin, Texas (LBJ)
National Archives of the United States of America, Washington, D.C. (NA [Washington])
Records of the Secret Service, Correspondence 1863–1950 (Re Spy Suspects during the Spanish-American War), National Records Center, Suitland, Md. (RSS)

Personal Communications

Powell, John. Interview with the author, Sudbury, Ontario, 21 August 1993.
Rostow, Dr. Walt Whitman. Interview with the author, LBJ Archives, Austin, Texas, 11 May 1993.
Rusk, Dean. Telephone interview with the author from Athens, Georgia, 13 July 1993.
Saurer, Axel, Third Secretary, German Embassy, Ottawa. Letter to the author, 3 January 1992.
Seaborn, Blair. Letter to the author, 21 June 1993.

Books and Articles

Adachi, Ken. *The Enemy That Never Was*. Toronto: McClelland and Stewart, 1976.
———. *A History of the Japanese in British Columbia*, in *Two Monographs on Japanese Canadians*, ed. Roger Daniels. New York: Arno Press, 1978.
Aglion, Raoul. *Roosevelt and De Gaulle: Allies in Conflict, A Personal Memoir*. New York: Free Press, 1988.
Andrew, Christopher. *Her Majesty's Secret Service: The Making of the British Intelligence Community*. New York: Viking, 1986.
Andrew, Christopher, and Oleg Gordievsky. *KGB: The Inside Story of Its Foreign Operations from Lenin to Gorbachev*. New York: HarperCollins, 1990.
Angevine, Robert G. "Gentlemen Do Not Read Each Other's Mail: American Intelligence in the Interwar Era." *Intelligence and National Security* 7, no. 2 (April 1992): 1–29.
Angus, Ian. *Canadian Bolsheviks: The Early Years of the Communist Party of Canada*. Montreal: Vanguard, 1981.
Aron, Robert. *L'Histoire de Vichy, 1940–1944*. Paris: Fayard, 1954.

Avery, Donald. "Allied Scientific Co-operation and Soviet Espionage in Canada, 1941–45." *Intelligence and National Security* 8, no. 3 (July 1993): 100–28.

———. "Canada's Response to European Refugees, 1939–1945: The Security Dimension," in *On Guard for Thee: War, Ethnicity, and the Canadian State, 1939–1945*, ed. Norman Hillmer, Bogdan Kordan and Lubomyr Luciuk. Ottawa: Minister of Supply and Services, 1988.

Azéma, Jean-Pierre, and François Bedarida, eds. *Vichy et les Français: Révolution Nationale*. Paris: Fayard, 1992.

Balawyder, Aloysius. *Canadian-Soviet Relations between the World Wars*. Toronto: University of Toronto Press, 1972.

Barrio, Antonio Marquina. "La Relative Neutralité Espagnole," in *Les États Neutres Européens et la Seconde Guerre Mondiale*, ed. L.E. Roulet. Neuchatel: Éditions de la Baconnière, 1985.

Barros, James. *No Sense of Evil: Espionage, the Case of Herbert Norman*. Toronto: Deneau, 1986.

Baudouin, Paul. *The Private Diaries of Paul Baudouin (March 1940 to January 1941)*, trans. Sir Charles Petrie. London: Eyre and Spottiswoode, 1948.

Beckett, J.C. *The Making of Modern Ireland, 1603–1923*, 2d ed. London: Faber and Faber, 1981.

Bell, J. Bowyer. *The Secret Army: The IRA, 1916–1979*. Dublin: Poolbeg, 1989.

Betcherman, Lita-Rose. *The Swastika and the Maple Leaf: Fascist Movements in Canada in the Thirties*. Toronto: Fitzhenry and Whiteside, 1975.

Bishop, Patrick, and Mallie, Eamonn. *The Provisional IRA*. London: Corgi, 1988.

Blake, Frances M. *The Irish Civil War*. London: Information on Ireland, 1988.

———. *The Irish Civil War and What It Still Means for the Irish People*. London: Information on Ireland, 1986.

Bothwell, Robert, and J.L. Granatstein, eds. *The Gouzenko Transcripts: The Evidence Presented to the Kellogg-Taschereau Royal Commission of 1946*. Ottawa: Deneau, 1982.

Bowen, Roger. *Innocence Is Not Enough: The Life and Death of Herbert Norman*. Vancouver and Toronto: Douglas and McIntyre, 1986.

Broadfoot, Barry. *Years of Sorrow, Years of Shame: The Story of the Japanese Canadians in World War II*. Toronto: Doubleday Canada, 1977.

Buck, Tim. *Canada and the Russian Revolution*. Toronto: Progress, 1967.

———. *Years in the Struggle: Reminiscences of Tim Buck*. Toronto: NC Press, 1977.

Campbell, Charles S., Jr. *Anglo-American Understanding, 1898–1903*. Baltimore: The Johns Hopkins Press, 1957.

Canada. Department of External Affairs. *Documents on Canadian External Relations*, 1909–53. Cited as *DCER*.

———. House of Commons. *Debates*, selected issues.

Canadian Annual Review, 1915.

Chapman, John W.M. "Tricycle Recycled: Collaboration among the Secret Intelligence Services of the Axis States, 1940–1941." *Intelligence and National Security* 7, no. 3 (July 1992): 268–99.

Churchill, Winston. *Their Finest Hour*. Boston: Houghton Mifflin, 1949.

Cleroux, Richard. *Official Secrets: The Story behind the Canadian Security Intelligence Service*. Toronto: McGraw-Hill Ryerson, 1990.

Coogan, Tim Pat. *The IRA*. Glasgow: William Collins and Sons, 1988.

Corson, William R. *The Armies of Ignorance: The Rise of the American Intelligence Empire*. New York: Dial, 1967.

Couture, Paul Morgan. "The Politics of Diplomacy: The Crisis of Canada–France Relations, 1940–1942." Ph.D. thesis, York University, 1971; Canadian thesis no. 51367.

———. "The Vichy–Free French Propaganda War in Quebec, 1940–1942." *Canadian Historical Association Papers, 1978*: 200–216.

Dawson, R. MacGregor. *Canada in World Affairs, 1939–1941*. London: Oxford University Press, 1943.

De Graff, Bob. "What Happened to the Canadian Personality Index?" *Intelligence and National Security* 7, no. 3 (July 1992): 317–26.

Doerries, Reinhard R. *Imperial Challenge: Ambassador Count Bernstorff and German-American Relations*, trans. Christa D. Shannon. Chapel Hill, N.C: University of North Carolina Press, 1989.

Dreyfus, F. Georges. *Histoire de Vichy*. Paris: Perrin, 1990.

Dupuy, Pierre. "Mission to Vichy." *International Journal* 20, no. 2 (Summer 1967): 395–401.

Eayrs, James. *In Defence of Canada – Indochina: The Roots of Complicity*. Toronto: University of Toronto Press, 1983.

———. *Northern Approaches: Canada and the Search for Peace*. Toronto: Macmillan, 1961.

———. "'A Low Dishonest Decade': Aspects of Canadian External Policy, 1931–1939," in Hugh L. Keenleyside et al., *The Growth of Canadian Policies in External Affairs*. Durham, N. C.: Duke University Press, 1960.

Elliott, Major S.R. *Scarlet to Green: A History of Intelligence in the Canadian Army, 1903–1963*. Toronto: Canadian Intelligence and Security Association, 1981.

English, John. *The Worldly Years: The Life of Lester Pearson, 1949–1972*. Toronto: Knopf Canada, 1992.

Farson, A. Stuart, David Stafford, and Wesley K. Wark, eds. *Security and Intelligence in a Changing World: New Perspectives for the 1990s*. London: Frank Cass, 1991.

Feis, Herbert. *The Spanish Story: Franco and the Nations at War*. New York: Knopf, 1948.

Ferguson, John H. *American Diplomacy and the Boer War*. Philadelphia: University of Philadelphia Press, 1939.

Fetherstonhaugh, R.C. *The Royal Canadian Mounted Police*. New York: Carrick and Evans, 1938.

Fisk, Robert. *In Time of War: Ireland, Ulster, and the Price of Neutrality, 1939–1945*. London: Paladin, 1987.

Foster, R.F. "Anglo-Irish Literature, Gaelic Nationalism and Irish Politics in the 1890s," in *Ireland after the Union*, ed. Lord Blake. Oxford: Oxford University Press, 1989.

France. Ministère des Affaires Etrangères. *Annuaire Diplomatique et Consulaire*, 1938–1964.

Frank, Robert. "Vichy et le Monde, le Monde et Vichy," in *Vichy et les Français: Révolution Nationale*, ed. Jean-Pierre Azéma and François Bedarida. Paris: Fayard, 1992.

———. "Vichy et les Britanniques, 1940–1941: double jeu ou double langage?" in *Vichy et les Français: Révolution Nationale*, ed. Jean-Pierre Azéma and François Bedarida. Paris: Fayard, 1992.

Gallo, Max. *Spain under Franco: A History*, trans. Jean Stewart. New York: Dutton, 1974.

Geyer, Michael. "National Socialist Germany: The Politics of Information," in *Knowing One's Enemies: Intelligence Assessment before the Two World Wars*, ed. Ernest R. May. Princeton: Princeton University Press, 1986.

Girard, Charlotte S.M. *Canada in World Affairs, 1963–1965*. Toronto: Canadian Institute of International Affairs, n.d.

Granatstein, J.L., Irving M. Abella, David J. Bercuson, R. Craig Brown, and H. Blair Neatby. *Twentieth Century Canada*. Toronto: McGraw-Hill Ryerson, 1986.

Granatstein, J.L., and David Stafford. *Spy Wars: Espionage and Canada from Gouzenko to Glasnost*. Toronto: Key Porter, 1990.

Grew, Joseph C. *Ten Years in Japan*. Westport, Conn.: Greenwood Press, 1944.

Hadley, Michael L., and Roger Sarty. *Tin-Pots and Pirate Ships: Canadian Naval Forces and German Sea Raiders, 1880–1918*. Montreal and Kingston: McGill-Queen's University Press, 1991.

Hannant, Larry. "Inter-war Security Screening in Britain, the United States, and Canada." *Intelligence and National Security* 6, no. 4 (Oct. 1991): 722–38.

Hicks, John D. *The Republican Ascendancy, 1921–1933*. New York: Harper and Row, 1960.

Hilliker, John. *Canada's Department of External Affairs, 1909–1946*. Montreal: McGill-Queen's University Press, 1990.

Hillmer, Norman, Bogdan Kordan, and Lobomyr Luciuk, eds. *On Guard for Thee: War, Ethnicity, and the Canadian State, 1939–1945*. Ottawa: Minister of Supply and Services, 1988.

Hinsley, F.H. *British Intelligence in the Second World War: Its Influence on Strategy and Operations*. Vol. 1. London: Her Majesty's Printing Office, 1979. Vol. 2. New York: Cambridge University Press, 1981.

Hobson, James A. *Imperialism*. 1902. Reprint. Ann Arbor: University of Michigan Press, 1965.

Horrall, S.W. "The Royal North-West Mounted Police and Labour Unrest in Western Canada, 1919." *Canadian Historical Review* 61, no. 2 (June 1980): 169–90.

Horrall, S.W., and Carl Betke. *Canada's Security Service: An Historical Outline, 1864–1966.* Ottawa: RCMP Historical Section, 1978.

Hoy, Claire, and Victor Ostrovsky. *By Way of Deception: A Devastating Insider's Portrait of the Mossad.* Toronto: Stoddard, 1990.

Jalava, Mauri. "Radicalism or a 'New Deal'? The Unfolding World View of the Finnish Immigrants in Sudbury, 1883–1932." M.A. thesis, Laurentian University, 1983.

Jeffreys-Jones, Rhodri. *American Espionage: From Secret Service to CIA.* New York: Free Press, 1977.

———. *The CIA and American Democracy.* New Haven: Yale University Press, 1989.

———. "The Montreal Spy Ring of 1898 and the Origins of 'Domestic' Surveillance in the United States." *Canadian Review of American Studies* 5, no. 2 (Fall 1974): 119–34.

Johnston, Hugh. "The Surveillance of Indian Nationalists in North America, 1908–1918." *BC Studies* 78 (Summer 1988): 3–27.

Kahn, David. *Hitler's Spies: German Military Intelligence in World War II.* New York: Macmillan, 1978.

Kealey, Gregory S. "State Repression of Labour and the Left in Canada: The Impact of the First World War." *Canadian Historical Review* 73, no. 3 (Sept. 1992): 275–314.

———. "The Surveillance State: The Origins of Domestic Intelligence and Counter-Subversion in Canada, 1914–1921." *Intelligence and National Security* 7, no. 3 (July 1992): 179–210.

Kealey, Gregory S., and Reg Whitaker. *RCMP Security Bulletins: The Depression Years, Part I, 1933–1934.* St. John's, Nfld.: Committee on Canadian Labour History, 1993.

———. *RCMP Security Bulletins: The Early Years, 1919–1929.* St. John's, Nfld.: Committee on Canadian Labour History, forthcoming.

———. *RCMP Security Bulletins: The War Series, Part I, 1939–1941.* St. John's, Nfld.: Committee on Canadian Labour History, 1989.

———. *RCMP Securtiy Bulletins: The War Series, Part II, 1942–1945.* St. John's, Nfld.: Committee on Canadian Labour History, 1993.

Keshen, Jeff. "Cloak and Dagger: Canada West's Secret Police, 1864–1867." *Ontario History* 79, no. 4 (Dec. 1987): 354–81.

Keyserlingk, Robert H. "'Agents within the Gates': The Search for Nazi Subversives in Canada during World War II." *Canadian Historical Review* 66, no. 2 (June 1985): 211–38.

Kitchen, Martin. "The German Invasion of Canada in the First World War." *The International History Review* 7, no. 2 (May 1985): 245–60.

Lacouture, Jean. *De Gaulle: The Rebel, 1890–1944.* New York: Norton, 1990.

Langer, William. *Our Vichy Gamble.* New York: Knopf, 1947.

Lenin, V.I. *Collected Works,* vol. 29. Moscow: Progress Publishers, 1965.

Leuchtenburg, William L. *The Perils of Prosperity, 1914–1932.* Chicago: University of Chicago Press, 1958.

Levenstein, Harvey. "Canada and the Suppression of the Salvadorean Revolution of 1932." *Canadian Historical Review* 62, no. 4 (Dec. 1981): 451–69.

Lingard, C. Cecil, and Reginald Trotter. *Canada in World Affairs, 1941–1944.* Toronto: Oxford University Press, 1950.

Lisée, Jean-François. *In the Eye of the Eagle.* Toronto: HarperCollins, 1990.

Littman, Sol. "Strong Vibes from a Quiet Source." *Canadian Dimension* 21, no. 7 (Nov.–Dec. 1987).

Lloyd, Alan. *Franco.* Marlow, U.K.: Longmans, 1976.

Lottman, Herbert R. *Pétain.* Paris: Seuil, 1984.

Lowenthal, Miller. *US Intelligence: Evolution and Anatomy.* New York: Praeger, 1989.

McCaffrey, Lawrence J. *Ireland: From Colony to Nation State.* Englewood Cliffs, N.J.: Prentice Hall, 1979.

Mackenzie King Diaries, typescript edition. Toronto: University of Toronto Press, 1973 (*1893–1931*) and 1980 (*1932–1949*).

McLin, Jon B. *Canada's Changing Defence Policy, 1957–1963: The Problem of a Middle Power in Alliance.* Toronto: Copp Clark, 1967.

Mahant, E.E., and Graeme Mount. *An Introduction to Canadian-American Relations.* Toronto: Nelson, 1989.

Mangold, Tom. *Cold Warrior: James Jesus Angleton – The CIA's Master Spy Hunter*. London: Simon and Schuster, 1991.

Marrus, Michael R., and Robert O. Paxton. *Vichy France and the Jews*. New York: Schocken, 1983.

Martin, Paul. *A Very Public Life*. Toronto: Deneau, 1985.

May, Ernest. *Knowing One's Enemies: Intelligence Assessment before the Two World Wars*. Princeton: Princeton University Press, 1986.

Miller, Carman. "English-Canadian Opposition to the South African War as Seen through the Press." *Canadian Historical Review* 55, no. 4 (Dec. 1974): 422–38.

Miller, Nathan. *Spying for America: The Hidden History of U.S. Intelligence*. New York: Paragon House, 1989.

Morn, Frank. *The Eye That Never Sleeps: A History of the Pinkerton National Detective Agency*. Bloomington, Ind.: Indiana University Press, 1982.

Mount, Graeme S. "Friendly Liberator or Predatory Aggressor? Some Canadian Impressions of the United States during the Spanish-American War." *North/South: Canadian Journal of Caribbean and Latin American Studies* 11, no. 22 (1986): 59–70.

———. "The Secret Operations of Spanish Consular Officials within Canada during the Spanish-American War," in *North American Spies: New Revisionist Perspectives*, ed. Rhodri Jeffreys-Jones and Andrew Lownie. Edinburgh: Edinburgh University Press, 1991.

Neilson, Keith. "Pursued by a Bear." *Canadian Journal of History* 28, no. 2 (August 1993): 189–221.

Newman, Peter. *Renegade in Power: The Diefenbaker Years*. Toronto: McClelland and Stewart, 1964.

New York Times, Editors. *The Pentagon Papers*. New York: Quadrangle, 1971.

O'Toole, G.J.A. *The Spanish War: An American Epic*. New York: Norton, 1984.

Paxton, Robert O. *Vichy France: Old Guard and New Order, 1940–1944*. New York: Knopf, 1972.

Pearson, Lester B. *Mike: The Memoirs of the Rt. Hon. Lester B. Pearson*, vol. 1. Toronto: University of Toronto Press, 1972.

Penlington, Norman. *Canada and Imperialism, 1896–1899*. Toronto: University of Toronto Press, 1965.

Pickersgill, Jack. *The Mackenzie King Record, 1939–1944*, vol. 1. Toronto: University of Toronto Press, 1960.

Popplewell, Richard. "The Surveillance of Indian 'Seditionists' in North America, 1905–1914," in *Intelligence and International Relations, 1900–1945*, ed. Christopher Andrew and Jeremy Noakes. Exeter: University of Exeter Press, 1987.

Porter, Bernard. *Plots and Paranoia: A History of Political Espionage in Britain, 1790–1988*. London: Unwin Hyman, 1989.

Possony, Stefan T., ed. *The Lenin Reader: The Outstanding Works of V.I. Lenin*. Stanford, Calif.: Hoover Institute, 1966.

Pringsheim, Klaus H. *Neighbours across the Pacific: Canadian-Japanese Relations, 1870–1982*. Oakville, Ont.: Mosaic Press, 1983.

Reischauer, Edwin O. *The Japanese*. Cambridge, Mass.: Harvard University Press, 1977.

Richelson, Jeffrey T., and Desmond Ball. *The Ties That Bind: Intelligence Cooperation between the UKUSA Countries – the United Kingdom, the United States of America, Canada, Australia, and New Zealand*. Boston: Allen and Unwin, 1980.

Ristelhueber, René. *Aventure de Fridtjob Nansen, Explorateur et Philanthrope*. Montreal: Les Éditions Variétés, 1945.

———. *"Dieu le Veut."* Montreal: Les Éditions Variétés, 1945.

———. *Histoire de France Illustrée*. Montreal: Les Éditions Variétés, 1946.

———. *Mission Française*. Montreal: Les Éditions Variétés, 1943.

———. *Les Traditions Françaises au Liban*. Paris: Alcan, 1925.

Robin, Martin. *Shades of Right: Nativist and Fascist Politics in Canada, 1920–1940*. Toronto: University of Toronto Press, 1992.

Roulet, L.E., ed. *Les États Neutres Européens et la Seconde Guerre Mondiale*. Neuchatel: Éditions de la Baconnière, 1985.

Rusk, Dean. *As I Saw It.* New York: Norton, 1990.

Sarty, Roger, and John G. Armstrong. "Defending the Home Front." *Horizon Canada* 8, no. 6: 2041–47.

Sawatsky, John. *Men in the Shadows: The RCMP Security Service.* Toronto: Totem, 1980.

Sherrin, P.M. "Spanish Spies in Victoria." *B.C. Studies* 36 (Winter 1977–78): 23–33.

Smith, Denis. *Diplomacy of Fear: Canada and the Cold War, 1941–1948.* Toronto: University of Toronto Press, 1988.

Sorensen, Theodore. *Kennedy.* New York: Harper and Row 1965; Bantam, 1966.

Speaight, Robert. *Vanier: Soldier, Diplomat and Governor-General.* Toronto: Collins, 1970.

Sunahara, Ann. *The Politics of Racism: The Uprooting of Japanese Canadians during the Second World War.* Toronto: J. Lorimer, 1981.

Suvorov, Victor. *Soviet Military Intelligence.* London: Hamish Hamilton, 1984.

Swettenham, John. *Intervention in Russia, 1918–1919, and the Part Played by Canada.* Toronto: Ryerson, 1967.

Taylor, Charles. *Snow Job: Canada, the United States, and Vietnam (1954 to 1973).* Toronto: Anansi, 1974.

Thomas, Hugh. *The Spanish Civil War.* London: Eyre and Spottiswoode, 1961.

Thomas, R.T. *The Dilemma of Anglo-French Relations, 1940–1942.* London: Macmillan, 1979.

Tournoux, Raymond. *Pétain et la France: La Seconde Guerre Mondiale.* Paris: Plon, 1980.

Trask, David F. *The War with Spain in 1898.* New York: Macmillan, 1981.

United States. Department of Commerce, Bureau of the Census. *Historical Statistics of the United States: Colonial Times to 1957.* Washington, D.C.: Government Printing Office, 1961.

————. Department of State. *Foreign Relations of the United States, 1900–1966.* Cited as *FRUS.*

Viñas, Angel. *Guerra, Dinero, Dictadura.* Barcelona: Critica, 1984.

Vincent, Carl. *No Reason Why: The Canadian Hong Kong Tragedy – An Examination.* Stittsville, Ont.: Canada's Wings, 1981.

Volkman, Ernest, and Blaine Baggett. *Secret Intelligence: The Inside Story of America's Intelligence Empire.* New York: Doubleday, 1989.

Vulliez, Wanda. *Vichy: La Fin d'une Époque.* Paris: Éditions France-Empire, 1986.

Wagner, Jonathan F. *Brothers beyond the Sea: National Socialism in Canada.* Waterloo: Wilfrid Laurier University Press, 1981.

Ward, Alan J. *Ireland and Anglo-American Relations, 1892–1921.* Toronto: University of Toronto Press, 1969.

Ward, Peter. *White Canada Forever: Popular Attitudes and Public Policy toward Orientals in British Columbia,* 2d ed. Montreal and Kingston: McGill-Queen's University Press, 1990.

Wark, Wesley. "Cryptographic Innocence: The Origins of Signals Intelligence in the Second World War." *Journal of Contemporary History* 22, no. 4 (1987): 639–65.

Whealey, Robert H. "Economic Influence of the Great Powers in the Spanish Civil War: From the Popular Front to the Second World War." *International History Review* 5, no. 2 (May 1983): 229–54.

Wilkie, J.E. "The Secret Service in the War," in *The American-Spanish War: A History by the War Leaders.* Norwich, Conn.: Chas. C. Haskell, 1899.

Wilson, Robert A., and Bill Hosokawa. *East to America: A History of the Japanese in the United States.* New York: Quill, 1982.

Winks, Robin. *Canada and the United States: The Civil War Years.* Baltimore: Johns Hopkins Press, 1960.

Witcover, Jules. *Sabotage at Black Tom: Imperial Germany's Secret War in America, 1914–1917.* Chapel Hill, N.C.: Algonquin, 1989.

Wright, Peter. *Spy Catcher: The Candid Autobiography of a Senior Intelligence Officer.* Toronto: Stoddart, 1987.

Xavier de Bourbon, Prince. *Les Accords Secrets Franco-Anglais de Décembre 1940.* Paris: Plon, 1949.

Index